W9-BSC-155

Where Basketball Is King—
Or Is It Knight?

Where Basketball Is King— Or Is It Knight?

Confessions of an Indiana Hoosier Fan

Louis Lemberger

VANTAGE PRESS
New York • Los Angeles

To Myrna, Harriet and Margo, my family and my best friends, who sometimes humored me but always shared my enthusiasm for "Hoosier Hysteria."

Contents

Acknowledgements

Writing a book on a topic you love is not a task but a pleasure. Publishing this work however provided a different challenge. To date, I have only written scientific papers and books based on my original research and on related issues, while this book is drawn on personal experiences. I hope others will enjoy reading it as much as I enjoyed writing it. It was with the encouragement and support of several people that this book was able to come to fruition. First I would like to thank my wife Myrna who agreed that this was something I wanted and needed to do and who provided the essential encouragement and the constant emotional support throughout. Likewise, my daughters Harriet and Margo who always provided additional positive input and did not object too vigorously when I included some of their escapades. I would especially like to thank Patricia Newman for all her efforts in the actual preparation of the manuscript and helping to make it a reality. Thanks are also due to my friend and colleague Emerson Houck who read an early draft and felt it was something that could be shared and enjoyed by others. His continued enthusiasm encouraged me on to get the book published. I am indebted to Bob Hammel, the sports editor of the Bloomington *Herald Times*, for taking the time to read the manuscript and for his constructive criticisms and commentary. For providing his editorial expertise and for being interested in me and this project, I am grateful. I am also most grateful to my friend Jeff Sagarin, a sports columnist for *USA Today* and a sports aficionado, who stayed up all night reading and commenting on an early draft, and who provided me with stimulating and enthusiastic support. I give special thanks to Myrna, for proofreading each draft and to my mother-in-law Sylvia Diamond for doing some additional grammatical editing. I would like to thank Neil Schor, whose encyclopedic sports mind was helpful in making sure I presented things accurately as particularly pertains to University of Michigan information. A very special thanks goes to Leonard Zimmerman and his colleagues at Vantage Press for their interest in this project, and for all their assistance.

Last, but certainly not least, I would especially like to thank Coach Bob Knight and the past, present, and future Indiana University basketball players, who have, and will continue to add a vast dimension of enjoyment, well defined as "Hoosier Hysteria" for me and my family and for untold numbers of fans everywhere.

Writing this book was an emotional catharsis. It allowed me to recall and relive portions of my life directly and indirectly related to basketball. It has been a fun and fulfilling experience.

Where Basketball Is King— Or Is It Knight?

Chapter 1
Prologue

In the game of chess, the king is the dominant piece. Other men include the queen, the castle, the pawn, the bishop and the knight. In another game—basketball, especially basketball in Indiana—for almost two decades the dominant piece appears to be the knight. That is, Bob Knight, coach of the Indiana University Hoosiers.

You're probably asking yourself: Why another book on basketball—especially on Indiana basketball, "Hoosier Hysteria." Let me tell you—there was a movie, *Hoosiers*, and books such as *Hoosiers, Hoosier Hysteria, I.U. Basketball, All the Way to the NCAA, Season on the Brink, Beyond the Brink with Indiana*, and probably a slew of others I haven't read or heard of. But this, I hope, will be different. This, I hope, will show you what basketball, as a spectator sport, in Indiana, is all about. It is told through the eyes of a transplanted family who adopted, and were then adopted by and became a part of Hoosier Hysteria. Although there are several levels of Hoosier Hysteria, I will try to relate the ultimate level, college basketball at Indiana University.

We moved to Indiana in 1971 from New York State via Bethesda, Maryland. At the same time another individual, from Orrville, Ohio, moved to Indiana after a memorable stop in New York State. This was the year that Bob Knight became the head coach of Indiana University after having spent time at the US Military Academy at West Point. This, in fact, is about thirty-five miles from where I grew up in upstate New York.

Although I hope to portray how a family had, and still is

1

having, a great deal of excitement and fun because of their love for the sport of college basketball, I must state at the outset that we are not unique. Perhaps just a little more fanatic than thousands of other families in Indiana, and, as I will show you, in New York. As a matter of fact, this type of fanaticism occurs in all of the hotbeds of high school and college basketball, encompassing small towns and large cities around the ACC, Big Ten, Pac Ten, Big Eight, Mid-American Conference, the Big East, et cetera. What I want to demonstrate is that fans are much the same all over the country, despite differing social strata. College basketball serves as a common bond and topic of communication between the rich and the poor, those with many years of formal education and those with none, those from the small farm communities and those from the the large industrialized cities, and those of all religions, races, and political convictions. It knows no boundaries. Basically, it probably all starts with a love for the sport and from an early exposure to basketball in grade school or early high school. In Indiana, they talk of Hoosier Hysteria. However, when I was growing up in New York in the Catskill Mountains (about ninety miles from New York City), it was no different, whether at state sectional time or during the regular season. Although the gyms of New York were smaller than those in Indiana, the enthusiasm was just as great.

I must tell you the area I was born in was somewhat special and unique. The Catskills are, as I mentioned, a small group of mountains of the Appalachian chain, about ninety miles from New York City. They are not that different from Indiana's mountains, except that the Catskills were a little higher than those in the Brown County region. Brown County is located in southern Indiana, near Bloomington, Indiana, the home of Indiana University and its Hurryin' Hoosiers. Both these areas share a similar terrain and foliage, and are dotted with small farms and small lakes. Let me tell you about the "mountains," as they are fondly known to New Yorkers.

Chapter 2
In the Beginning: 1937–51

I was born in 1937. At that time the Catskills were famous for four things: (1) good hotels, serving plenty of food featuring a kosher cuisine. World-famous examples of these hotels were Grossinger's and the Concord; (2) the *Frische Luft*, translated, for those unfamiliar with Yiddish, as "the fresh air." This, in fact, was a major reason why New York City residents—people from Brooklyn, the Bronx, Queens and Manhattan—traveled a full day's journey by car or hackie on old Route 17 over the Wurtsboro Mountains to such places as Fallsburg, Woodridge, Liberty, Monticello, Parksville, and Ellenville; (3) being the birthplace and nurturing environment for such famous comedians and entertainers as Jerry Lewis, Buddy Hackett, Eddie Cantor, Milton Berle, Jackie Mason and Alan King, just to name a few, who all "grew up" in the mountains. Moreover, many other entertainers were discovered here. Last, but certainly not least, the Catskills were famous for (4) college basketball. This was a place where college athletes worked in hotels as waiters, busboys, bellhops, and lifeguards during the day and played basketball in a summer league to entertain the hotel guests in the evening. They could earn money for their college tuition and other expenses while they honed their basketball skills in a competitive environment. At that time there were no Pan Am games, no World Basketball games, nor any other modern-day opportunities for talented college basketball players to "strut their stuff."

The Catskill Mountains were fondly known as the "Borscht

Belt" or the "Jewish Alps." In addition to hotels, there were many bungalow colonies and roominghouses, also known as *Kuch-aleins* or Cook-alones. Woodridge, the small village in which I grew up, had a total population of about 500 in the winter, which mushroomed to several thousand inhabitants in the summer. Woodridge was located in Sullivan County, jokingly referred to as "Solomon" County. The county had a population of about 45,000 in the winter, which approached 2 million during the summer months. Each town usually had at least one hotel. The major one in our village was called the Alamac Hotel. This was a typical Catskill Mountain establishment, characteristically made up of a huge main house with large blue spruce trees on the expansive front lawn, a large swimming pool off to one side, and a wood-frame social hall on the opposite side.

Directly across the road from the social hall was a black-top basketball court with an expansive modern pavilion extending behind it. On those evenings when games were played, both teams' benches were set up at courtside in front of this pavilion. Across the court were the spectator stands, usually filled with enthusiastic partisans cheering for their own staff. Several large floodlights were located at the periphery and others hung on wires high above the court so that the hotel guests could view the night basketball games. Here in the early forties basketball was king. The entertainment in the social halls with the up-and-coming comedians clearly took a back seat and was the secondary act. These acts usually performed either on nights not devoted to basketball, the premier event, or after the games were completed.

The owners of the Alamac, Max and Gussie Shapiro, had twin boys, Charles and Walter, who were two of my best friends. Thus I spent a great deal of time at the hotel. My father's name was also Max. He was in the dry cleaning business, and he and my mother, Ida, who also helped in the shop at times, worked very hard in the summer season, as did all the residents who were dependent upon the tourists for their livelihood. As my father often used to tell me, "If you don't make it in the summer, you will have to eat snowballs in the winter." Thus, as a young boy I was free to visit with my friends, especially in the summertime, when my parents were very much involved with their seasonal business.

The Shapiro's lifestyle was completely different from that of my parents, but because I was outgoing and never felt inferior to anyone, I wasn't bothered and fit in well with the twins and their family, as well as with the "city" people, i.e., the hotel guests. The twins had an Uncle Dave—Dave Weiss—whom I remember as being very friendly with some of the coaches and "big shots" in college and professional basketball. As a result, these celebrities visited the hotel and I had the opportunity to "hang around" them. In retrospect, knowing what I know today about some of the people and their reputations, I guess I should have been intimidated. But you know how pesky kids can be, especially when they have a personality and reputation that compares with that of Dennis the Menace. I was short for my age (about ten to twelve years old at that time) and did not reach any kind of growth spurt until about fifteen years of age. However, even at age ten I liked to play basketball and to be part of the activities with the "older guys."

What was it like growing up as a kid in the mountains? Well, we were involved in many activities—swimming, playing softball (in organized leagues and many times we played against adults from various hotels and roominghouses) and, of course, playing, and especially watching, basketball.

As you could imagine, in my hometown basketball was the center of activity when I was a youngster. Each village had its own school and each school had its own team and gym—just as depicted in the movie *Hoosiers*, showing life in Indiana. Villages such as Fallsburg, Woodridge, Mountaindale, Woodbourne, and Hurleyville and larger towns such as Monticello, Ellenville, and Liberty all played each other. The rivalries were intense and were a matter of civic pride. For Woodridge to beat the much larger towns like Monticello, Liberty, or Ellenville was commonplace. This was all part of our bragging rights. I remember as a child sitting on the stage in the school gym and watching some of the games. You see, every basketball gym doubled as the

5

school auditorium, with the stage at one end of the basketball court. When a village civic event or school program was planned, the basket was elevated.

It was considered a big honor for the young kids to be allowed to keep score. The scoreboard was made of wood and the numbers were wooden figures that had small holes at the top so they could be placed over a hook. Now, thanks to television and the extensive coverage given to the University of North Carolina basketball program, everyone is familiar with this type of scoreboard, since a similar one is still in use at the Dean Smith Center, or "Deandome" in Chapel Hill. Thus, at UNC, even in this modern era and technological age, they still keep score on an old wooden scoreboard, in addition to the elaborate electronic scoreboard. It is nostalgic and reminds one of bygone days. I can certainly relate to the youngsters who have the honor of keeping score in this old-fashioned manner.

After World War II, several of the school systems in New York State centralized, and as a result, some bitter rivals and adversaries found themselves playing and cheering for the same team. This was the case between the villages of Woodridge and Fallsburg. Instead of hating the opponents' ball players, we now were united and thus rooted for each other. As the old expression goes, politics make strange bedfellows. As you can see, this can even occur in basketball.

Another phenomenon occurred after the war. In 1945–46, when the young boys returned from Europe and the Far East, basketball teams cropped up in all of the towns in the Catskills. In our area, a league was formed with teams from Woodridge, Middletown, Monticello, et cetera. Woodridge, one of the smallest towns in population to participate, had a team known as the AVC, short for the American Veterans Committee. Thus, each town had its own team and the rivalries continued, not only at the high school level, but now at a higher level. Most of these young men never attended college, but some of them were pretty good ball players and therefore the league was very competitive. Woodridge won the championship several times consecutively, playing to packed gyms filled with the town's faithful. Although the crowds and the gyms were small compared to what I later was exposed to in Indiana, to me they were large since I never had any means of comparison. Nevertheless, there was tremendous team spirit and enthusiasm. At the high school level, many of the townspeople would follow the team bus to the away games, forming a caravan similar to that depicted in the movie *Hoosiers*.

I attended Fallsburg Central High School (the result of the merging of five schools—Woodridge, Fallsburg, Mountaindale, Woodbourne, and Hurleyville–Loch Sheldrake), one of the smallest schools in the ten-team DUSO league, the conference in which we played. This league consisted of schools from Dutchess, Ulster, Sullivan, and Orange Counties, thus the name DUSO, and was composed of small schools such as Fallsburg and large city schools such as Newburgh, Kingston, Middletown, and Poughkeepsie. While a freshman in high school, I recall a group of guys piling into Ed "Red" Hedman's car and driving to a game at Beacon, New York, a city directly across the Hudson River from Newburgh. In those days the New-burgh–Beacon bridge on Interstate Route I-84 did not exist, and thus we needed to take the ferry across the river. It was a cold, snowy, wintery night, but still Fallsburg Central High School had a respectable crowd cheering them on.

In my sophomore year, as a member of the junior varsity team, the team bus traveled with the players, coaches, and cheerleaders to Poughkeepsie to play the "big city boys" in their "bandbox" gym. This gym, located below ground level, was extremely small and had a very low ceiling. For me, this outing was indeed a big adventure. In retrospect, one aspect which sticks out in my mind entails watching their varsity center. I guess he was about six foot, four inches, with a prominent square jaw. He was a good basketball player and I saw him again when he played first base for their baseball team. Since we were a small school, we participated in varsity soccer rather than football, as was the case with many small schools in New York State. However, this high school athlete from Poughkeepsie was also a class football player and later went on to star for the San Francisco Forty-niners. It was not until years later while living in Indiana that I again heard the name of that basketball center—Monte

Stickles. Some other people from our league played at the college level, including Ed Weaver from Kingston (he went to the USMA at West Point) and Mickey Bartkowski from Newburgh Free Academy (he later played for Manhattan College), but by and large, none ever made it big nor achieved fame as hoop stars.

The Catskills, and New York State in general, were big on sports, especially basketball. In those days there were many players and owners of Jewish background who were associated with the sport at both the collegiate and the professional level. The combination of the ethnic background of the Catskills and the love of these individuals for basketball made it natural for New Yorkers, Philadelphians, and people from the East Coast in general to spend their vacations in this area. In fact, this was the heyday of the Catskills, the days before air travel to such exotic places as Las Vegas, San Francisco, Hawaii, Miami, the Caribbean, or Europe. It was also the era before air conditioning and before people moved to private homes in Long Island, Westchester, and Rockland County. Thus the day-long journey to the Catskills on Route 17, which now takes only about two hours on super highways, is a journey into a lost, bygone era. A recent motion picture depicting this decline in the popularity of the Catskills and the ending of an American institution is entitled *Sweet Lorraine*, starring Maureen Stapleton. This movie was filmed in South Fallsburg, New York, in the heart of the Catskills.

Chapter 3
Meeting the Legends

Have you ever visited the Basketball Hall of Fame in Springfield, Massachusetts? About twelve years ago, my wife Myrna and daughters Harriet (then age twelve) and Margo (then age nine) spent a delightful few hours there. It brought back many fond memories of delightful aspects of my youth. It also brought together these aspects with my current life. It connected my past and all of the joys associated with growing up in the Catskills in the heyday of basketball with the present—basketball in Indiana. Names out of my past, such as Chuck Cooper, Clair Bee, Eddie Gottlieb, Haskell Cohen, Dudey Moore, Bob Cousy, and many others were all represented there. So were names I had recently become familiar with, such as Paul "Tony" Hinkle, Phil Eskew, Branch McCracken, Everett Dean, Scott May, and Kent Benson.

Now that you know that I grew up in the Catskills, I hope you have some understanding and appreciation for the area and its love for college basketball. At the Alamac Hotel I had a unique opportunity to meet some of the greats in college and professional basketball. One of the first individuals I can recall meeting was Chuck Cooper from Duquesne University in Pittsburgh. He was tall and solidly built. I didn't realize it until I visited the Hall of Fame, but in 1950 he became the first black player to be admitted into the National Basketball Association (NBA), when he started playing with the Boston Celtics. In Springfield they had his uniform on display and there was a whole section devoted to him. I remember hanging around with him and I recall that he was always cordial to me and the Shapiro twins. He sometimes took us on his daily work-related drives and played catch with us. He was truly a nice guy. I have recollections of two other basketball players from that time. They were Paul Senesky, from St. Joseph's of Pennsylvania in Philadelphia—I remember hearing that his brother George was playing in the professional ranks and would later go on to coach the Philadelphia Warriors—and Ray Knight from the University of Notre Dame in South Bend. Ray Knight was a waiter and was also very friendly to us. Little did I know that about twenty-five years later I would also be living in the Hoosier State. If you had told me this even when I was thirty, I would have thought you were demented! To me, at that time, the picture of the USA as seen in the *New Yorker* magazine was just a little too restrictive. Instead of civilization ending at the Hudson River, it really terminated just beyond the Catskills.

The college ball players in the hotel summer league were just kids—about nineteen to twenty-one years of age—but to me they were grown men. I was four feet, five inches tall, and they ranged between six feet to six feet, eight or nine inches. However, I didn't realize what tall was until several years later when I met Ray Felix. He was really tall—about seven feet. At that time, he also was a bellhop at the Alamac Hotel and would soon become a member of the Baltimore Bullets as a result of Mr. Clair Bee's leaving college coaching and assuming the job as head coach with Baltimore's professional team. Ray Felix was one of the early seven-footers in the sport, being preceded by Walter Dukes from Seton Hall, Bob Kurland from Oklahoma A & M, and only a few others. Ray Felix later went on to play for the New York Knicks, but like his predecessors, really did not achieve stardom in the pros, although he had an excellent rookie season.

During that summer, Clair Bee brought him to the Alamac and introduced him around. One incident particularly stands out in my mind. We had a theater in Woodridge known as the Lyceum. In the winter, that is, after Labor Day, it was closed, but in the summer it did a booming business. One evening I saw this poor chap, seven feet tall and skinny as a rail, sitting on the aisle, trying to jam his long body into the relatively small theater seat. He almost appeared to be folded in half, as his knees were almost touching his chest. I said hello to Ray and was delighted and honored that he remembered me and returned my salutation. For a young boy, this friendly gesture on his part went a long way to make me feel good and important. Who watched the movie? I sat the whole evening watching Ray's every move as he tried to get comfortable.

Certainly the highlight of these summer evenings was watching the "visiting" hotel teams play at the Alamac Hotel, starring such greats as Bob Cousy of Holy Cross and the Tamarack Lodge in Greenfield Park, and Paul Arizin of Villanova and the Nevele Country Club in Ellenville. Arizin was renowned for introducing and perfecting the one-hand jump shot. In addition, there were Sherman White of Long Island University and Grossingers Hotel in Ferndale and George Mikan, who was now playing professionally but who was still associated with Klein's Hillside Hotel in Parksville, New York. My friends and I and the other kids always flocked around Mikan, just to touch him and get his autograph, since even then, he was a well-known star. In those days it was easy to get close to the ball players and the stars. Mikan, who played his college basketball at DePaul for Coach Ray Meyer, went on to be selected as the best player of the half-century in basketball.

It is of interest that all of these players went on to distinguish themselves in the pros, all, that is, except Sherman White, who unfortunately became one of the scapegoats of the basketball scandals of 1951. He was ultimately banned from playing professional basketball. It is said by some that he may have been the best college basketball player of his time. Just as it was very easy for kids like myself to get next to those superstars, I guess it was also easy for gamblers to influence these naive young men.

I had another opportunity to watch several other players who were involved in the infamous scandal. In the winter, it was customary for several New York City high schools and colleges to spend a weekend in the Catskills playing exhibition games. I recall Boys High, now Boys and Girls High, from Brooklyn coming to play at Fallsburg Central High School. In addition, CCNY (the City College of New York), coached by Nat Holman, played

11

an exhibition game in our gym. Their players were all famous and would become the first and only team to go on to win both the NCAA and the NIT in the same year. They included Ed Roman, Al Roth, Ed Warner, and Irv Dambrot, just a few of those who were involved in the scandal of 1951.

Holman, the coach of CCNY, was a very good friend of Max (Mickey) Kinsbrunner, another full-time resident of the Catskills. Kinsbrunner was a collegiate star at St. Johns University and later was one of the original Celtics. He and Nat Holman were teammates on that famous team. This world-renowned team included another great player named Joe Lapchick, who went on to coach St. Johns University and later the New York Knickerbockers. When I was growing up in the Catskills, Mickey Kinsbrunner was the athletic director at the Concord Hotel and his children attended Fallsburg Central High School. His son Jay was a few classes below me and also played basketball, but unfortunately he did not have the natural ability that was attributed to his father. He had a tough time in school sports, considering he had to try to live up to his father's reputation. However, this did not affect him academically since, after high school, he went on to college and graduate school and received a Ph.D. Not bad for a kid from the country.

Another player that I met in the mountains was the two-time All-American Sihugo Greene from Duquesne. During my Christmas vacation in December 1955 I saw him play in the Holiday Festival Tournament in Madison Square Garden. Also playing in that tournament were the San Francisco Dons, who with their superstars Bill Russell and K. C. Jones dominated college basketball that year. About 18,000 others packed the Garden that night to watch them play. Greene's coach was a relatively short, well-built man named Dudey Moore. He also hung out at the Alamac Hotel in those days.

Yet another coach who was prominent in the summers at the Alamac was Eddie Gottlieb, owner of the Philadelphia Warriors. I remember him as being a robust individual with a pot belly who always carried a big cigar. It is interesting what you remember when you are ten years old. I also recall, however, that he was a gentleman with the youngsters, always saying hello and joking with us. As I mentioned earlier, while on our visit to the Hall of Fame I saw material about him describing his early involvement with the Philadelphia Spha's—this was a team in the Philadelphia Jewish League, and Spha's was the abbreviation for South Phildelphia Hebrew Academy. Mr. Gottlieb is described in the Hall of Fame as a super promotor of basketball and was one of those responsible for helping salvage the pro game and for being instrumental in forming the NBA. His Philadelphia Warriors won the first NBA championship in 1946– 47. He was also described as a "great promotor of honor and integrity." Well, what else would you expect? You can usually judge a man's character by the way he treats children and how they respond to him. As I told you, I thought he was truly a gentleman. Seeing his picture in the Hall of Fame and viewing this part of the museum brought back fond memories as I related my own childhood experiences to my children.

At the Hall of Fame, there was a very special section depicting the relationship between Maurice Stokes of St. Francis of Loretto, Pennsylvania, and Jack Twyman, who played his college ball at Cincinnati. Twyman had set up a fund to help defray the medical expenses incurred by his teammate Maurice Stokes of the Cincinnati Royals professional team. Stokes had had a mysterious bout with encephalitis (sleeping sickness). This is not uncommon in the Midwest, where several varieties of this disease exist, such as Western Equine Encephalitis and St. Louis Encephalitis. In Stokes's case, it was thought to be related to head trauma secondary to his hitting his head on the floor during a basketball game. Coincidentally, the administrator of this Maurice Stokes fund was Haskell Cohen, who had been the head of public relations for the National Basketball Association. As I mentioned earlier, he was a good friend of the Shapiro twins' uncle, Dave Weiss. Thus the connection to such basketball celebrities as Eddie Gottlieb and others who had found their way to the Alamac Hotel now became clear to me. This special display also gave me another opportunity to share my childhood with Myrna, Harriet, and Margo.

Speaking of Maurice Stokes, I remember a time in 1955, when I was about seventeen years old, sitting with a group of friends in Gary Slater's car, hovering over the car's radio as Maurice Stokes led St. Francis of Loretto, Pennsylvania, in scoring in the NIT semifinals. He had a fantastic night; despite their 79–73 loss to Dayton, he scored forty-three points and completely dominated the game. Although his team finished in fourth place, he was named the most valuable player of the tournament. He went on to play basketball for the Rochester Royals, who soon moved to Cincinnati, then later became the Kansas City Kings, then moved to Sacramento. Well, I guess this sort of tells you what has happened to pro basketball! It clearly is a business with very little allegiance to the fans. This is a point I will discuss later in explaining my love for college basketball and its inherent stability, while contrasting that to professional sports with their "couldn't-care-less" attitude regarding the faithful fans.

Now, Maurice Stokes and Jack Twyman developed a unique relationship when they played together. This subsequently strengthened after Stokes's tragic illness. Twyman set up a special fund to help support Maurice's medical expenses. One of the primary activities to raise money for the fund was an annual basketball game which continued until Maurice's death. Now, where would you expect such a game to be played? You're right! In the Catskills. A famous hotel known as Kutsher's Country Club located near Monticello, New York, the county seat and the heart of the Catskills, was chosen as the site. Here, NBA greats and graduating college players would play against each other to help one of their own. Even today, Kutsher's is the site of an annual benefit basketball game. One individual who regularly attends these games is Coach Bob Knight of Indiana University.

Another great in the field of basketball not only attended these games until his death, but after his retirement actually made his home at Kutsher's in Monticello. This giant of a man, in fact, was quite short in stature considering that basketball is a "big man's" game. This individual, Clair Bee, was a unique individual, one in a million. He was gentle, intelligent, soft-spoken, and I would guess stood only about five feet, six inches. At least that was my impression the first time I met him in 1947 at the Shapiro's house at the Alamac Hotel when I was about ten years old. It was in the springtime, and Clair and Mrs. Bee had come to make final arrangements with Max Shapiro regarding the summer basketball camp which he held for youngsters and teenagers at the hotel. I recall that he was wearing a white shirt and clean-laundered and pressed white slacks. He was always well groomed. This was the first time I had met him, and little did I know that I would have many future opportunities to hear that name during my college days as well as after moving to Indiana.

This larger-than-life individual was the coach of the Long Island University Blackbirds, who played their home games in either Madison Square Garden, or, more often, on the fifth floor of the formidable building known as Brooklyn College of Pharmacy, a division of Long Island University located in the Bedford-Stuyvesant section of Brooklyn. At that time, LIU, which was physically located about five miles away, had no campus or gym of its own. In fact the building that housed LIU was more famous for housing one of the most reowned theaters in New York City. This was the Brooklyn Paramount—a showplace in its day, comparable to Radio City Music Hall on Sixth Avenue and Fiftieth Street in Manhattan, and the Roxy, a famous theater in Times Square. Today, only Radio City Music Hall still exists, the Roxy and the Paramount both having closed their doors.

Many knew of Mr. Bee simply as a great college basketball coach, first with Rider College, then with Long Island University. He won 95 percent of his games there and is still one of the all-time leading coaches with the best percentage won-lost record. Incidentally, Bob Knight is not too far behind Mr. Bee. Clair Bee's Blackbirds were one of the premier college teams of that era, that is, before the scandals. They held the record for the longest winning streak for a team on their home court, fondly known as the "Druggists' Den," which was often referred to in the press as the Blackbirds' Bandbox. It was a small gym with a bank of stands on one side and folding chairs on the other. It didn't look much different from the average high school gym in

New York State. As a matter of fact, my high school gym probably held more people. The floor was dark and the whole atmosphere did not go along with what might be expected of a major college team. When I attended Brooklyn College of Pharmacy (BCP) in 1956 and first set foot on that floor in those hallowed surroundings, I was in awe of the history that I knew surrounded me. Subsequently, as a player in that gym, the feelings were even more intense. Just down the hall from the basketball court was the laboratory of one of my pharmacology professors, Dr. Shirley Kraus. This was also the place where I started my career as a researcher, working in her lab.

Clair Bee rose within the ranks of LIU from basketball and baseball coach, to athletic director, and then to become assistant to the president. His teams were always well disciplined, and he stressed defense and teamwork. This was certainly a part of basketball with which I would later become very familiar as an adult living and cheering for Indiana University's Hurryin' Hoosiers under Coach Robert Montgomery Knight.

Actually, the name Hurryin' Hoosiers was a misnomer, as I soon found out when I arrived in Indiana. This was the style of play under the former Coach Branch McCracken when they won NCAA championships in 1940 and 1953. However, things changed in Bloomington under their new coach. He, in fact, had just moved there from Army, the US Military Academy at West Point, which was located on the Hudson River in Orange County, New York. It is interesting that just down the road, about five miles to the north, was a small college preparatory high school known as New York Military Academy, which had as their basketball coach this older individual. Yes, you guessed it, Clair Bee was just the proverbial stone's throw away from Bob Knight, and I am sure must have had a tremendous positive influence on young Coach Knight's development. Knight went to West Point at the age of twenty-three to do his military service and to serve as an assistant coach to Tates Locke. When Locke moved on, Knight stayed there to become one of the youngest head coaches of a major college basketball program.

Clair Bee had found his way to Cornwall on the Hudson via

Baltimore. After the basketball scandals of 1951, he was devastated and disillusioned with the influence that gamblers had on college basketball. In 1952, he left LIU, where he had achieved such success, and where he coached great ballplayers such as Sherman White, to assume the head coaching job of the Baltimore Bullets. After several mediocre years in the professional ranks, he left and went to Cornwall-on-the-Hudson. After his retirement he then moved about thirty to forty miles to Monticello, New York, where he still remained active and interested in college basketball until his death on May 19, 1983, at the age of eighty-seven. Just like Eddie Gottlieb, Clair Bee was a gentleman in the truest sense—a gentle man and, of course, a true genius.

Many people are aware of Clair Bee's classical basketball books on coaching, drills, and the defensive techniques of the game. These collectors' items were published as a series of four books by Barnes and Company. However, few people are aware of the other side of Mr. Bee. He also authored the Chip Hilton Sports Series, a series of fictional books for young boys. The books deal with such sports as basketball, football, and baseball. I started collecting this twenty-three-book series about eight to ten years ago. Besides the personal pleasure and satisfaction in the discovery of these rare finds, it gives me something to do and keeps me out of trouble when my wife Myrna takes me to flea markets and garage sales. I spend some of my time trying to add to my collection. I consider each acquisition, no matter what condition or which specific publication series, a real find. It recently became clear to me that these books are hard to find and clearly collectible. In my case, it's mainly for sentimental reasons.

Clair Bee's basketball camp at the Alamac Hotel was one of the forerunners of what now occurs on every college campus. Coaches and ex-players direct basketball camps for youngsters during the summer months. The situation in our town in 1949 was similar to that depicted in the movie *Breaking Away*. I was one of the "townies," a group of kids from varying backgrounds and socioeconomic levels, who were somewhat envious of the "rich" city boys who came to spend several weeks learning and playing basketball under the tutelage of greats such as Clair Bee. We relished the opportunity to play pick-up games with them in their off time, but these opportunities seldom occurred, which was further cause for frustration.

It's not every youngster growing up in a hamlet with a population of 500 who has an opportunity to personally meet the world-famous Harlem Globetrotters. Boy, was I lucky. The Globetrotters were presenting a benefit game at the Alamac Hotel. The Harlem Globetrotters, with such greats as Marques Haynes and "Goose" Tatum, were there with their owner and leader, Abe Saperstein, and his family. Mr. Saperstein's son Jerry was a year or two younger than me and the Shapiro twins, and so we all hung around and played together during their weekend stay. Jerry introduced us to the players and to his father, and I got their autographs. I also got Jerry's autograph since I thought it was "neat" that he was a normal kid even though his father was Abe Saperstein and he was in such close contact with the most famous basketball team in the history of the sport.

Even today, when I attend an IU basketball game, I am reminded of those days. You see, the IU pep band, and I am sure every other band as well, plays "Sweet Georgia Brown" as the team is warming up. This, in fact, was the trademark and calling card of the Harlem Globetrotters as the players stood in a circle passing the ball around. Nothing gets your blood heated up and your brain ready for a good basketball game like sitting through a few choruses of "Sweet Georgia Brown." It is an IU tradition that always returns me to those bygone days at the Alamac Hotel in Woodridge, New York, and to my home in the Catskills. I can assure you these fond memories of my youth can never be displaced.

Chapter 4
The Learning Years: 1954–71

The college basketball scandals, which had a devastating but fortunately only a temporary effect on the game, took place in 1951. They essentially broke when a young man named Junius Kellogg from Manhattan College notified the New York City district attorney's office that he had been approached to "shave points" in some of their games in Madison Square Garden, or "the Garden," as it is fondly known to New Yorkers. The Garden in those days was located on Eighth Avenue and Forty-ninth Street. It took up a whole city block and was the home of the New York Knickerbockers professional basketball team, the New York Rangers professional hockey team, and the Ringling Brothers Barnum & Bailey Circus when it was in town in the spring. It was also the "temporary" home for several local college basketball teams and, last but not least, it was the host site of the well-known National Invitation Tournament, better known as the NIT. At that time this tournament was one of college basketball's premier events. It was every young athlete's dream to someday play in Madison Square Garden; however, this honor was reserved for only a few.

The Garden was a place where the bookies would meet and greet each other and was a place loaded with excitement. Outside, under the overhanging marquee, scalpers would be hawking tickets and crowds would gather to enter the arena to root for their team. It was guaranteed that the partisan crowd was rooting for the New York team because only a few seats were available for visitors, and New Yorkers were, and still are, strong supporters of their teams. Even to this day, with such poor standings in the leagues as some of their teams have exhibited, the fans are still 100 percent behind their heroes.

Well, to get back to the original thought, after Junius Kellogg broke the story, the DA made many arrests, including such prominent players as Sherman White, Ed Roman, Al Roth, Floyd Layne, Irwin Dambrot, Leroy Smith, all from the New York area, and several players from outside New York. Of course, players from outside New York were not immune, and, as one might have anticipated, a few were also involved in the scandal. These included several players from Adolph Rupps'—the Baron's—prominent University of Kentucky Wildcat NCAA championship team of 1949, notably Ralph Beard, Alex Groza, and Dale Barnstable, as well as Gene Melchiorre from Bradley University in Peoria, Illinois.

As a result of the embarrassment and guilt associated with this series of events, many basketball coaches refused to let their teams play in New York, especially in the Garden. This became a time of retrenchment for college basketball, especially in the East. Fortunately for sports fans, East Coast basketball would eventually be revived and regain its level of prominence. This culminated with the founding of the Big East basketball conference in 1979 under its new commissioner, Dave Gavitt, of Providence College. The Big East basketball conference consists of such powerhouses as Georgetown, St. John's, Providence, Seton Hall, Pittsburgh, Connecticut, Syracuse, Boston College, and last but not least Villanova. Recent successes in the NCAA tournaments speak well for the Big East conference. In 1985 there were three teams from this conference in the final four, and in 1987, they progressed two teams to the final four. Well, it shows that college basketball is alive and well in the Mid-Atlantic region in the East.

At about this time (i.e., 1954), I graduated from high school and planned to start college at Albany College of Pharmacy, a division of Union College. Unfortunately, my father's dry cleaning business was suffering a questionable future after some problems when his partners, whom he had just bought out, decided to go into competition. As a result, my entrance into college was postponed and I worked with him in the dry cleaning business for two years. At this time, it again became financially stable and it was now feasible for me to go off to college. During this interim period I played basketball on our town's team, which was sponsored by the local American Legion Post. In the summer of 1954 I met my future wife, Myrna, an event which modified my future college plans and, of course, my whole life. Instead of attending college in Albany, I went to New York City and enrolled at Brooklyn College of Pharmacy (BCP), part of Long Island University.

By now I had grown more than a foot and was about five foot eight or five foot nine and much more developed. On my second day of college I decided to go out for the school's basketball team, which played competitively in an established pharmacy school league. I was directed to the gym where the trials were taking place, and there I met the coach, who was a fellow by the name of Saverio Picariello. He also served as an assistant coach at Long Island University, first under Coach Clair Bee and later under Bee's successor, Buck Lai. Mr. Picariello was short and stocky and was quite a disciplinarian. He was fondly known as "Pic." It is of interest because during the two years I worked and toiled in my father's "sweatshop," pressing clothes, driving a delivery truck, making repairs on machines, and loading and emptying the laundry and dry cleaning vats, I played baseball with a team known as the Monticello Clothiers, named after their sponsor, Hammond and Cooke, a men's haberdashery in Monticello. A teammate and friend on that team, Ralph Hirsch, who was serving as the basketball coach for Fallsburg Central High School, was a Brooklyn boy and a friend of Mr. Picariello. Thus, when I arrived at BCP, I was instructed to give Ralph's regards to him.

I enjoyed the first few days of practice and made some good friends, with whom I would be in close contact over the next three to four years. I made the team and was looking forward to having this as a means of keeping in shape and relaxing from my study schedule and from my frequent trips to the Bronx to see Myrna. Unfortunately, the school's administration decided to discontinue the extramural basketball program shortly thereafter and that was the last time I had any contact with Pic. BCP did, however, continue their intramural basketball program, and thus I now played against the upperclassmen, who, instead of being my teammates, were now the competition. In addition to our intramural games, on occasion we would schedule an exhibition game against other pharmacy schools such as Columbia University. We played all of our games in the same gym I had heard and read so much about—the Long Island University Blackbirds Bandbox. Now it became clear to me why it was called the "Druggists' Den" since, in fact, it was where pharmacy students like myself played.

A famous financial planner, Venedda Van Caspell, author of a series of books with titles such as *Money Dynamics*, *Money Dynamics in the 80s*, et cetera, divides life into three portions: the learning years, the earning years, and last, either the golden years or the yearning years. Her premise is that those who plan well can retire with financial independence and those who don't plan well go through their retirement in a less stable situation. A lot depends on the learning years. Not only do I collect books as a hobby, but I also collect sayings from Chinese fortune cookies that I think are applicable. One which I obtained in 1956 and still to this day save in my wallet says, "Money spent on the brain is never spent in vain." From my personal experience, truer words were never uttered. Thus, while in pharmacy school I studied hard and then went on to graduate school at Albert Einstein College of Medicine in the Bronx, first for my Ph.D. in pharmacology and then for my M.D. It was relatively easy for me to do well since Myrna and I continued to date, and then got married in 1959, during my last year at BCP. She was always very understanding and supportive, emotionally, psychologically and, early on in our marriage, financially as well. As I progressed, I was able to provide our support by acquiring scholarships, fellowships and of course student loans.

Our first daughter, Harriet, was born in 1965, just prior to my starting medical school, and three years later our second daughter, Margo, was born. After medical school, I completed my medical internship in New York City and spent two years in the United States Public Health Service at the National Institute of Health in Bethesda with Drs. Julius Axelrod and Irwin Kopin. These were very exciting times. While I was a fellow in this laboratory, we conducted experimental research in the fascinating area of drugs of abuse and tried to unravel the mysteries of how the brain and the nervous system functions. During my tenure, Dr. Axelrod won the Nobel Prize, based on work he had done earlier.

During my "learning years," I had little time to avidly pursue my love for college basketball since I had to face reality and hit the books and work in the summers, either in my father's dry cleaning business or in scientific research laboratories. This was necessary to make ends meet to support my family, and to continue my education. I knew that with the opportunity to go to college went the commitment to succeed. This, I felt, was my first obligation, since the alternative might be working in the sweatshop pressing pants for the rest of my life. Thus, while I was busy trying to meet my own goals, I missed a whole lot of what was happening around me and I must admit, college basketball was one of those areas sorely missed.

During this period, some of the greats of college basketball were strutting their stuff and taking center stage or, more appropriately, center court. These included such giants (literally and figuratively) as Lew Alcindor, also known as Kareem Abdul-Jabbar, from New York City's Power Memorial High School and then UCLA; Jerry West from West Virginia, who then attended West Virginia University; Wilt Chamberlain from Philadelphia, who attended Kansas University for two years; and last but not least, Oscar Robertson from Indianapolis, who attended the University of Cincinnati. Although I occasionally watched them on TV and read about them in newspapers and sports magazines, I did not have the time to devote to this interest with the same intensity I did in high school. One exception was Wilt Chamberlain, whose career I followed closely, since he spent his summers working as a bellhop at Kutsher's Country Club in the Catskills.

After the drought during graduate school, medical school, and my internship, I again had an opportunity to play basketball and to watch college ball while at the NIH. We played at the offic-ers' club at the Pentagon, and in my spare time I watched ACC basketball on television while living in the D.C. and Maryland area. Since this was ACC country, I saw such schools as UNC, North Carolina State, South Carolina (at that time they were still in the conference), and Maryland. However, in those days there was no ESPN and no cable TV and therefore very few other con-ferences were seen on a regular basis. One day in 1970 I heard some of the staff and research technicians talking about the NCAA finals, which were being played at Cole Fieldhouse on the campus of the University of Maryland in College Park. In my younger days, or certainly at the present time, I would have tried to scrounge a ticket by either staying in line all night or by buying a ticket from a student or a scalper. However, at that time I was busy with my wife and young family, trying to spend every avail-able opportunity with them when I wasn't working on my re-search project.

My research was directed at determining how marihuana—actually its major psychoactive component, delta-9-THC—af-fected the body as well as how the body affected delta-9-THC. That research encompassed such questions as how human be-ings metabolized or disposed of and eliminated marihuana from the body after it was smoked or ingested. In fact, one of my major areas of research interest while at the NIH, and even before com-ing to the NIH, was the study of how drugs of abuse affected the body. Little did I know, at that time, that about fifteen years later Len Bias, one of the foremost college players to ever play in Cole Fieldhouse, would set the college basketball world, and the sports world in general, on its ear because of his tragic and un-timely death due to the pharmacologic and toxicologic proper-ties of another drug of abuse—cocaine.

In the late 1960s and early 1970s, marihuana and delta-9-THC were the drugs that researchers in the drug-abuse field were trying to understand. Cocaine, because of the monetary expense associated with its use, was a drug not commonly used by "aver-age" abusers, but was reserved only for the rich. Boy, how things have changed! Cocaine became more accessible and more affordable to many more individuals, and has become a major social problem. It is currently the drug towards which extensive research in the field of drug abuse is directed.

While serving my military service at the NIH, I received an invitation to present a seminar in Indianapolis by Dr. Bill Martz from the Lilly Laboratory for Clinical Research, a division of Lilly Research Laboratories of Eli Lilly and Company. This is a large pharmaceutical corporation whose headquarters are in Indianapolis. The Lilly Laboratory for Clinical Research, known as the Lilly Clinic which is located on the medical school campus of Indiana University, enjoys a reputation as one of the most famous clinical pharmacology research units in the world. I accepted the invitation and visited Indianapolis.

Coming from New York, and generally having never left the state until I moved to Bethesda, I admit I didn't know much about Indiana or what to expect on my visit. Like most people who are sports enthusiasts, I was aware of three things relating to Indianapolis and Indiana University. First, this was the site of the Indianapolis 500, a fact that everybody the world over knows. Second, they had a good basketball team with a longstanding tradition. And third, they had an excellent swimming team. It's a shame to admit that, and the fact that Eli Lilly and Company was a leader in the pharmaceutical field (which I learned from my training in pharmacy, pharmacology, and medicine) was the extent of my knowledge of Indiana. As a matter of fact, my pharmacy school class had visited Lilly over the Lincoln's Birthday holiday vacation break in February of 1960. Since Myrna and I had just gotten married two months earlier, and since we did not have a honeymoon at that time (she went back to work after our one-day vacation in the city and I went back to classes), we decided to take those few days as our honeymoon and spend a long weekend in the Catskills. Well, isn't that where everyone from New York City went for their honeymoon in those days?

In October of 1970 I flew to Indianapolis and gave my seminar. Much to my surprise, I was offered a permanent position with Lilly. Being relatively naive, I had no idea when I accepted

25

the invitation that a job offer might have been the purpose of the invitation. I did fall in love with the Lilly Clinic and the idea of its proximity to, and interaction with, the Indiana University Medical School. As a result, I was quite impressed with the potential this could offer me as a place to develop as a researcher for the next two to three years.

I returned to Bethesda and told Myrna about the trip. I asked her what she thought of Indiana. She responded quickly, "What is it?" She accused me of being crazy and having lost my marbles. "There is no way that a bunch of dyed-in-the-wool New Yorkers are going to be able to adjust to and be happy in Indiana," she stated. The following month we both flew out with the children and went house hunting. She reconsidered and we decided we would at least give it a chance for a few years. I was still in the service—the United States Public Health Service—a uniformed service into which doctors and scientists who were interested in research and health-related areas could apply in lieu of some other military branches. I was thirty-two years old at the time of my entry into the USPHS, married with two children. I thought this was a good way of doing my military service as a physician. I had enlisted in the navy when I was seventeen years old, between high school and college. As a single young man, I felt that I would like to be in the service. However, I was rejected at that time, having failed the physical at 39 Whitehall Street (the army induction center for the New York area) because of poor vision when not wearing glasses.

So here I was with nine months left in the service and a job offer in a place my wife and I were not convinced we would like. In fact, we were almost positive that we would not like the Midwest. However, since both of us are impulsive and adventuresome, Myrna and I decided to accept the job. In just one weekend while on our house hunting trip, we bought a lot, found a builder, and contracted to have our house built. In fact, Myrna basically designed the house and made all the necessary decisions through the mail and over the telephone. Interestingly, we essentially never saw the house until it was completed, when we arrived in Indianapolis at the end of June in 1971. To give you an idea of the sendoff that we received from Bethesda, one of my colleagues told Harriet and Margo that he hoped they would be happy in Indian-no-place.

Chapter 5
The Transition Years: 1971–75

The transplants from New York City arrived in Indianapolis in late June of 1971. Between finding out the best way to get to work, working on the lawn, and getting integrated into the community, the first few months passed quickly in our new hometown of Indianapolis.

Each day, on the route to the hospital (Marion County General Hospital, formerly known as Indianapolis City Hospital), I would pass by an old school complex known as Crispus Attucks High School. It was named after a runaway Negro slave who was the first man to be killed by the British in 1770 during the Boston Massacre. This school was located about a half-mile from the hospital. The Attucks Tigers, as their teams were called, were basically composed of black students. Crispus Attucks High School had been well known and respected throughout the state for their successful basketball programs, first under Coach Ray Crowe, and later under Coach Bill Garrett, who incidentally was the first black player to don a red and white uniform at Indiana University. I was told that Coach Crowe worked with the younger boys in the neighborhood while they were in elementary and junior high school and thus developed them as fine young men as well as good basketball players.

Throughout the 1950s, Attucks's teams were not only in the heat of Hoosier Hysteria, but reached the pinnacle by winning the boys state championship on three occasions, 1955, 1956, and 1959. I had heard the name of one of Crowe's young prodigies many times before—Oscar Robertson, also known as the Big O. This was the same Oscar Robertson who led the University of Cincinnati to the NCAA final four in 1959 and 1960. Another participant in that 1960 final four was intrastate rival Ohio State, the eventual NCAA champion that year, with IU coach-to-be Bob Knight as the sixth man. This was the same Oscar Robertson who went on to star in the National Basketball Association (NBA) with the Cincinnati Royals and Milwaukee Bucks and who was said by some to have been among the best players in college and professional basketball.

Every day, driving to work, I would be reminded of the fine basketball tradition of Indiana. Perhaps this made it easy for a transplanted New Yorker who loved the sport to feel at home in this new city. When we first moved to Indianapolis, it was very provincial—certainly a stark contrast from New York City or Washington, D.C. One of my friends and co-worker who grew up in Boston said, "You should have seen it five years ago!" Well, Indianapolis has certainly changed during the time we have lived here. It is now quite cosmopolitan and is a lovely place to live and raise a family. It has been termed the Amateur Sports Capital of the Nation and recently was the topic of articles entitled "A Diamond in the Rust" in *National Geographic* magazine and "Indy's Image is Aglow" in *Smithsonian* magazine. The terms *Indian-no-place* or *Naptown* certainly no longer applied.

My first few days at the Lilly Clinic at Marion County General Hospital (now known as Wishard Memorial Hospital) were filled with a variety of new and exciting encounters. Since this was basically my first job—not counting medical school, internship, and the military—everything was really a new experience. I had met many people during my initial interviews and visits; however, Dr. Bill Martz, my new boss, now introduced me to those people that I would be working with permanently. So many new faces to try to associate with names. One individual I particularly took note of was Bob Jewell, a medical technologist in the hematology laboratory. He was about six foot six, softspoken, and a very gentle man. He was prematurely grey and very distinguished looking.

At that time I did not realize that he was one of the stars of the all-Negro Crispus Attucks teams that had participated in the high school state finals. I also didn't know that he had won the coveted Arthur L. Trester Award for mental attitude in 1951. This award is given to one of the players of the Final Four teams who exemplifies the tradition of Mr. Arthur Trester, the first commissioner of the Indiana High School Athletic Association, and incidentally a member of the Basketball Hall of Fame in Springfield, Massachusetts. It wasn't until several years later that I learned that Bob Jewell, who I sometimes referred to in my own mind as a gentle giant, was so honored. Little did I realize that he was imprinted in the annals of Indiana high school basketball forever. This became clear to me when I noted several years later, in the *Indianapolis Star*, a list of previous Trester awardees. There was the name of my friend, Bob Jewell. He was the first black player to whom this honor was accorded. When we first arrived here, Bob's girls and my daughters were involved together in the Brownies and Girl Scouts, and Margo went to the same elementary school as one of his daughters.

By the time I got my "feet on the ground" in Indiana, the leaves were falling off trees, the autumn was coming to a close, and I was discovering that the onset of winter also signaled the onset of the basketball season. I would soon feel as at home here in Indiana as I did growing up in the Catskill Mountains.

Bill Martz, a typical Hoosier, was born in Anderson, Indiana, and lived in the small town of Brownsburg, Indiana. He knew of my love for and interest in basketball, and he and his wife Mary invited us to attend a high school basketball game with them at the Brownsburg gym. What a delightful evening. Bill's son David was a starter for the Brownsburg team and their whole family was involved in the sport. David's girlfriend Sandy was a cheerleader, and she and Bill's daughter Sharon took our daughter Harriet, then only six years old, onto the court and got her involved with the cheerleaders. Harriet immediately started emulating them, doing cartwheels and participating in the cheers. Myrna and I were delighted and beaming as we watched from the bleachers. Margo, who was only three years old, also participated with them, as best as a three-year-old can. The gym was packed, and the fans were screaming, yelling, and cheering for the hometown boys. It's hard to imagine that this

Friday evening ritual was going on all over the state in large- and small-town gyms. This was our first real taste of Hoosier Hysteria—not unlike that in which I personally had witnessed and participated in New York State. It was clear that this was going to be a significant part of our future life in Indiana.

Bill Martz tried to convince me that the Indiana-style high school playoff system was superior to that practiced in New York State. In New York and various other states, the schools participating in the playoffs are divided into classes and sections. For example, Class A sectionals might be for schools with the largest enrollment—usually schools in the larger cities—whereas Class D might include those schools with the least enrollment, generally in the rural areas. The New York City schools had their own tournament. Thus, in New York State there were many champions: one for each section within each class. In contrast, Indiana utilizes an open system where all of the approximately 400 schools in the state are placed in the same pot and each school, regardless of its size of enrollment, has a chance to be crowned the state champion. The initial competition is at the sectional level. This progresses to the regional level, then to the semi-state, and finally the final four, which culminates in the state championship game. These latter two events until recently were played in Market Square Arena in Indianapolis in front of 17,000 screaming partisan fans. This is Hoosier Hysteria at its best. For many years, the final four was played in Hinkle Field House on the campus of Butler University in Indianapolis. Then, for a brief period (just a few years), the games were temporarily moved to Indiana University's Assembly Hall in Bloomington. In 1990, they were played in the Hoosier Dome in Indianapolis before a record crowd of about forty thousand fans.

The excitement of the progression from the sectionals to the finals was recently depicted in the movie *Hoosiers*, in which a fictitious team named Hickory High won the state championship in Butler Fieldhouse. This movie, as I interpret it, is basically a combination of two events: 1) the 1954 State Championship won by Milan, a small farm community in southeastern Indiana whose players represented the rural aspects of the state;

31

and 2) the coming of Bob Knight to the state of Indiana. Although "fictitious," this movie is the cinema's version of an actual team from Milan, Indiana, which did win the state championship in a contest against a large city school on a last second shot by a player named Bobby Plump. This David-and-Goliath analogy has been told and retold in Indiana folklore since 1954 and holds out hope to those small high schools that they too may be the champions! To tell you the truth, I also have become a believer in the Indiana system. It is much more exciting from the fan's point of view, and must be incredibly satisfying for the athletes.

Speaking of Hinkle Field House (formerly called Butler Fieldhouse), this is the home of the Butler University Bulldogs basketball team. Since our home is about two miles away, we go there frequently to see special basketball events, Butler basketball, and, of course, the high school sectionals. There I have watched some of Indiana University's greats, such as Landon Turner, when he played for Tech High School, and Mike Woodson, when he was at Broad Ripple High School. The field house was renamed to honor Paul D. "Tony" Hinkle, who for many years was the coach and athletic director of Butler and who is a member of the Basketball Hall of Fame. Butler is also well known for its fine music school, where Harriet and Margo took clarinet and flute lessons, respectively. When I drove them to their lessons, I would sometimes go over to the field house just to pass the time watching Butler's team practice or looking in on some of the local amateur and professional players.

It is of interest how some parents differ. In New York it was a great satisfaction to have your children advance in school, graduate early, and going on to high school or college ahead of time. Precocity was rewarded by having such programs as the "rapids" in elementary school, allowing children to skip years of school to recognize those who excelled academically. In contrast, until recently in Indiana, it was in vogue to purposely hold the athletically gifted young boys back, repeating years in elementary school or junior high, to allow them to reach their full growth potential while they were still attending high school. Thus young boys entering high school were more physically mature, stronger, and most important, taller—all of the attributes which make for a better basketball player. My wife and I were astonished when our home builder told us that his son repeated a year in junior high school to develop into a taller basketball player for his high school years.

This philosophy was recently challenged in the Indiana courts. The Indiana High School Athletic Association (IHSAA), the governing body for high school sports, attempted to prevent Richie Mount, the son of former Purdue All-American Rick Mount, from intentionally being held back for one year, even though he had successfully completed that grade. The court voted in favor of the youth and his parents, thus allowing him to be held back. However, as a result of this case, the Indiana High School Athletic Association passed a new ruling making this practice unacceptable, assuring that in the future youths would be penalized for this practice, and their years of eligibility for playing basketball at the high school level would be limited.

As you might imagine, it took several years for us to get situated in Indianapolis, adjusting to the neighborhood, to work, and to getting the children set in their schools and their social activities. It wasn't until the fall of 1972 that I ventured from Indianapolis to Bloomington and got season tickets to watch Indiana University's football games. It wasn't hard to get football tickets. However, getting basketball tickets was another story. Indiana University has always had a great basketball tradition, with coaches such as Everett Dean and Branch McCracken. Coach McCracken, in fact, led them to NCAA championships in 1940 and 1953. Thus, with the Hoosier's basketball tradition, and with the new coach and the new arena, my chance of obtaining basketball season tickets was remote. The football team's defensive safety, a young man from Thornbridge High School in a Chicago suburb, was not only exciting the football fans, but also the roundball fans, since he was also a star basketball player. That superstar, named Quinn Buckner, played football for only two years. He then committed himself solely to the basketball program. That winter and for the next few years, we watched Indiana University basketball on TV and enthusiastically rooted for them. We faithfully wore our red garments while sitting in our family room glued to the TV set as we cheered them on.

In the 1972–73 season, the Indiana team gelled and made it to the final four in St. Louis. I remember standing on a corner in the French Quarter in New Orleans while attending the annual meeting of the American Society for Clinical Pharmacology and Therapeutics (ASCPT), discussing the upcoming final four with Roger and Lois Maickel from Bloomington. After the meeting, they were going to St. Louis to watch the game and give moral support to the Hoosiers. I recall how fortunate I felt they were and how envious I was. Imagine going to the final four as a spectator and cheering for your team. What a thrill. This team, coached by Bob Knight, included Steve Downing, Steve Green, Jim Crews, John Laskowski, Quinn Buckner, and John Ritter, to name just a few. During the semifinal game against UCLA, it is said a single call might have been responsible for dictating the final outcome. IU's center Steve Downing had three personal fouls and Bill Walton, the UCLA center, had four fouls. A block was called against Downing, and he fouled out only a few seconds later after scoring twenty-six points. At that juncture, the game was very close. Partisan Indiana fans thought it should have been called a charging foul on Walton. Had this been the case, he would have fouled out and Indiana might have rallied, possibly winning an NCAA championship for Coach Knight, on his first attempt. However, this was not to be, and the Hoosiers and Coach Knight returned home from St. Louis and continued to build.

The 1973–74 season was also very special and successful for IU fans. Indiana finished the Big Ten season tied for the title with Michigan. IU had won twenty games and lost only four games (two preconference: one to Notre Dame at home and one to Oregon State away; and two Big Ten games: Michigan, away, 73–71, and Ohio State, away, 85–79). The NCAA rules stated that only the Big Ten conference champion could represent the conference, and since Michigan and Indiana had tied for that honor, a playoff game was necessary. This was scheduled to be played on a neutral site and Illinois' Assembly Hall was chosen. Since IU had lost to Michigan away 73–71 but won in Bloomington 93–81, it looked as if IU would stand a good chance of winning the tiebreaker. Myrna, the girls, and I listened to the game on the radio that late winter evening since we had some school-related activity to attend. When the activity was over, we drove to the Pizza Hut for a snack. It was nearing the end of the game and IU was on the short end. I remember us sitting in the car on the side of the restaurant eagerly antipating IU's every basket. Unfortunately, they didn't come often enough and IU lost 75–67.

Michigan went to the NCAA and Indiana went to the runnersup tournament, the newly created Collegiate Commissioners Association Tournament (CCA) in St. Louis. They probably would rather have gone to the NIT in New York, but that was not to be. Indiana beat Tennessee, the Southeast Conference (SEC) runnerup, 73–71, then beat the Toledo Rockets, the Mid-American Conference runner-up, in an overtime game 73–72. They then made their way to the championship game where they were to meet the University of Southern California (USC), the PAC-10 runnerup. Indiana played the Trojans close for the first eleven minutes and was trailing by several points when Coach Knight protested the officials' failure to call a violation on the USC center for carrying the ball. For this, Knight was assessed a technical. From the fans' vantage point, it appeared that the "General" got several additional technical fouls to shock his troops, and he was ejected from the game. He was forced to watch his team play from a seat in the stands, along with the other 4,700 regular paying fans. On TV, the cameraman periodically showed Coach Knight watching the game. It appeared to me that that act—their coach being ejected—must have awakened the team because they played with a vengeance, outscoring Southern Cal by a 65–36 margin and winning by a final score 85–60. Because of the small attendance, the future of the CCA was in question, and eventually it was decided to discontinue the CCA and expand the NCAA field. As a result, Indiana University has the distinction of being the only college to have won the NCAA, the NIT, and the CCA.

I continued to try, unsuccessfully, to get season tickets for

Indiana basketball so that I could be a real full-fledged spectator, not just a TV participant. I was told that my name was on a waiting list and that I should be patient. Patience is not one of my better virtues.

The 1975 season was indeed a season to be remembered. Again, we watched IU play on the boob tube. That starting team consisted of Scott May, Quinn Buckner, Bobby Wilkerson, Kent Benson, and Steve Green, and the sixth man, who came off the bench, "supersub" John Laskowski. They were dynamite. They were undefeated throughout the regular season. As they made their way through the preconference and Big Ten season, everyone, including our household, expected IU to win the NCAA. Then, as we watched TV in February of 1976, shock and despair filled our family room. In the closing minutes of the first half of their game against Purdue at Mackey Arena, forward Scott May broke his forearm. We thought he was gone for the rest of the season. Despite May's absence, Indiana won the Big Ten, and then won their first NCAA game. Next, they faced Kentucky at Dayton, Ohio. Coach Knight started Scott May, who played with his arm in a cast. It had been pinned to stabilize it, enabling him to participate. He played, but clearly wasn't in his top form. After only a couple of minutes, Knight realized that May would be more of a detriment than a contributor and took him out of the game.

Late in the game, Indiana was down by approximately ten points with time running out. I can recall where I was at that exact moment. I was listening to the game on a portable radio while my older daughter was competing in the science fair at her elementary school. To give you an idea of the magnitude of this game, and the interest of the average Hoosier fan, I spent a great deal of time doing my own play-by-play for bystanders and other parents who also had to miss the game because they couldn't watch it on TV due to this higher commitment. In the remaining time, Indiana gallantly fought back, cutting the deficit from ten to eight to six. However, time ran out when we were only two points behind. Had there been just a little more time, no one doubts that Indiana would have been victorious and again gone on to the final four. We all—probably the whole state of Indiana, including, I would imagine, many Purdue fans—were frustrated and devastated. As you can imagine, Kentucky, the border state to the south of Indiana, is not often the recipient of cheering by fans from the Hoosier state. I can assure you the feeling from Kentucky fans is mutual. This is a classic college rivalry and, moreover, an interstate rivalry.

To be sure, it was a long summer, not only for Coach Knight and the basketball players, but also for the fans. We kept wondering what the final outcome would have been had that fateful moment in February, when Scott May broke his arm, not occurred. Well, injuries do occur, and they can't be factored into the equation. But do they have to happen to Indiana with such regularity? What a damper for such a successful season. Well, hopefully that should make future victories all the sweeter.

At the end of this season, Bob Knight received a philosophical, morale-building letter from Clair Bee, the former Long Island University coach and superb writer, who was now in his late seventies. It started, "Take a deep breath. Get your bearings. Set your sights on even greater heights and start all over again." It ended with "He will be back," in reference to the young leader. Coach Knight was to actively respond to this letter during the following season.

Chapter 6
Oh What a Perfect Season: 1975–76

St. Louis, November 29, 1975. Indiana University 84–UCLA 64. Boy, were we invincible! In the fall of 1975, the UCLA Bruins, the previous NCAA champions, couldn't hold a candle to the Hurryin' Hoosiers. We all lamented about what last season's NCAA tournament would have been like if Scott May hadn't broken his arm. Well, that was now in the past. Now the team and all of the fans had to look forward to the future and to what promised to be an exciting season. Well, that was the good news. Now for the bad news. The Lembergers still didn't have season tickets for Indiana University basketball. Well, it was banishment to the TV in the family room again. Every Thursday and Saturday we would don our red outfits and root, root, root. The rest of the family rooted, but I was more emphatic and animated. I would yell at the TV, at the referees, at Coach Knight, and at the ball players from my seat on the carpeted floor. To say I am a hyperactive, emotional fan is putting it mildly.

Early in the season I got a call from Roger Maickel, a friend of mine who was a pharmacology professor in the Indiana University Medical School program in Bloomington. In 1973 Roger and his wife, Lois, both diehard Hoosier fans, were fortunate to attend the NCAA final four in St. Louis. Roger, whom I have known for years, left the NIH in Bethesda in the mid-sixties and joined the pharmacology and psychology departments in Bloomington. A mutual friend, Ronnie Kuntzman, a dyed-in-the-wool New Yorker, said that Roger went out to "Bloomingdales." The purpose of Roger's call was to ask me to do him a favor. He wanted me to serve as an outside reader on a doctoral thesis for one of his graduate students. This request included that my wife and I go down to Bloomington, and then out to dinner with the Maickels after the thesis defense. He stated that I would also get an honorarium, which I couldn't accept anyway.

Well, for those who know me, my response was predictable. "I'll gladly do it! Forget dinner! Forget the honorarium! Just get two tickets for Myrna and me for the Notre Dame–Indiana basketball game." Roger persuaded some members of his department to donate their tickets to the cause and the date was confirmed. To be honest, I would have done it even if he didn't take us to a game. We left the children with friends in Indianapolis and early that morning journeyed to Bloomington, full of excitement and anticipation. Myrna and Lois spent the day getting to know each other, while Roger and I participated in the student's thesis defense. Later, we all met and then it was a quick snack and off to the game. Adrian Dantley was a junior and Notre Dame was certainly going to be a good test for the highly touted and number-one ranked Hoosiers. IU won, 64–60, but it was a hard-fought game with Adrian Dantley scoring nineteen points, and Indiana's victory coming on two foul shots by Quinn Buckner in the last few seconds.

What excitement! Seeing the Hoosiers in person! Scott May, Quinn Buckner, Tom Abernethy, Bobby Wilkerson, and Kent Benson. What a lineup! Well, I guess it's back to the TV set. When we left Bloomington, I told Roger to call us any time there was an opportunity for us to get tickets, night or day, and we'd be on our way.

IU completed the preseason undefeated. Each subsequent game became more and more of a challenge as, at their away games, the opposition's fans tried to spark their own team to victory.

I would have just two other opportunities to see that great 1975–76 team play in person. The next game that I saw was in mid-January in Jenison Field House in East Lansing, Michigan. Gerry Gebber, a classmate of mine from my Brooklyn College of Pharmacy days, who was now a professor, was in charge of the pharmacology department seminar series at Michigan State University. In early fall of 1975 he called and asked if I would give the department a seminar on my marihuana research. He cited some possible dates. I quickly took out my planning calendar and asked if January 12, 1976, was available, since this coincided with the IU–Michigan State basketball game. See, that's the purpose of a daily planner—to allow you to plan ahead for important events! We agreed on that date, and to my great pleasure, IU was still undefeated when January 12 rolled around.

I arrived in East Lansing in the morning and gave my seminar that afternoon. I was given a tour of the department and went one-on-one in discussions with several faculty members. I then went to dinner at the Kellogg Center Student Union with Gerry, Ken Moore and Ted Brody, the Chairman of the Department. We discussed science and medicine, and, of course, I managed to interject some basketball talk. You see, the Michigan State fans were not very excited about basketball at that time. Football had always been their big thing. Well, you guessed it. Of course, this was before the days of Earvin "Magic" Johnson. The rest is history. He singlehandedly changed the town from a football empire to a basketball-conscious campus in just two short years. Unfortunately for them, but fortunately for IU and the rest of the Big Ten basketball fans, he left after only two years. The pendulum swung back, and Michigan State has again become a football power, as exemplified by the Spartans winning the Big Ten and the Rose Bowl in the 1987–88 season.

After dinner, we walked across the campus to the field house and sat in the balcony near half court. I screamed and cheered as Indiana put State away. To this day, Ken Moore still teases me about that evening. As he tells the story, "I could understand how Lou would cheer when IU did something good, but did he have to cheer when Michigan State did something bad?" I tried to explain to him that Indiana's greatest strength was its defensive game. It's great to watch a quick guard steal the ball, or a center or forward jump into the passing lane and pick off a pass and convert it into a fastbreak goal. With the era of Bobby Knight, we all—not just Indiana fans, but college fans nationwide—became conscious of the importance of defense.

Indiana won that evening by a handsome score (69–57), and Dr. Moore still tells me how he feared for my life at the hands of the Michigan State University fans, who found me totally obnoxious. Well, I never said I was a normal fan. That trip to East Lansing started something which our family and the Gebber family enjoyed for many years. We would spend the weekend at the Gebbers', attending the IU–Michigan State games (when they were on Saturdays), and they would reciprocate, coming down to Indianapolis for Thanksgiving weekend, which included, of course, a trip to Bloomington to see the season's opening game.

The last game that we would attend in person that season took place one week later. On Monday, January 19, 1976, I got a call at work from Roger Maickel. A severe snowstorm was expected to cover Indiana in a few hours and Dr. Lyle Beck, a semiretired, elderly pharmacologist, and his wife didn't want to venture out in the storm. He asked Roger to offer the tickets to us. I enthusiastically accepted, then called Myrna from work. She was very receptive and that triggered off a frenzy of activity as she got my red sweater out of the drawer, hopped into the car with the girls, and picked me up at the hospital. I was waiting downstairs, and when she arrived, I quickly jumped into the car, took over the wheel, and headed down Route 37 with the girls giggling in the back seat of our 1974 Oldsmobile. The snow was already beating against the windshield, but with studded snow tires and four eighty-pound bags of salt in the trunk, the car drove like a tank. When we arrived in Bloomington, we drove directly to the Maickels' house, where we quickly introduced our girls to theirs, and the four of us departed for the game. It was another exciting evening. The IU–Purdue basketball games are always classics. No matter who is ranked higher or who is favored, all bets are off when it comes to this rivalry. Whether it's basketball or football, Indiana versus Purdue is something else. If you got the impression that IU—Kentucky was important, the IU–Purdue rivalry has the magnitude of a world war. This, of course, involves the bragging rights for most of the state's residents, a goodly number of whom are pro-Purdue, although I suspect the majority are IU faithful.

We were very happy and delighted since Indiana won the

game. We returned to Roger's house to pick up Harriet and Margo and then ventured out into the cold night air. We were in the midst of the snowstorm, which would eventually dump ten to twelve inches of snow on central and southern Indiana. What a beautiful sight. The headlights reflected off the glistening, virgin snow as we drove home on the yet undisturbed highway. The headlights also lit up the oncoming falling snowflakes, giving the impression that they were large pieces of confetti and streamers being thrown at us in celebration of the evening's victory.

Well, that was it for watching the Hurryin' Hoosiers play in the flesh and in person. Actually, the Big Ten season had started earlier with an away game at Ohio State. The Hurryin' Hoosiers had remained undefeated to this point, however, they won a close game in their conference opener versus Ohio State in Columbus. We watched this game on TV and it was clear that although they were great, they were not invincible. Indiana had a tough time beating Ohio State and eventually won by a score of 66–64. That victory almost got away from them. I can assure you, the floor of our family room got a beating that day. We got out of St. John Arena by the skin of our teeth, and I was just thankful that we emerged with a win. This was the opening game of the Big Ten season, and we knew that no victories would come easy.

Although I had to watch this game on television, the following year I made every effort to get to Columbus to see the Ohio State–Indiana game in person. Since I was a visiting professor at Ohio State and had to lecture to the medical students during the second semester, what better time to arrange for these lectures than concomitantly with the Indiana–Ohio State game in Columbus. Dr. Joe Bianchine, chairman of the pharmacology department at Ohio State at that time, and a good friend, was amenable and set up my lectures to be given either on the Friday before the upcoming Saturday night game, or on the Monday morning following the game. That year (1977), Ohio State was not doing well in the Big Ten Conference because it was in a rebuilding period. Therefore, Joe had no trouble getting tickets for my whole family as well as tickets for his own family. Joe was a novice basketball fan, and I tried to teach him the nuances of the game. He learned his lessons well and we subsequently made my lecturing at the time of the IU game in Columbus a regular event. Myrna and I reciprocated by having him visit with us when Ohio State played in Bloomington, which was usually the final game of the Big Ten season. Thus, having missed the Hoosier's exciting 1976 season opener in Columbus in person, I was hopeful that I could attend IU's road games in the future.

Bob Knight was always at home in St. John Arena, having played his college ball there. It is of interest to note that over the years we visited Columbus, we sensed that the fans had several different responses to him and his presence. For example, in 1981, a local radio/TV commentator tried to start a fad, encouraging fans to give Knight the old Bronx cheer as he entered the playing court. This loud reception of boos was quickly countered by a much less vocal group of Ohio State fans who cheered for him. I was one of the few fortunate Indiana fans there, all who loudly cheered for him. On another occasion, when he entered the arena, the Ohio State fans reacted as if the prodigal son had returned. One thing is for sure: Ohio State can be proud of what they turned out. Knight, in my estimation, is a caring, honest individual with integrity and concern for his players, who just happens to be the best coach in college basketball history. What, me biased? But I think future history will bear me out. That's not to say that he doesn't have faults. In fact, many of them are known worldwide because of his antics that have received considerable media coverage.

After a while, we would visit Columbus just to see the games, even if they didn't coincide with the medical students' lecture schedule. When we embarked on these annual treks, I would take some vacation time and we would leave early in the day and check into the Holiday Inn across from St. John Arena (coincidentally, the same hotel in which the ball players stayed) the evening before the game. In 1977 we arrived before the team did and were in the lobby when their bus pulled up in the driveway. Margo, who was about eight years old at the time and a "peanut," walked up to Kent Benson, who, in fact, was her "heart throb" and said, "Oh, you're so tall." Harriet's favorite at that time was Jim Wisman, who could probably be on the Wheaties package cover substituting for Jack Armstrong, the all-American boy.

As a matter of fact, Jimmy was a celebrity in his own right, having been on the front page of many newspapers in America during the 1976 season when a famous shirt-pulling incident occurred. It took place in Bloomington during the second of the classic IU–Michigan battles that year. Earlier in the year in Ann Arbor, Indiana had defeated Michigan 80–74. In the return match at Bloomington, Michigan's strategy included using a full-court press. Wisman, the player responsible for inbounding the ball, threw the ball away two or three times in a row. You could imagine me, sitting in front of the TV yelling at Wisman, then yelling at Knight to get him out of the game. Well, Knight did it, and unfortunately it made all of the headlines—as they say, a picture is worth a thousand words. Indiana finally won the game in overtime by a score of 72–67. The overtime situation was set up after a dramatic tip shot at the buzzer in regulation time by Kent Benson. This was facilitated by a tip up to the basket by Jim Crews. This team effort tied the game and enabled IU to maintain its unblemished record.

Earlier in the 1975–76 season, the perfect season, another exciting last-second shot also allowed them to tie a game and go on to win in overtime. This event occurred in December 1975, in a game against Kentucky, when Kent Benson tipped in a shot a few seconds ahead of the buzzer. This shot tied the game in front of a packed house in Louisville's Freedom Hall, and allowed IU to stay in the battle. They eventually went on to a 77–68 overtime victory. At the time, we were in Florida visiting Myrna's mother and father in West Palm Beach for the Christmas vacation period. I can recall listening to this game while sitting in Myrna's mother's "Florida" room, sort of like a back porch, since that was the only place our radio got a strong enough signal for us to hear.

Another close game that I remember vividly from that year

occurred later that month when IU was in the Holiday Festival Tournament in New York's Madison Square Garden. IU advanced to the final game and was playing St. John's University, the hometown favorite. Myrna, the girls, and I were driving back from a daylong trip to Miami and were working very hard trying to get the game on our car radio. At times we were quite successful and able to get good reception on WOWO, the "power" station from Ft. Wayne, Indiana that broadcasts IU basketball games. At night, the transmission from this station can be heard for extremely long distances. As the score of the Indiana–St. Johns game became closer, we became more involved. I recall pulling off onto the shoulder of the road so that we could listen and concentrate, and most of all "help them." I tell you, it's not easy being a fan, and I am sure many people who follow their favorite sport can also attest to this. When your team wins, you share in the great feeling. However, when your team loses, it's as Myrna and I aptly put it, "a downer." You get emotionally involved, and the energy expended is almost comparable to personally playing in the specific game. Indiana finally won in a very close game, the outcome being decided during the last minute. Of interest was that this game was being played in front of nearly 20,000 people, reportedly one of the largest crowds to view a college game in the Big Apple. This in itself gave us some positive feelings, since the team from the heartland had performed well in our hometown.

Indiana continued to do well in the Big Ten conference and remained undefeated. The Hoosiers entered the NCAA tournament as the favorite, expected to win by both the media and especially by their fans. They got by their first opponent, St. John's, whom they played at Notre Dame's Convocation Center and who, you might recall, had given them a tough game in the Holiday Festival Tournament, in New York City at Christmas. We watched this game on TV, and in contrast to the game against St. John's earlier in the season, this one went pretty easily. Despite this, we sat in front of the TV on pins and needles, because the NCAA format is devastating for the teams and the fans alike. With the single elimination, it makes it very stressful. It's not like the playoffs or the World Series in baseball where the best three of five or four of seven decides who progresses to the next stage or who is champion. There, in fact, is *no* tomorrow.

The Hoosiers went on to the regionals in Baton Rouge, Louisiana. Bob Knight surrounded himself with some of his friends and the finest coaching minds in the country. One of these was Clair Bee, who now was in his eighties. I had to go to Seattle, Washington, for the annual meeting of the American Society for Clinical Pharmacology and Therapeutics and therefore I could not watch the next game against Alabama. You see, out on the West Coast the television station had different priorities and they were more concerned about the Pepperdine game. Well, I never said life was fair or that everyone knows a good thing when they see it. After the conclusion of the day's scientific sessions and other planned activities, several of the fellows from Indianapolis came to my room, where I called Myrna to find out the score of the Alabama–Indiana game, which I thought had been played earlier in the day in Baton Rouge, Louisiana (due to the time difference on the West Coast). She refused to talk to me since the game was still in progress and, as she described it, was a "barn burner." I instructed Myrna to set the telephone in front of the TV set and for the next ten or fifteen minutes we all sweated together—Myrna, Harriet, and Margo in Indianapolis and my colleagues and I in Seattle. I could hardly hear the TV and Myrna would periodically break in and fill us in with the details. I would then relate them on to my friends. I specifically recall, with Alabama ahead by one point, Leon Douglas taking two foul shots and missing them, as IU was fighting desperately to tie the score and come back from the slight deficit. This they did when Scott May scored with two minutes to go. Indiana finally won the game 74–69 in the final minutes as their defensive effort held Alabama scoreless for the last four minutes of the game. Indiana went on to beat Marquette in the next game, a contest in which Al McGuire got two technical fouls at critical times. Indiana won that game 65–56 and thus made it to the final four.

For me, it was back home again to Indiana. For the Hurryin' Hoosiers it was on to the Spectrum in Philadelphia, the city of brotherly love. As Knight stated at the finals in Philadelphia, "I went into this game thinking about so many people who had invested so much of themselves in our program. I think of an eighty-year-old man sitting up in the mountains of New York watching this game on television. Nobody has been more influential on my basketball life than he has been." This eighty year-old man watching TV was Clair Bee and the mountains Coach Knight was referring to were the Catskill Mountains. I could have assured him at that very moment that a thirty-eight-year-old transplant from the same Catskill Mountains, dressed in red garb and sitting on the edge of his seat in Indianapolis, was also watching TV and preparing to root the Hoosiers on to victory, albeit long distance.

The final four consisted of Indiana, UCLA, Michigan and Rutgers. Indiana had met and beaten UCLA at St. Louis for their season opener, but we certainly didn't want to take them for granted. This evening, I recall Richard Washington leading UCLA in scoring and offense and drawing two fouls on Kent Benson in the first minute, when Coach Knight switched Tom Abernethy onto him. Tom shut him down for nearly thirty minutes before he had to leave late in the game with a knee injury. But by then, IU was leading by ten points. As before, IU defeated UCLA (65–51), and we all breathed a sigh of relief. The next game pitted Indiana against Michigan. We had beaten them twice before—once in the overtime contest in which IU tied the score at the buzzer. Myrna, the girls, and I sat on the floor in front of the TV that evening, which incidentally was Myrna's birthday. When the game started, we were excited because we had beaten them before, and we knew we could at least be competitive. However, we were apprehensive since the odds were clearly in Michigan's favor. After all, how many times in one season can you beat someone of Michigan's caliber?

The game started and unfortunately Indiana got off to a slow start. Then it happened: About two minutes after the tipoff, Wayman Britt drove hard to the basket. Bobby Wilkerson tried to take the charge, but was accidentally hit in the head with Britt's knee or an elbow. Myrna and I looked at each other in shock. Of course, we were all concerned about Wilkerson's health and condition. But we also had visions of Scott May's mishap last year, which in all likelihood had cost us the national championship. Without Spiderman, the nickname affectionately given to Wilkerson for his tenacious defense and excellent rebounding, it looked as if we were finished. The General, as Al McGuire calls Bobby Knight, tried several substitutions at the guard position. First Wayne Radford, then Jim Wisman. Wisman did the job. He penetrated, dished off, and got the ball to the scorers. This was the same Jim Wisman who, earlier in the season against the same Michigan team, was jerked off the court by his jersey. Clearly he had learned his lessons well from his coach and will always be remembered in our household as having played a key role in the 1976 NCAA championship win, as Indiana defeated Michigan 86–68. We were all elated, hugging and kissing each other. They announced on TV that the team would be flying back to Indianapolis the next day and that a victory rally and celebration would take place in Bloomington's Assembly Hall in the evening.

The basketball players landed at Indianapolis International Airport (actually, at that time it was called Weir Cook Airport) with a large crowd of avid fans awaiting their flight. I had to be at work at the hospital that day, but Myrna went to greet them at the airport. She waited for the team to board the IU bus for Bloomington, and spent a few minutes talking with, and congratulating, Wayne Radford. This was our first association with an NCAA championship team. Indiana had won the title in 1940, which was just before Myrna was born, and again in 1953, long before we even knew where Bloomington, or more realistically where Indiana, was.

Later that afternoon, Myrna, Harriet and Margo picked me up at the hospital and we all took the trip down to Bloomington, where we met the Maickels. At this time it was not to see a basketball game, but to be part of the celebration for the *champs*! It was nice to hear the band play their usual repertoire: the old classic "Sweet Georgia Brown," the Indiana fight songs, including "Indiana Fight," "Indiana Our Indiana" and those mainstays of this year's season, "Bennie and the Jets," especially for Kent Benson, "The Mighty Quinn" for Quinn Buckner, and of course, "We Will, We Will Rock You," with its familiar finishing line, "We Are the Champions—of the World!"

Margo and Harriet were dressed in red and white outfits, befitting the occasion. Harriet and Carolyn Maickel stayed in the stands and, leaning over the railing, watched the activities from that vantage point. However, Carolyn's older sister Nancy took Margo down onto the basketball floor. Before long, eight-year-old Margo, who was wearing a red sweater with a white vest and looked like a miniature cheerleader, was surrounded by an enthusiastic group of students and was the center of attention. They put her on their shoulders and paraded her around. Little did she know that eleven years later she would be playing these same songs as a member of the Marching Hundred at football games and on occasion in the IU basketball pep band.

In time, the basketball players, managers and coaches came onto the floor and walked onto the stage. The festivities included introductions by Coach Knight and speeches by the players. Last but not least was the unveiling of the NCAA first place trophy and plaque to the fans. This was met with thunderous cheers and applause. Buckner and May were in all of their glory, joking with Knight and the fans. What an evening!

After the formal celebration and the frolicking was over, Coach Knight set up a chair on the stage and stayed to sign autographs for the fans. A group of youngsters from about four to eighteen years of age lined up near the stairway leading onto the stage. This group of kids included Margo and Harriet, who were positioned somewhere in the middle of the line. Myrna and I stood back and watched with much delight. During his earlier talk, Knight had announced that he had just arrived from Washington via Philadelphia and that he had a cold. Although it was obvious he was very tired, he stayed and signed autographs for about two hours, until the last kid on the line was accommodated. When Margo got to him, she told him that he was very cute. He smiled, gave her his John Hancock and a pat on her derriere, and sent her on her merry way. What a day that was. During the evening, I overheard Coach Knight ask his wife Nancy to order pizza and to invite the whole team over to their home. He told her that he would join them later. We left Assembly Hall late that evening to go back to Indianapolis, and I guess the players went to the Knight's house to continue their unofficial victory party.

Since 1976 we have relived the memories of that season many times. I bought a phonograph record of the original broadcasts by Don Fischer, the play-by-play radio announcer for the IU basketball games, depicting the highlights of that basketball season. In addition, I taped the TV highlights, since the local TV stations replayed portions of that season's road to the NCAA. More recently, ESPN, the sports TV channel, had a half-hour segment on each of the recent NCAA final four and championship teams. I can tell you that watching the 1976 edition of the Indiana Hoosiers is still very exciting. Do you know the last college basketball team to have gone through the regular season undefeated and win the national championship? You're right. It was the 1975–76 edition of the Hurryin' Hoosiers. Thirty-two wins and no losses. This *was* the perfect season. Not only for the team, but for the fans, and especially for our whole family.

Chapter 7
Bloomington or Bust: 1976–79

In basketball, the championship is won on the court, in the heat of battle, unlike in college football, where the number one team is chosen by the coaches or media by a poll. In March, Indiana University won, and was crowned the NCAA champion with a record of 32–0. To our great surprise and delight, that fall we received a letter stating that season tickets to the Indiana basketball games had become available, and that we would be able to purchase two. We couldn't believe it. The team has its best season and some people were giving up their cherished tickets. You never know what makes people tick. Well, their loss was our gain. Hooray! The Lembergers would be a part of IU basketball. How exciting. When we took the twice weekly trip to Bloomington, we sometimes left the children at the Maickels, and other times we tried to buy tickets for them outside the arena from entrepreneurial students. You might be surprised, but we were always successful.

Our seats for the 1976–77 season's games were in the faculty/staff section, but unfortunately, they were in the next to the last row. Well, beggars can't be choosers. We were just glad to be a part of the festivities. When we did get tickets for the children, they would either sit on our laps or sit in the aisle in the last row. In general, the 1976–77 season was a downer compared to the previous few campaigns. With the graduation of four of the five starters from the 1976 NCAA championship team, the season was difficult at best, and then with an injury to Kent Benson (he sustained a back injury midway through the Big Ten competition), it was hard to salvage. With Kent Benson's injury, the heralded freshman, Derrick Holcomb, demonstrated his potential as Benson's replacement and certainly as a potential future superstar.

Unfortunately, the next year, he decided to leave the IU program and return to his native Illinois under Coach Lou Henson—probably the biggest mistake he would make. He had to red-shirt for one year, and I remember when he returned to Assembly Hall in Bloomington in 1979. It was the first game of the Big Ten conference season, and the game was being played the first week of January. We planned the return trip from our Florida vacation to include stopping off in Bloomington before driving home to Indianapolis. That evening, when the Illinois players were being introduced, there was the usual silence. I recall screaming at the top of my lungs, "Welcome home, Derrick." Although Holcomb was sensational during Illinois' pre-conference games, he didn't have a good game against IU. Despite that, Illinois won. In general, Holcomb's college career was relatively mediocre, which some attributed to a problem with his feet. My personal opinion is, had he stayed at IU and been committed to Coach Knight, he would have become a college superstar. I guess we will never know.

That fall, I received an invitation to be a visiting professor in Brazil. This was to be for a one-month period, with my lectures being scheduled to be given in February and early March. I was to leave on February 18th, and we were planning a birthday party for Harriet, whose birthday is February 17. When asked what she wanted, she stated she wished to see the Indiana–Illinois game in Champaign–Urbana, a request I quickly agreed to. Despite the inclement weather and Harriet feeling somewhat under the weather, possibly coming down with the flu, the four of us drove to the University of Illinois. I got tickets for us in the last row. We were elated as Kent Benson and the Hoosiers took a commanding halftime lead of about 20 points. During the intermission, the Illini mascot Chief Illiniwek took to the court and stirred up the hometown fans. When the Hoosiers returned, it was as if they had been chewed up by a buzz saw. As the Illini slowly cut into the lead, their fans became more supportive, and it was like a vicious cycle, the team and the fans feeding off each other. The few Hoosier fans, including Governor Otis Bowen, couldn't help our team as our cheers were drowned out by the Illini faithful. IU lost in what ended up to be a very close game (IU 69–Illinois 73).

In retrospect, since IU was not really in contention and didn't get an NCAA or NIT bid, I guess this was as good a time as any for my trip to South America. During my absence, Myrna and the girls continued to go to the games and kept me updated.

That year, one of the first rounds of the NCAA was to be held in Bloomington, and so I ordered advance tickets, hoping Indiana might be playing. As it turned out, Michigan played Holy Cross and UNC–Charlotte, with Cedric "Cornbread" Maxwell, played Central Michigan. In an attempt to see the games with the family, I flew through the night from Sao Paulo, Brazil, to Miami, and then on to Indianapolis. Myrna and the girls picked me up at the airport, and it was off to Bloomington. We rooted for Michigan, since they were the Big Ten representative. They won. After the game, Harriet and I took a walk through the corridors of Assembly Hall, where we saw Johnnie Orr, the Michigan coach. I stopped to congratulate him—as any IU fan would have done. He thanked me, and with a gleam in his eye and a smile on his face said, "This was my first win in Assembly Hall." I quickly responded, "That was because this was another first. This was the first time that I ever rooted for Michigan in Assembly Hall." He laughed and we exchanged salutations and he continued on his way.

It seemed like only a short time before the start of the next basketball season. In fact, everyone was anticipating the 1977–78 basketball season, since Indiana fans usually did not have much to cheer about during the football season. For as long as I can remember, the Hoosier fans' motto has been, "Wait, 'til basketball season." So when Michigan and Ohio State demolished us on the gridiron, we always could take solace that we would get our revenge on the hardwood floor. We hoped the 1978 season would be more exciting than the previous year's.

Happily, we now moved down about ten rows and I found out what makes the world go round. You guessed it. The green stuff. With that revelation, I increased my contribution to the Varsity Club and joined one of the major contributor categories, which entitled me to consideration for two tickets, if, in fact, there were any available. Fortunately, there were, and thus we now could legitimately sit together as a family. No more uncertainty and apprehension that the kids might have to be dropped off at a friend's house, as in the past. Thus, even for the soldout games such as Notre Dame, Kentucky and Purdue, Harriet and Margo had their own seats. For these games the average fan couldn't afford to buy tickets from the students or the scalpers. At times, they would ask five to ten, or even twenty times the face value. There is no doubt Hoosier basketball, let me correct that, college basketball in general, is big time. This is not unique to Bloomington. Unfortunately, it is one of the sad facts about sports in our society. Sports, in general, has become a big business, both aboveground, through legitimate channels, and via the "underground."

The Hoosier basketball team played well throughout the season, and we all traveled to East Lansing, Columbus, and Ann Arbor, but most importantly to Bloomington. Harriet was really into the game, but Margo could take it or leave it. She usually brought along books to read and humored us by seeming interested at times. Boy, was this all going to change. After the Big Ten season concluded, IU got a bid for the NCAA and the first game was to be played against Furman in Charlotte, North Carolina. That year we also had another Big Ten team in the NCAA by the name of Michigan State, led by the Magic Man, Earvin Johnson. Since they won the Big Ten championship, they got the privilege to play in the Midwest first-round regionals, which just happened to be in Market Square Arena (MSA) in Indianapolis.

Earlier in the year I had ordered tickets for this event for our family and for the Gebbers. They drove down from East Lansing for the weekend and we all went to the game on Saturday afternoon. That year, Michigan State beat Providence in MSA on their way to their loss to Kentucky in the regional. (Kentucky eventually became the NCAA champions.) As soon as the State—

Providence game was over, the Gebbers went back to our house to stay overnight, and the Lembergers jumped into our 1974 Oldsmobile and headed for Charlotte, North Carolina, to watch the Indiana game, which was to be played on Sunday. We drove for several hours and stopped near London, Kentucky, about 250 miles from home. The next morning we got up early to get an early start on the road. Everything seemed in order until we had driven about one hundred miles from Charlotte. Then, the generator light went on—at least, that's what they used to call it. Now they call it by a fancy name; I think it's called a Delcotron. Regardless, you get the picture. The car was giving us mechanical trouble.

It was about 10:00 A.M. and tipoff was scheduled for 1:00 P.M. We drove off the interstate and up a ramp to a nearby service station in Mooresville, North Carolina, where we were informed by the garage mechanic that the car needed a Delcotron. He informed me that he didn't have one in stock, but assured us that he could get one in about a half hour and put it in in a similar time frame. I paced in front of that garage's door like a caged tiger while they got the part and while the fellow was installing it. Everything looked good, but that was only on the surface. He couldn't get the thing to "sit" just right and decided it was the wrong model. I almost died. He removed it, went back to his supplier, got another model, and commenced to reinstall it. You could imagine my level of anxiety and my level of hyperactivity. It was now about 11:30 A.M. and we were "fit to be tied" and every other cliche you could think of.

When the job was finally completed, I quickly paid him and we were on the way. Since this was a period in our nation's history when the CB radio was at the peak of its popularity (it was actually a fad) and enjoying its heyday, we could take advantage of this modern-day technology located under the dash. Myrna, also known by the handle of "Kitty Cat," manned the CB and communicated with the truckers. My handle was "High Flyer," based on my previous scientific research involvement with marihuana. Harriet and Margo carried out their assignments from the rear seat positions. They were instructed to watch the ramps for any "Smokies" or "Bears." In retrospect, I have to admit that this was a highly irresponsible act on my part, and something a somewhat intelligent, sometimes mature individual should not have done. Surely it was something I would not do, nor would I want my children to do, in the future. But IU basketball is IU basketball, and besides, this was going to be the first NCAA game in which we could actually root for Indiana in person.

I zoomed down the highway, concentrating solely on the driving, and we arrived at the Charlotte Coliseum at 1:10 P.M. Myrna and the kids jumped out of the Oldsmobile with their tickets in their hands, and I quickly parked the car. Fortunately, the Charlotte Coliseum is not too large and our seats were easily accessible. With the playing of the national anthem, the player introductions, the TV commercials, and so on, I missed only about twenty seconds of actual playing time from the tipoff. What a relief to be actually seated at the game. Considering all the trials and tribulations of getting there, it was a pleasure to watch the game, which, in fact, was very exciting. Wayne Radford, who had been one of the team leaders all year, also played well in this game. IU pulled the game out by only a single point (IU 63–Furman 62). This was a game where many times it looked like we wouldn't be victorious. As we were celebrating this victory, little did we know what awaited us on the way home.

After the game we started the long journey, expecting to drive most of the way that day and evening, and planning to get up early, be on the road by 4:00 or 5:00 the next morning and thus arriving home by 8:00 A.M., just in time to get the kids to school. Well, as Robert Burns wrote, "The best laid plans of mice and men often go astray." Fifty miles from Charlotte a big explosion (well, maybe it was a little bang) occurred, accompanied by a puff of smoke that emerged from under the hood. I pulled off the road by an exit and parked on the shoulder. About one hour transpired while I tried to hitch a ride. I was finally successful and was able to get a tow truck to stop and take the car, and more importantly, the family, into the local town.

To make a long story short, the garage in Mooresville that

connected the Delcotron had connected the belts wrong. It adversely affected the battery, which was in essence destroyed. I was informed by the mechanic on duty that the whole job would take several hours to complete. As a result, we stayed in North Carolina that evening and leisurely drove home the next day. We all joked about our mutual experience, and the family became a lot closer as a result of our ability to come through this adversity together. After the car was repaired, the remainder of the trip home was fun. We called the school that morning and explained the situation, stating that the girls would be absent that day. I think both of them also had the sniffles and a slight cold, or some similar ailment! What is that, you don't believe that? What a cynic. I called in myself and took a day's vacation.

The next week, IU was to meet Villanova in Providence, Rhode Island. Since I had to be in Washington, D.C., on Thursday for business at the Food and Drug Administration, I decided to take Friday as a day's vacation and to go to Providence. Myrna reserved a hotel room for me, and everything went smoothly. She's the best travel agent I know and she gets the best air fares, room rates, et cetera. Over the years she has learned to understand the system and has mastered it. It's hard to know what the lowest airfare is or what specials the hotels are offering unless you are patient and can deal with all the bureaucracy. Ironically, while in Providence, I stayed at the Holiday Inn, next to the Civic Center, the site of the game. This was also the hotel in which the team was housed. It's interesting, because the tours sponsored by the university's Alumni Association had to stay in Boston and commute to the game.

This time, IU came out on the short end of the stick. Villanova 61–IU 60. At the Providence site, Duke subsequently defeated Villanova, winning the regional and advancing to the final four, where they lost to Kentucky, the ultimate NCAA champion. Since IU had lost and was not going to play in the Sunday game (there being no consolation game), I decided to leave very early on Saturday morning. I arranged for a cab at 5:00 A.M. to take me to the airport to catch the 6:00 A.M. flight to Indianapolis. I shared the cab with an interesting man, dressed in a

57

business suit and carrying a portable typewriter. During the ride to the airport I found out that his name was Max Stultz. I didn't realize who he was until we talked further. He was a sportswriter for the *Indianapolis Star* who covered Indiana University and Purdue University sports, and whose articles I had been reading and enjoying for years. I must have read his columns hundreds of times, but I admit that I didn't connect the name with the profession when he first introduced himself. I guess in those days I didn't pay much attention to bylines.

We discussed the game, and I must say his views were very professional and quite unemotional. He said the Hoosiers went about as far as, or further than their abilities could take them. Thank goodness run-of-the-mill fans like myself don't think like sports writers. If we were so logical, analytical, and calculating, a great deal of the joy, excitement, and enthusiasm would be missing from the game. It's the unpredictability of collegiate sports that sets it apart and gives the underdog and the never-say-die fan hope. The idea of a team coming from behind, in what otherwise would appear to be a fait accompli, a foregone conclusion, is what makes college basketball unique.

For example, in 1979 the Northwestern Wildcats, the perennial doormat of the Big Ten, beat the unconquerable Michigan State Spartans by about twenty points, whereas during the same season Indiana lost to Michigan State three times by significant margins. Incidentally, Indiana massacred Northwestern just prior to the Wildcats upsetting State. Similarly, consider the fate of North Carolina State (1983), Villanova (1985), or Kansas (1988) on their roads to successfully winning their NCAA crowns. We could all think of many examples where David beat Goliath, but if we thought of this in advance and addressed it analytically, we probably would miss good basketball games, and, more importantly, a great deal of surprises in life in general.

In the fall of 1978, as the weather turned cold just prior to the start of the 1978–79 season, things actually heated up for us. We were notified by the athletic department's ticket office that they were moving our seats, and that we would now be closer to the court. The seats were really choice ones—just opposite the

Indiana bench and Coach Knight—at the foul line extended. They were close enough to court level to see the players and Bob Knight's facial expressions, but high enough up so that we could see and monitor the whole court, and thereby watch the plays and the patterns developing. In my estimation, these are the best seats in the house, but, you know, I'm biased. Seriously, these seats are good!

Perhaps the most valued aspect associated with these seats is that we are in the middle of an eclectic group of diehard Hoosier fans. Behind us sit the rock specialists—that is, several members of the geology department and their wives and/or children. There is Professor Dave Towell and his wife Lindsey, who, incidentally, are both originally from New York State. Then there are the Suttners, Professor Lee and his wife Ginny. Lee grew up in Wisconsin. Behind Harriet and Margo are Professor Don Hattin, also with the geology department, and his wife Marge. Now, in my opinion, this group exemplifies the term *fan*. They are all extremely knowledgeable about the sport of basketball, and are very enthusiastic. Moreover, they, and we, all tend to be biased, thinking Indiana University can do no wrong. At times we feel the officials are turkeys and dead wrong if their call is against IU, but feel they are very knowledgeable and doing a superb job if the call is in our favor. Well, this is a natural response, isn't it? I'm sure this is not only true in Bloomington, Indiana, but also in Chapel Hill, North Carolina; Lexington, Kentucky; Lawrence, Kansas; and, I can assure you, in Madison Square Garden, too.

In the seats directly in front of us sit a lovely couple—Bernie and Marge Clayton. Marge is what the dictionary defines as a *lady*—gentle, considerate, a controlled fan, although at times she does let her emotions get the best of her in the midst of some of IU's basketball battles. Her husband Bernie is a real gentleman. He is not only an enthusiastic, ardent IU fan, but is also one of the world's foremost authorities on the baking of bread. He has published the definitive book on bread baking, entitled *The Complete Book of Breads*.

Our first encounter with the Claytons was not very pleasant.

Here we come, the new people on the block. Moreover, here am I, with a loud voice and a big mouth, a rabid fan who screams and yells. It probably could be said that you wouldn't need a public-address system at the game, and that they could just let me do the job. Bernie, who sat directly in front of me, was very patient and put up with me for the first few games, then he finally resorted to putting cotton in his ears and giving me all sorts of dirty looks, which I must admit made me quite uncomfortable. We finally solved the problem. He and his wife changed seats. He now sits in front of Harriet rather than me. In addition, I agreed to be a little more considerate. I have to tell you, it was not an easy adjustment, trying to cheer at a lower decibel level, but I did. Of course, sometimes I can't help myself, but at those times, Marge and Bernie are also cheering at the top of their lungs. We have developed a lovely friendship on our twice-a-week visits to Bloomington. Several years ago, Bernie gave us an autographed copy of his book, and he inscribed it, "To the Lembergers—without whom IU basketball wouldn't be IU basketball." We were deeply touched by this gesture and we cherish their friendship.

Directly to my right sat the Meinscheins, Mary and Warren. He was a professor in the geology department and also an ardent basketball fan. Now, directly in front of me sat the two most interesting people in our section. These men, both in their mid-thirties, were classmates at Massachusetts Insitute of Technology (MIT). Wayne—Wayne Winston—originally from New Jersey, has a Ph.D. and is a computer specialist in the IU Business School. He authored a text on systems and management decisions and is highly respected in his professional circles. His sidekick, Jeff Sagarin, is originally from New Rochelle, New York, and was a graduate student at Indiana University. Jeff's name may be familiar to you. He was once referred to in a *Sports Illustrated* article on college basketball by Curry Kirkpatrick, a well-known sports writer, as the "Wizard of Bloomington." He is what you would term a computer nut and is responsible for the computer power ratings for basketball and football in the widely distributed newspaper *USA Today*, and has a column in a variety of syndicated newspapers. It is interesting for me to read his weekly ratings, especially when I am traveling overseas. For example, on recent trips to Oslo, Norway, and Sydney, Australia, I picked up *USA Today* and was delighted to find Jeff's column there. It's sort of having a bit of home along with me.

Jeff is something else. He's the nicest guy you want to meet, but a throwback to the fifties and sixties. He loves "Leave It to Beaver" and "My Little Margie." We often confer on various aspects of sports nostalgia, quizzing each other and trying to stump one another. I have to admit that he is often the winner. However, as good as he is regarding sports, and considering that setting point spreads is his profession, he can't beat Myrna. Every game Myrna "bets" our house on whether Indiana will win or lose and by how many points. Myrna, being another diehard fan, always takes IU as the favorite and, more often than not, beats his special point spread. Recently, Jeff and Wayne and a friend of theirs put together a computer-based basketball game called "Hoops." They got Billy Packer to help them rate the players defensively and to help promote this unique undertaking. It's a great, fun game. After receiving a copy from them, I played it on my IBM PC and found it fascinating.

When we first showed up in our new seats, Jeff and Wayne didn't seem to be getting into the games or cheering much. They would sit with computer books or with a pad and analytically follow the game. To Lee Suttner and Dave Towell, the fellows sitting behind me, and to me, this was somewhat disconcerting, so I would periodically give these computer geniuses a hard time. Eventually they left their extraneous materials home and got more involved in the game and its associated activities. They even progressed to the point where they occasionally stood up to cheer when the Indiana band played its fight song, in an attempt to stimulate the crowd to cheer.

Now, the girl who usually sat to my left was a special fan. This is my daughter Harriet. Although at that time Harriet was only in elementary school, she had a special affinity and interest for Indiana and Big Ten basketball. She followed the newspaper accounts and was almost like an encyclopedia when it came to facts and trivia about IU basketball. At school, her male class-

61

mates in the fifth or sixth grade were very impressed with her knowledge level and therefore she often became the resource person when a group debate arose. I must admit that even I would often have to confer with her to answer some of my own questions about the team. Myrna sat next to Harriet with Margo's seat being to the left of Myrna's. At this stage, i.e., 1978, Margo was not very enthusiastic about basketball games, but this was to change with time, as she eventually developed into a fervent, rabid, fanatic—just like her father.

Early in the season, we received an omen that this would be a fun group of people surrounding us, and that this basketball experience would be great for our family. During the first game of the regular season, the official failed to make a call after an Indiana player was obviously fouled under the basket. The foul was obvious to all 17,200-plus fans, but as is often the case, the refs missed it. One of the people in our immediate group stood up and shouted, "What are you doing under the basket, ref? Picking your nose?" With that, Margo, who at times was indifferent about the games, leaned over to her mother and said, "You know, I think I may enjoy this season after all."

Since then we have had several opportunities to move closer to courtside, but have always declined. Where else could you enjoy the game and basically have an extended family? All of our group are just that. One happy family with a common bond: IU basketball.

Well, as you can see, 1977 and 1978 were good years for us as a family. We had developed and nurtured an interest in college basketball which kept us all talking to each other, kept us doing things together, and most of all, kept us all loving each other and thankful that we had one another. The other love it gave us was that for IU basketball. We were now an ingrained part of Hoosier Hysteria and the IU basketball tradition. There was no question where our allegiances lay between New York and Indiana. IU and Indiana won hands down.

Chapter 8
Back Home Again in Indiana.
Oops! I Mean, New York:
1979–80

Well, as you already heard, we had good seats in Assembly Hall and were excited to have a delightful group of people surrounding us at the games. Even before the first home game was played, things were buzzing in Bloomington—as a matter of fact, throughout the state and country. Bob Knight was making history. You see, the Indiana Hoosiers had been participants in the Seawolf Classic, also known as the Great Alaska Shootout, hosted by the University of Alaska-Anchorage. In the fall of each year, they invite several of the top teams in the nation to travel to the north. These extra games are not counted against the team's allotment, as dictated by the NCAA, and thus are considered as additions to their regular season. Indiana was one of those selected this year. IU finished the 1978 season with a 21–8 record and made it to the NCAA regionals. They were also supposed to be pretty good this year. Our family all sat around the TV in our red outfits and were stunned when IU lost to Pepperdine 59–58 in their season opener in Alaska. However, the real shocker came the next night when they lost to Texas A & M 54–49. Two losses in a row! Starting the season 0–2! This was unheard-of.

They appeared to overcome their problem and won the next game against Penn State before returning home for their regular season opener in Bloomington. There was mass confusion. The newspapers said Coach Knight had kicked three players off the team and put five others on probation. Knight had discovered that several of his players were smoking the original weed—you know, pot, Mary Jane—while on the Alaska trip—no pun intended. Well, with his dedication to running a clean program, and with his commitment to right, and to the parents of the boys he recruited, he discharged several of his players. One individual who was involved in this incident, but who admitted his participation and indiscretion, was the freshman Landon Turner. He was reprimanded by Coach Knight, placed on his best behavior, and allowed to stay with the team. Turner's impact on Indiana's basketball during the next few years would be legend and would become a part of IU history. Thus the Great Alaska Shootout was a disaster and was jokingly referred to as the Great Alaska Smokeout by some of the fans.

Despite this ominous beginning, the team rallied from adversity and basically held together. This team had the unenviable distinction of having to play Michigan State three times that year, once in Oregon at the Far West Classic where we lost 74–57, once in East Lansing where we lost 82–58, and finally in Bloomington where we again lost 59–47. Because of our friendship and relationship with the Gebbers, we went to the away game in Michigan, where the enthusiasm amongst their fans was great. They were indeed excited and effervescent about their team. They, in fact, still had the Magic Man, "Magic" Johnson, who was setting the league on fire. During that season, Myrna and I, and Gerry and Sandy would constantly call each other or send each other limericks through the mail. Some of them were classic. For example, one that Myrna wrote after the Northwestern-Michigan State game I particularly enjoyed. It goes:

There once was a team in confusion
Who suffered from one grand delusion
The team was called State
They thought they were great
But found Magic was just an illusion.

This interfamily, cross-state rivalry made the season that much more enjoyable and a whole lot of fun.

Indiana always plays Kentucky in a December game. This year, Kentucky was one of the top-rated teams in the country. They had just won the NCAA national championship (1978) and, as always, were loaded with talent. I had to attend a meeting of one of the scientific groups of which I am a member, the American College of Neuropsychopharmacology (what a mouthful), whose meeting was in Maui, Hawaii, that year. The weather was generally good, with lots of sun and ocean breezes, so my friends and colleagues thought I was crazy when I told them I was leaving on Friday evening (rather than staying over the weekend) to fly home to see a basketball game. Well, they were probably right, but, you see, this was not just any ordinary basketball game. It was Indiana against Kentucky. This is what it's all about. I took the red-eye and flew through the night, arriving in Indianapolis about 11 A.M. Saturday morning.

Although I was tired from the night flight and was hurting from my sunburn, I looked forward to seeing Myrna and the girls and to the thought of watching the game. They picked me up at the airport and we drove down good old Route 37 to Bloomington, arriving as usual in time for the pregame practice. I always like to get to the game about thirty minutes before tipoff to watch the teams warm up, to "kibitz" with our extended family, and just to know that we are safely in the arena and in our seats at tipoff time. This is better than being caught in a traffic jam or in the parking lot, trying to make our way to the game in time. The trip from Hawaii through the night was well worth it. The game was clearly Kentucky's. They led most of the way, but IU players responded to the home crowd's encouragement and to the circumstances, and soon closed the gap. With essentially no time left, Mike Woodson got the ball, came across the keyhole in front of the IU basket, and, as he had done numerous times in the past, put up a soft shot, which went "swish" through the net, tying the score and forcing the game into overtime. What excitement! Everybody around hugged each other and cheered heartedly for IU's gallant effort. In the overtime, IU eked out a 68–67 victory. What a day! It was well worth the trip back and sacrificing a little of the Hawaiian sun.

Later in the season our family journeyed to Columbus, Ohio,

as part of my teaching arrangement. We had good seats for the basketball game, near the court, and were really enjoying the game. We cheered loud and hard as we were confident that IU was surely going to win. They had an eight-point lead with one or two minutes to go. Steve Risley had just stolen the ball and was driving down the center of the court for an easy layup with two Ohio State warriors in pursuit. Now, as you know, Myrna and I are objective individuals—not at all biased. Risley was clearly fouled, and, as a result, missed the shot. Ohio State got the ball and immediately scored. The crowd went wild, and subsequently Indiana self-destructed as Ohio State kept fouling and the Indiana players consistently blew their free throws, allowing Ohio State to continue to score. This resulted in the game being tied 55–55 at the end of regulation play, and with all the momentum going toward Ohio State, they were able to win the game 66–63 in overtime. Now, if you think this was a bummer, you're right. As the old expression goes, "We was robbed." The after-the-game dinner with the Bianchines was full of the usual personal post-game analysis but nothing changed the outcome. IU lost a tough game. But as things go, there is always tomorrow. The season continued, and Indiana eventually split their games with Ohio State and Purdue. The Purdue rivalry was as intense as ever. We beat them by nine points at home and they beat us by seven in West Lafayette.

At the regular season's end, the NCAA field was selected and we were hoping that we would at least be candidates for selection by the NIT, considering that we did have twelve losses. As luck turns out, we got into the NIT tournament and went into what Coach Knight terms his third season. First is the preconference season. Second is the Big Ten conference season, and if the team and fans are lucky, we go into the third season, tournament play. This year, the Big Ten was well represented in the NIT (Indiana, Purdue and Ohio State). Indiana first played Texas Tech at Lubbock, a game that we watched on TV as the Hoosiers demolished the Red Raiders. The second game was scheduled in Bloomington against Alcorn State, an all-black school with a good basketball tradition and a very successful basketball program. They had just entered the NCAA Division I category, so initially there was a question as to whether they would be invited to participate in the NIT. Fortunately, they were. The game was billed as a contest between David and Goliath. Myrna and I and the girls sat very close to court level, and we were almost in shock as David almost pulled out the upset of the year. They had two guys who were very thin—actually, they were as skinny as rails. However, these two individuals totally dominated the backboards and pulled down most of the rebounds. We won 73–69, but only by the skin of our teeth, and primarily due to our facility at making our foul shots near the end of the game.

Now the excitement really started. We had made it to the next round, the semifinals in New York's Madison Square Garden. Harriet and Margo stayed with friends of ours, and Myrna and I went "home"—back to the Big Apple, back to Knickerbocker, back to Gotham, back to New Amsterdam. To say we were really excited is an understatement. We had two signs that we had gotten from the varsity club several years ago. One poster said, "Beat Ohio State"—our first opponent in the Garden—and the other sign, imprinted in red and white, was inscribed "Go, Indiana." We hung them in the car windows and started our journey east, Myrna wearing her red "Go Big Red" beret with its white pompom, and me in my red Indiana shirt.

We drove across Ohio and Pennsylvania and into New York State. This was a trip we had taken many times, but I must admit, this time it was really exciting for us since it represented the first time we personally were going to the finals of a tournament like the NIT. As we ventured across western Pennsylvania on Route 80, conversing with the truckers and other motorists over the CB, we noticed a station wagon loaded with people carrying a "Go, Ohio State" sign and a sign singling out a specific Ohio State player, Mike Cline, with his number on the sign. As it turned out, this car was also going to Madison Square Garden and contained his parents and family. Myrna carried on a long conversation with them on the CB radio as we traveled alongside each other on the highway. We wished them good luck and we both concluded that "May the best team win."

When we arrived in the city, we went to IU ticket manager Bill King's room in the Statler Hilton to get our game tickets. We then stopped for a quick bite, and went on to the game. Our seats were in the Indiana section behind one of the baskets in the temporary stands. It was exciting for us just to be a part of the festivities, and this was magnified by being so close to the game's action. The four participating schools that had survived to this point were Indiana, Ohio State, and Purdue, all from the Big Ten, and Alabama from the Southeastern Conference. Each had cheerleaders, a small pep band, and of course, a representative group of rabid fans.

Myrna and I screamed and yelled. It was gratifying to see Myrna so enthusiastic, since at times I almost felt she went along just to keep me company, but was not really into it. At the game, I sat next to a thin, grey-haired, distinguished looking gentleman named Herschel O'Shaughnessey, who, I learned, was an executive with Cummins Engine, manufacturers of diesel engines in Columbus, Indiana. He and his wife Mary were ardent Hoosier fans, but he had to admit that he had never come upon any fan as loud, determined, and persistent as I was. When it came to cheering, he commented on my stamina and how it was an attribute—that is, when he wasn't protecting his eardrums. Well, Indiana beat Ohio State 64–55, and Myrna and I felt relieved. This compensated for the loss we sustained to them in Columbus earlier in the year. If we got robbed before, I guess someone decided to make it up to us and to right the previous wrong. I could think of no better time than then, in a national tournament.

Now the final game of the NIT, the championship game, was all set to be played the following evening. Indiana was to meet Purdue. This would give my people—the native New Yorkers—a taste of Hoosier Hysteria and a feel for the intense rivalry that I had been trying to relate to some of my New York friends for years. Unfortunately, I would not be able to see this classic game in person. Strange as it may sound, I screwed up. You see, I was the chairman of the executive committee of the division of clinical pharmacology of the American Society for Pharmacology and Experimental Therapeutics (ASPET). Little did I know two months before, when I had arranged this meeting to be convened at the annual meeting of the American Society for Clinical Pharmacology and Therapeutics in Kansas City, that IU would be playing in the final game of the NIT against Purdue in New York City that very night. I either didn't have confidence in IU at the time or I was stupid. One thing is clear and that is that I am not clairvoyant.

After the Ohio State game, Myrna and I had arranged to stay in a hotel at the Newark Airport where the next morning at 6 A.M. I had to catch a plane to Kansas City for the ASCPT meeting. I had several committee meetings to attend during the day, but the important committee that I was scheduled to chair was meeting at 6 P.M. (Kansas City time) in one of the hotel's conference rooms. Well, enough is enough. I may have had to be in Kansas City and miss the game in person, but I certainly am not a masochist. I searched for and found some chalk, and then wrote a note on the blackboard in the conference room stating that the meeting site had been changed to my room in the hotel. I then went upstairs, put on my red shirt, and parked myself in front of the TV. Fortunately, the game was being televised by a national TV syndicate (Mizlou Network) and could be viewed across the entire country.

When the other members of the committee trickled into the room, they were astonished. They all were good sports and allowed me to conduct the meeting with breaks and interruptions at critical times during the game. One of my friends and a member of the group was Dr. Arthur Hayes, Jr. Arthur went on to become one of the best commissioners of the Food and Drug Administration, serving from about 1981 to 1983. He always teases me about that meeting in my room, and, I am sure, as a result of that evening he too has a warm spot in his heart and a better appreciation for Indiana basketball. As the final two to three minutes of the game approached, I suspended the meeting temporarily. I could not take it any longer. There is a limit to one's ability to deny himself his need for expression. Thus, everyone sat in front of the TV, either on the floor or on the bed, wherever the eight to ten people could get comfortable.

At that point the score was close, but Purdue was leading with only a few minutes left. Indiana had the ball, and a pass to Mike Woodson under the basket had just been stolen. Now Purdue had the ball, and it was freeze time. At that time, in the history of college basketball, there was no 45-second shot clock rule, and it looked like it was all over for IU. Purdue took a time out with little precious time remaining in the game. This was followed by Bob Knight calling three time outs in succession to prepare his team and set up the last series of plays. When play resumed, Purdue again reinstituted the freeze, utilizing a four-corner offense. Knight's strategy was that when the ball got into Purdue center Joe Barry Carroll's hands, IU would quickly foul him, hoping that he would miss the foul shot. He did, and Indiana got the rebound and possession.

Now Indiana was trailing by only one point and they meticulously worked the ball around, I expect trying to get it to Mike Woodson, their leading scorer. Well, it was obvious that this was not going to occur due to intense defensive pressure that Purdue was applying to him. Butch Carter decided to take the shot with about four seconds left on the game clock. He took an eighteen-foot jumper from the top of the keyhold. The ball hit the rim and eventually went through the net. With this, pandemonium broke out in my room. IU was ahead by one point, 53–52, with two seconds left. But I knew it was not over yet. As Yogi Berra said, "It ain't over till it's over." Purdue inbounded the ball and got it into the hands of Jerry Sichting in the corner, at the baseline at the far end of the court. This was exactly where Purdue wanted it. Sichting, an excellent shooter who went on to play with the Boston Celtics, let loose with a jump shot from the corner. The ball just hit the rim and bounced away. Close, but fortunately for the IU faithful not good, and certainly no cigar. Now, pandemonium really broke out. I was screaming and cheering and my friends and colleagues, eight to ten of the world's leading clinical pharmacologists, and Kay Croker, the executive secretary for ASPET, were all cheering along with me.

Now, that's what I call good friends. They all took pleasure in sharing my elation.

But what was going on back in New York? Since I could not attend the game, Myrna asked Bruce Reines, a young sculptor who had lived with us for two years in Indianapolis, to go along with her. Myrna and I had helped Bruce get settled and find direction when late in his teens he was having some difficulties. He was now living in Connecticut with his family, and so he met Myrna in New York. As Myrna related it, when she and Bruce showed up at the gate, Mr. O'Shaughnessey warned Bruce that he would have to fill a big pair of shoes—or, more appropriately, a big mouth—and that he was required to cheer loud to make up for my absence. Just the way I was elated and cheering wildly in Kansas City, Myrna and Bruce were at the same time in Madison Square Garden. We spoke on the phone later that night and relived the game and the evening's events. Well, when Myrna and I, the transplants from New York, each returned home, we knew that we clearly identified ourselves as Hoosiers, and that, in essence, New York was a nice place to visit, but Indiana was home. You know, as the song states, "Back Home Again in Indiana."

Shortly after the season ended, rumors surfaced that Coach Knight had been approached by Arnold "Red" Auerbach to coach the Boston Celtics in the professional ranks. Because of Bob Knight's friendship with Red Auerbach and John Havlicek, this was a distinct possibility, and thus these stories were taken seriously. Of course, all the Hoosier fans were apprehensive, but were relieved when Knight stated that he couldn't see himself as a professional basketball coach. He did state that he would not rule out some other career besides coaching, such as doing television color commentating—a profession that he, in fact, does well at, as was evident when he did some analysis during the NCAA tournament. With his declining of this Celtic job offer, the fans in Indiana breathed a sigh of relief. Now the fans and the coach could concentrate on the next year's prospects for success in Bloomington.

The spring, summer, and fall passed quickly. During the fall of that year, all the loyal IU fans kept busy cheering on their

71

gridiron heroes, who were improving. As a matter of fact, IU's football team, under the mentorship of Coach Lee Corso, did exceptionally well and would be playing against Brigham Young University in the Holiday Bowl in San Diego. This was to be IU's first bowl appearance since they went to the Rose Bowl in 1967. It is of interest because people say that I somewhat resemble Lee Corso. I guess it may be true. Three separate incidents to support and substantiate this allegation come to mind.

Each fall the athletic department combines an IU football game with an evening basketball game in which Knight's warriors play a visiting international team—such as the Russians, the Korean national team, or the Czechoslovakian team. Between the afternoon and evening games, our family and some friends went to the Pizza Hut for dinner. We were sitting near the salad bar when some of the IU football players walked by and said, "Hi, Coach!" You can imagine how that quickly became the topic of discussion over dinner. On another occasion, we were at an Ohio State–Indiana University basketball game in St. John Arena in Columbus. Myrna, the girls and I had seats in the front row of the stands by the railing. It seemed as if we were the only IU fans there. You see, by then Ohio State had become a power (with Clark Kellogg and Herb Williams), and now even the fairweather fans jammed the arena, making seats very difficult to obtain for the visiting team's fans. There I was, cheering and screaming as usual when two guys from Ohio State came up to us, leaned over the railing and asked if I was Lee Corso, the IU football coach. A similar incident occurred one Saturday as we were leaving Crisler Arena in Ann Arbor, Michigan, after an IU–Michigan basketball game. Can you imagine my disappointment when Lee Corso was fired? I could no longer be a "celebrity." I do have to admit that I was one of the fans who, in fact, wanted his head.

In early November, the college basketball issue of *Sports Illustrated* hit the stands. The cover simply had an Indiana jersey with the number one on it. This was certainly going to be the year of the Hoosiers. We had all the starters returning from the NIT championship team. Moreover, we would be adding one of the most heralded high school basketball players in the nation, Isiah

Thomas from Chicago. Isiah was said to be a six foot, two inch guard (actually, he appeared shorter) who was smart, talented and extremely personable. The other major high school player entering college basketball that fall was Ralph Sampson, who had elected to attend the University of Virginia. Late in the spring of 1979, the United States Pan American Team held try-outs in Bloomington, Indiana. This site was chosen because Bob Knight was the coach of that year's team. The Pan Am games themselves were to be played that summer in San Juan, Puerto Rico. Only two high school players made the team—Thomas and Sampson. In addition, there were two current IU players—Mike Woodson and Ray Tolbert—who also had the honor and privilege to represent the US. A few weeks after the final selection of the team, they held an exhibition game in Assembly Hall with the Pan Am team playing a group of IU alumni (Scott May, Quinn Buckner, Kent Benson, et cetera). As expected, the crowd went wild when Isiah was introduced. We all anticipated his playing permanently in Assembly Hall wearing red and white in lieu of the blue USA uniforms. I am sure he got a special feeling as the 17,000 fans gave him a special acknowledgement.

Well, that US Pan Am team went to San Juan and won the gold medal. But the trip was not without incident and controversy. Everyone is familar with the story regarding Coach Knight and the policeman. It was alleged that an altercation between the coach and a San Juan policeman occurred relating to the practice time for the US team in a local gym. Witnesses supported Coach Knight's account, but the policeman pressed charges anyway. However, the hearing never came to fruition.

Well, the entrepreneurs in Bloomington capitalized on this. One of my colleagues brought me a red T-shirt which had inscribed on one side, "Remember San Juan." On the other side it read, "Free Bobby Knight." I never wore it, since I keep it as a memento. It is a classic. In our household, there was no doubt that this whole incident was a setup and that Bob Knight was, in fact, an innocent victim. That is not to say that he may not have overreacted, but we certainly felt that the issue was blown out of proportion.

When the season started, all of the fans were proud of our returning heroes—Knight, Woodson, Tolbert and the new kid on the block, Isiah Thomas. This, plus the preseason number-one rating and the anticipation of a dynamite season, had us all excited. We started the season by winning our first four games by comfortable margins. The air was filled with optimism as we sat in the family room in our red outfits watching Indiana play Kentucky in Lexington. Then lightning struck and the tides turned. As in 1975 when Scott May was injured, the Hoosiers' fortunes changed. Lightning would strike twice, or possibly three times, in the same place for the Hoosiers. During the game, Randy Wittman began to limp—a twisted ankle, we thought. In fact, it was much worse. He had a broken foot and was out for the season. Well, déja vu. We were in shock, as, I am sure, was the team. This may partially explain why they lost to Kentucky by eleven points.

Shortly thereafter, they were scheduled to play the North Carolina Tarheels. Dean Smith's teams are perennial powers, and this was the first time they would be playing in Bloomington. Moreover, the game was to be viewed on national TV. It was scheduled just at the start of our kids' Christmas vacation. We were all looking forward to an exciting game as we purposefully delayed our trip to Florida to make that Saturday game an integral part of our vacation. We packed the car with our suitcases—summer clothes for the south and winter clothes for the trip down and back—and we started for West Palm Beach, Florida, via Bloomington, Indiana. Not the usual route, but hopefully one which would start our vacation off on a high note. Just prior to the game we found out that Mike Woodson would be sidelined and out of the lineup due to a pinched nerve in his back.

IU played valiantly, but lost. On the trip to Florida, we all imagined what the outcome of that game might have been had Wittman and Woodson been healthy and able to play. Well, that's life! While we were sunning in Florida and seeing the usual tourist attractions, such as the Monkey Jungle, the Parrot Jungle, et cetera, for the umpteenth time, the team was in San

Diego, California playing in a Christmas Holiday Tournament (the Cabrillo Classic). Each of the evenings that IU played, Harriet and I drove around the West Palm Beach area trying to find the ideal spot to get the best radio reception. After considerable searching, we settled down and listened to their game against Tennessee. We were elated when we heard the announcer state that Jim Thomas just made his second free throw, with only twenty-four seconds left, to take the lead. Tennessee tied it, and with two seconds left, Isiah Thomas made a layup, allowing Indiana to defeat Tennessee 70–68. The game against Brown the next night was much easier on our hearts, and as a result, IU won the Invitational after beating the Ivy League school 61–52.

The news seemed good until the team returned to Indiana, at which time information was communicated in the news media that was, at best, disastrous. Not only had we lost Randy Wittman for the year (fortunately, he could be red-shirted and thus was eligible to play another season), but now Mike Woodson, who didn't play in the North Carolina game because of a pinched nerve, was diagnosed as actually having a herniated disc and had to undergo back surgery. Since he had already played six scheduled games, there was to be no next year for Mike since the NCAA rules clearly stated that he could not be red-shirted. Thus it was almost positive he would be out for the whole season, and in his senior year to boot. What a way to end a college career. Poor Mike! Gloom hung over the heads of the IU faithful. Did the team have a little black cloud hanging over their heads? From the heights of elation after being on the cover of *Sports Illustrated* in November to the depths of despair just six weeks later.

While Mike Woodson had his surgery and was recuperating, the Hoosiers were just a mediocre team. In the first twelve games of the Big Ten conference season without Woodson, Indiana won seven and lost five.

One of these victories occurred on February 7, 1980. In fact, this turned out to be Coach Bob Knight's 300th career victory. Thus, at age thirty-nine, Knight became the youngest coach of a big-time college program to achieve this milestone. Unfortunately, it was a bittersweet evening. With a crowd of over 16,000 people, on a cold, winter evening, more controversy entered the scene. That evening, we drove down from Indianapolis in the chilling cold weather and settled into our seats in pleasantly warm Assembly Hall prior to the tipoff. I must tell you that the seats in Assembly Hall are theater-type seats. They are cushioned and quite comfortable. I guess, with the cold outside, the pleasant temperatures inside, and the combination of the comfortable seats and the thought and anticipation of a lackluster effort by the opponent, Northwestern, the fans decided to relax and just sit back and watch. During the player introductions, there was very little cheering. I must admit that, contrary to my usual enthusiasm, this evening I also was a little complacent.

Well, Coach Knight, being an astute individual, noted the lack of emotion by the fans and, despite the fact that the score at the half was 39–27, Indiana having a comfortable twelve-point lead, he angrily went to the microphone and publicly chastised the IU faithful. The crowd, displeased with this, booed the coach. When he went to the locker room for the halftime, his wife took the microphone to try to rationalize the coach's reaction. By now, the fans were somewhat hostile and, unfortunately, she got a response similar to that which he had gotten earlier. In fact, she then left the arena and did not return to see the completion of the game. To be perfectly honest, Myrna and I were not pleased with the fact that we were being lectured to for not being enthusiastic enough. Here, the one time in I don't know how many years, or how many games, that we don't get into the game, we get yelled at. Myrna was furious. She told me, "I am not a child that has to be reprimanded when I don't cheer." As a matter of fact, she almost refused to go to other games that season, and I had to coax her along. In retrospect, she was pleased she went, but still, the situation that evening was not pleasant. I had to feel sorry for Coach Knight who, I am sure, was expecting his 300th win to be taking place in happier circumstances.

One week later, almost as if a miracle had taken place, it was announced that Woodson, who had undergone an accelerated rehabilitation program, might return. It soon became definite that he would return for the Iowa game in Iowa City. That evening, we again sat in front of the TV set, going through our ritual of wearing red. Superstitious? Who says we're superstitious? At that time, the Iowa Hawkeyes were in the heat of the battle for the Big Ten championship, and it was obvious that Indiana was in for a tough battle. At the tipoff, Indiana—I mean, Mike Woodson—took off like he was shot out of a cannon. He made his first three shots in a row. Pandemonium broke out in our family room. We had the feeling that the Hoosiers were reincarnated and had just gotten an injection of adrenalin or some magic potion.

With Mike Woodson in the lineup, Indiana went on to win its next five conference games. One of these was part of a very exciting weekend for all of us. On Friday, February 22, we drove to East Lansing, Michigan, to visit the Gebbers. The evening before, Mighigan State and Indiana had fought a tough battle in Jenison Field House. The Hoosiers eventually won, 75–72, but the lead changed hands numerous times, and it was, in fact, a classic, exciting college basketball game. However, this Friday evening, we all gathered around the TV in the Gebber family room to watch another significant sporting event. The Winter Olympics were taking place in Lake Placid, New York, and this evening, the US Olympic hockey team was playing the Russian team. After a long, hard battle, which brought out a great deal of nationalistic feelings from everyone in the room and, I am sure, everyone in the nation who was watching, the US team defeated the Russians.

On Saturday, we all traveled to Ann Arbor to watch Indiana play Michigan. The Hoosiers, who were tied for first place, were in a must-win situation and were put to the test by the Wolverines. Indiana eventually won in the closing seconds by a score of 65–61 in what was a very exciting game. We all spent the rest of the day in Ann Arbor and then drove back to East Lansing that evening.

The next day, Sunday, February 24, we were supposed to leave early in the afternoon for our return trip home. However, our departure was postponed for several hours so that we could all watch the finals of the Olympic hockey tournament together. The US was playing Finland for the gold metal. What a thrill! Both of our families sat literally glued to the TV set as the US team defeated Finland. We all shared in the victory and felt proud when the crowd chanted USA! USA! USA! and when the goalie, Jim Craig, draped himself in Old Glory. It was indeed a proud day for the US of A.

Indiana's final Big Ten game was to be played against Ohio State in Bloomington. Harriet and I went with Dr. Bianchine and his daughter, Christine. In fact, this game was for all the marbles, since IU and Ohio State were tied for first place. The winner would be the Big Ten champion and get an automatic berth to the NCAA. It was a typical Ohio State–IU game, down to the wire and then some. It went into overtime, at which time Indiana won by the narrow margin of 76–73. What a comeback from a season that was filled with ups and downs. It was one in which Coach Knight and the Hoosiers, including, of course, the fans, could have easily given up just from sheer frustration, but instead went from the heights of euphoria after being rated number one pre-season, to the depths of despair mid-season, back to the heights of esctasy at the season's finale, by winning the Big Ten championship.

Since Coach Knight arrived, the tradition in Assembly Hall has been for him to let the seniors address the fans after the last home game of the regular season. After this emotional victory, many of the students and other fans reacted spontaneously and stormed the court. The public address announcer was trying to clear them from the floor to progress with the planned program. This spontaneous outpouring of fan enthusiasm delayed the traditional speeches for five or ten minutes. Harriet was furious. She was screaming, "Forget about the fans," as she chanted with the crowd. "We want Woodie! We want Woodie! Let's hear Woodie." Lee Suttner behind me was also irate. He was screaming, "Let the fans stay on the court and let them be a part of it.

They would never kick them off at Notre Dame." Well, finally Woodie did speak. The fans expressed their appreciation for his determination and for his devotion to them and to the team by responding to his every phrase with loud, thunderous applause and whistling. His extra efforts and commitment to his physical rehabilitation program had paid off.

Indiana was now solidly in the NCAA tournament and progressed on to the regionals by defeating Virginia Tech in the first round. That game was hosted by Western Kentucky University in Bowling Green, Kentucky, and was sold out. I tried to get tickets, but was told IU's allotment was only 250 seats, and so we had to watch it on TV. Next, IU was going to Rupp Arena in Lexington, Kentucky, a facility which seats 25,000 people, to play their instate rivals, the Purdue Boilermakers. Same problem—IU's allotment was small and so we also watched the IU–Purdue game on TV. The other teams included in that regional were Duke and the University of Kentucky. There was a great deal of resentment from most of the fans that Kentucky would be playing in the regional on their home court. I felt confident that we could beat Purdue and then felt we would unfairly be faced with having to play the Kentucky Wildcats. There was a very good possibility that we would be defeated by them on their home court, in their friendly surroundings. Thus, we felt Indiana would be cheated, never making it to Market Square Arena in Indianapolis, the site of the final four. This scenario was very unsettling.

Well, we had no need to worry. Everything went contrary to all my predictions and expectations. The good news was Kentucky was beaten by Duke, but the bad news was that Purdue beat Indiana handily by the score of 76–69. As you could imagine, we were all depressed for days. As Coach Knight stated, Woodie took us about as far as was humanly possible. Fatigue and exhaustion had finally caught up with him and the team. Even super efforts by Mike and Isiah Thomas couldn't avert the inevitable. We were depressed, not simply because IU lost, but because it was Purdue—our archrival—who would now play Duke for a chance to go to the final four in Indianapolis.

Well, let's face it. Purdue is from the Big Ten, and from the state of Indiana, and some of my best friends graduated from there, and, of course, they diligently root for the Boilermakers. In contrast, Duke is from the ACC. It was obvious who our household would be rooting for. It's like one's immediate family. You can call your brothers and sisters all sorts of names, but just let an outsider do that. At times like this, you realize where your real allegiances are and react accordingly. As the old expression goes, blood is thicker than water! I guess it holds for basketball as well, since we cheered Purdue on and they did get to the final four, along with Louisville, UCLA and Iowa. Imagine, Iowa and Purdue in the final four—two teams we beat for a total of three of four games during the regular Big Ten season. Is there no justice?

To even make it worse, here the final four was in Indianapolis, Indiana, my adopted city, and I couldn't even get a seat to see any of the games. One year earlier I had sent an application to the NCAA and enclosed my check for tickets to the game, along with 50,000 other fans. In essence, this represented approximately 200,000 requests in an arena that seats about 18,000 people. Fat chance! There was no surprise when my letter was returned with the check. I did try to pull strings to get tickets, but these efforts were also unsuccessful. If I had been a subscriber of season tickets for the Indiana Pacers, who regularly play in Market Square Arena, I might have had some chance of obtaining tickets for the NCAA final four, but since I was not, no dice.

Don't get me wrong with what I'm about to tell you, but personally, I wouldn't go around the corner to attend a professional basketball game, although I must admit I do watch the playoffs on television. That's just a personal bias and not to say that others wouldn't find professional basketball enjoyable. When I was a kid growing up in New York State, I loved the Knicks and I remember on rare occasions rooting for Bob Cousy and the Boston Celtics, or for Paul Arizin and the Philadelphia Warriors and rooting against the Syracuse Nationals and the Minneapolis Lakers. But something changed. Maybe it was because the Rochester Royals became the Cincinnati Royals, or is it the Kansas City

Kings? Or the Sacramento Kings? Or maybe it's because the Syracuse Nationals became the Philadelphia 76ers? Or that the Philadelphia Warriors moved to San Francisco and then became the Golden State Warriors? Or was it because the Minneapolis Lakers became the Los Angeles Lakers? Or the Fort Wayne Pistons moved to Detroit? Or was it because the Tri-Cities Blackhawks moved to Milwaukee as the Hawks, and then moved to St. Louis. Then they upped and left and moved to Atlanta to become today's Atlanta Hawks. Boy, am I confused. I imagine you must be also.

Maybe it's just the big, long season, and then the playoffs. Maybe it's drugs in the NBA. Or just the high salaries the players get. I don't know what it is, but I just don't enjoy professional basketball. Maybe, deep down, it's because I was a diehard Brooklyn Dodger fan, and as a teenager was devastated when they left Brooklyn and Ebbets Field to go to Los Angeles. With this move, they demonstrated no allegiance or commitment to the fans and fortified in most fans' minds that professional sports are just a business. Big business! I can assure you, Notre Dame is and always has been in South Bend, the University of Michigan has always been in Ann Arbor, and Indiana University has always been in Bloomington. I guess I like stability.

As I told you, I wouldn't go around the corner to see a professional basketball game (and we live only about fifteen minutes away, and I work less than five minutes away from Market Square Arena), but I drive about 140 miles, twice a week, to see Indiana's Hurryin' Hoosiers play. This is because, in my mind, there is nothing in all of sports that can compare with college basketball. It's alive. The kids play their hearts out. An example in point is the saga of Mike Woodson's senior year. Moreover, nothing can compare with the fans' involvement (student, faculty and alumni alike), the overall atmosphere (the band, the cheerleaders, the pompom girls, et cetera), and the overall excitement associated with college basketball.

Even watching the Indiana away games on TV has some beneficial attributes. Both the Indiana home and away games are televised. One of the sponsors of these shows has been State

Farm Insurance Company. Their commercials are classics. First, the telecast starts with a woman, dressed in a maid's outfit and carrying a broom, sweeping the hallways of Assembly Hall. This woman is singing to herself as she sweeps. As she nears, her voice gets louder and lo and behold, she is singing the IU fight song. In real life, this woman is Martha Webster, an opera singer from Chicago. One evening, she showed up in person at Assembly Hall and, with her broom, swept a path across the basketball court. Seventeen thousand happy fans, who usually only see her on TV for the away games, joined in the chorus. Another interesting aspect of watching the away games on TV is seeing the clever commercials depicting "another Indiana legend." These in fact, highlight the backgrounds of some interesting people who were born in the Hoosier State and achieved prominence. These skits are very popular and quite enjoyable, and include segments on Garfield and his sidekick cartoonist Jim Davis, John Wooden, Oscar Robertson, Hoagy Carmichael, James Dean, and Tony Zaleski, also known as Tony Zale, the boxer, who, incidentally, used to have his training camp in the Catskill Mountains.

As an aside, the TV announcer Chuck Marlowe also serves as the host or moderator for the Bob Knight Show, usually seen on Sundays during basketball season. I never realized, until reading about the passing of a Mrs. Marlowe in the obituaries, that Chuck's mother taught at a local private school, the Orchard School, and that she was, in fact, the delightful woman who was Margo's preschool teacher. It sure is a small world. Over the years, her son has worked hard to bring pleasure to our household by helping us to enjoy the Hoosiers and their coach, even while they are in such faraway places as Iowa, Minnesota, or non–Big Ten states where the team might be playing.

The Hoosiers of 1979–80 traveled a rocky road, but still gave the fans their money's worth. Well, since you know I was a fanatic Brooklyn Dodgers fan, I will give you the old cliche that I used to employ ad nauseum every fall. Wait till next year!!

Chapter 9
Good *and* Lucky—Philadelphia Revisited: 1980–81

We were disappointed that IU did not get an opportunity to play in the final four in Indianapolis. However, we realized that this was the start of another year and a new season, and that Philadelphia, the City of Brotherly Love, the site of the NCAA in 1981, was going to be good to IU fans. Fortunately or unfortunately, as the case may be, in the preseason ratings, in contrast to the previous year, the media didn't think IU had the ability to go all the way. At times, neither did the fans. It was a tough time for us in particular.

The Hoosiers started off the season with two wins and then had the pleasure of hosting Kentucky at home. We trailed most of the game. Near the end, with about two minutes left and the score tied, Isiah lofted an Alley-Oop pass to Ray Tolbert. It was perfect. Right above the basket and the cylinder. Ray got it in perfect position and slammed it down. Surprise! He jammed it into the back of the rim, and the ball caromed out near half court into Kentucky's possession. They scored an easy basket to take the lead. They held off IU and won 68–66. IU went down to a hard defeat. I can assure you it was a quiet ride home in our car. Not much humor. Not much joy.

Indiana also lost its next game, to Notre Dame in South Bend, and then won a few contests over marginal opponents. We then lost to North Carolina at Chapel Hill and finished the preseason at the Rainbow Classic Tournament in Hawaii, losing first to Clemson and then to Pan American University. Who? Yes, you read it correctly—Pan American University. As a consequence, we finished pretty low in that tournament's standing. It became obvious to those in our household that we had a big problem. Our overall preseason record was seven wins and five losses. Not very good since we didn't beat anyone who was ranked, and lost to some teams with far less talent and lesser reputations than ours. It has been said that when they returned from Hawaii, the team rededicated themselves. It also is rumored that at that time, Coach Knight decided to give Isiah a free rein, to allow him to improvise and sort of be a free spirit. Whatever it was, it worked. They were 15–4 during the Big Ten conference season, and won the Big Ten championship on the last day of the season. They were good, but boy, were they lucky. I kept my fingers crossed the whole season.

In mid-January of 1981, Myrna and a girl friend went on a cruise on the QE II. Since I travel extensively, I thought this was only fair, and so I stayed home with the girls and tried to plan enjoyable activities for us. It just so happened that Indiana was playing Northwestern in Evanston during that period. I called my brother, David, in Milwaukee, and a friend of the family who had moved to Chicago and who just happened to also be an IU alumnus, and invited them to join Harriet, Margo, and me, first for dinner in a Japanese steak house, and then the basketball game on Saturday night.

Not realizing that the restaurant didn't start serving until 6:00 P.M. and that tipoff at McGaw Hall in Evanston was at 8:00 P.M., you can imagine my anxiety in the restaurant as time kept moving and I knew we had yet an hour's drive to Evanston. I finally rushed the waitress to get us our check as we all gobbled down our desserts and hurried out the door. She followed us and told Margo, "Your father crazy, rush, rush, rush."

We got into the car and headed towards Evanston. When we got within a few miles of the arena, the traffic became very heavy. Whenever Indiana plays at Northwestern, there are a substantial number of IU fans who attend, since it gives them an opportunity to get seats and see the Hoosiers, and also because there are a lot of IU alumni in the Chicago area. This year, there was yet another attraction and reason for interest in IU, that being Isiah Thomas, who was from the Chicago area. Thus, his friends and followers all wanted to watch him.

Well, you could imagine my dismay at being caught in traffic several blocks from the arena with tipoff just a few minutes away. I parked the car on a side street and led the charge as we all ran alongside the traffic for the two or three blocks to the game. We arrived a few minutes late, and to our amazement, there were two to three times more fans wearing red than were wearing Northwestern colors. Indiana won the game, Isiah played well in front of his hometown fans, and a good time was had by all. After the game, we went out for a snack and returned to our hotel. A few weeks later, Myrna returned to find Harriet with the flu and Margo on crutches with a broken toe. Boy did I hear how incompetent a "baby" sitter I was.

When Myrna returned, the Hoosiers were doing well in the heart of the Big Ten battles. We desperately needed to win the Big Ten title in order to be seeded in the Midwest. This would give us a chance to play in the regionals being hosted by none other than Indiana University in Bloomington. You know, somehow I would not be too upset if they got to play on their home court. Forget what I said previously about Kentucky having gotten to play in Rupp Arena. I didn't really mean that it was unfair for a team to play on its home court in the NCAA. I was just kidding.

Well, to be perfectly honest, this thought process was all conjecture and wishful thinking, because realistically, back in January, the chances of IU winning the Big Ten conference looked quite remote. Iowa had beaten them twice in conference play and was leading the league. Thus, with only a few games remaining, all looked lost for us to win the conference outright. Going into the final two conference games, Iowa was one game ahead in the standings. The Hawkeyes had to play Michigan State in East Lansing on Thursday evening, and then Ohio State in Columbus, their final game. Two relatively easy opponents. So it looked like a sure thing for them. We also had to play on the road, first Illinois on Thursday, and then Michigan State the following Saturday. Even if we won both games, we probably couldn't win the championship outright anyway. Right? No, wrong.

Well, we were very lucky. On Thursday, Michigan State upset Iowa, and Indiana played well and beat Illinois. Myrna, I and the girls were fortunate because we had planned to visit the Gebbers that weekend. We would go cross-country skiing together during the day, and go to the basketball game in the evening. On Saturday morning, Gerry and I went to Jenison Fieldhouse and watched the IU practice. Bob Knight and Jud Heathcote were sitting near us in the empty bleacher seats, joking with each other. The Hoosiers looked good, and I kept thinking what would happen if IU won, and if Iowa lost to Ohio State. I quickly returned to reality convinced that this would never happen since Ohio State was having an off year, and because Iowa was loaded with talent. Certainly, Iowa would rebound after Thursday evening's defeat, realizing that the championship was at stake.

In the afternoon, we watched the Iowa–Ohio State game on TV in the Gebber's family room and with a few minutes to go, Ohio State had about a ten-point lead. It looked like all our prayers had been answered. This, in fact, was the last game for some of the Ohio State seniors, one being Herb Williams, and he and his colleagues decided to "hot dog" it near the end of the game—behind-the-back passes, fancy shots, et cetera. Ohio State lost possession of the ball several times in this stretch of time, and Iowa looked like they might make a run. As the cliche goes, they might snatch victory from the jaws of defeat. There I was, sitting on the floor screaming and cursing at the TV and the Ohio State players, especially at their coach, Eldon Miller. I always said he could never control them or make them play disciplined ball. Well, Iowa lost and now IU had to win. Our fate was in our own hands. If we did win, we would have the championship outright. However, if we lost, we would be tied with Iowa and they would probably be selected in the Mideast because they had beaten us twice during the season.

That evening, Indiana was invincible. The help defense was superb. Landon Turner, Ray Tolbert, Ted Kitchel on the baseline and Isiah Thomas and Randy Wittman as the guards with Jim Thomas and Steve Risley coming off the bench. Since our seats were at courtside, we could appreciate their efforts. It's an experience to watch ten young men, all ranging in height from six feet, one inch to six feet, ten inches tall, standing near you. You certainly get a different feel and perspective for the game from this vantage point. Indiana won 69–48, and were on their way to the NCAA. We waited eagerly by the TV the next day to see where IU would be assigned. Would they go to the Mideast regional, or would the selection committe make an example of IU and send them to another region so they would not have the opportunity of playing on their own home court? Well, the selections and pairings were out, and Indiana did get a reasonable seeding in the Midwest regional. Again, that's the good news. The bad news was that DePaul, the number one rated team in the nation, highly ranked Kentucky and Maryland, and other great teams were also assigned to that regional. It was by far the toughest of all the four regionals.

I was able to get only two tickets for the first-round game being played in Dayton, Ohio. IU was scheduled to play on Saturday against the winner of the Thursday night game between Maryland and the University of Tennessee–Chattanooga. Harriet, who had another commitment, couldn't go, but we "forced" Margo to come along with the hope and expectation that, if we arrived early, we might be able to buy a ticket outside from a scalper. This was our intention, and we were right, and, of course, lucky. Tickets were still available outside from enterprising "fans." Since our original seats were in the upper level, we took Margo with us, and she sat in an empty seat in the row behind us. At Dayton the court is made of a composition material and looks similar to terrazzo. It is not wood, as most basketball courts are, and it is painted a shiny tannish-orange. From our seats it was as if we were watching the game from the Goodyear blimp. Regardless, just being there was exciting, and we wouldn't have traded it for the largest screen television. There is no thrill comparable to being at an important game in person.

We played our first game of the regional against Maryland. This was, in fact, scheduled as the second game that afternoon. The first game featured DePaul, of Chicago, the top-ranked team in the nation. During the pregame, the DePaul fans were already shouting in unison, "We are DePaul! We are DePaul!" and "We're number one. We're number one" in anticipation of their upcoming game. We sat back and watched DePaul, the highly favored team, play St. Joseph's of Pennsylvania. We watched the game intently because we would possibly be playing DePaul next week. Their fans were now shouting, "We are DePaul! We are DePaul!" at the top of their lungs in a thunderous chorus.

Three students from St. Joseph's were sitting behind us next to Margo. One kept saying, "I can't understand how I let you guys talk me into coming here. We're going to get killed." As the game progressed, it surely appeared that way. Then St. Joe made a game of it. Now this young boy started to comment, "Well, it's not such a bad game after all, at least we're not getting blown out or embarrassed." Near the end of the game it became a very close contest. DePaul was ahead by one point and had one of their stars on the foul line with only twelve seconds left. The shooter, Skip Dillard, missed the foul shot. A St. Joe player rebounded it and dribbled through several DePaul players. As he approached the basket, he passed to a teammate, and the DePaul defense closed in on him. With this, this player recognized what was happening and dished a pass off to another teammate who was free under the basket and who made an easy shot at the buzzer. Final score: St. Joseph 49–DePaul 48.

Mark Aguirre, DePaul's All-American "superstar," picked up the loose ball and walked off the court in a daze. The DePaul fans were stunned. We were stunned. The three kids from St. Joe were elated and were in disbelief. Margo, who eventually recognized that this was a historic game, was cheering with them. The boy from St. Joe who didn't want to be there from the start was now shouting to his friends that he wouldn't have missed that game for the world. So, as is often the case in the NCAA tournament, the highly rated team underestimates its opponent and takes them for granted. As a result, DePaul went back to Chicago and beautiful Lake Michigan and the next week St. Joseph's would be playing in beautiful downtown Bloomington.

Now, Margo really got into the Indiana game, despite the circumstances of being "forced" to attend. This, I am sure, was related to the excitement of the first game. Our opponent, Maryland, who didn't do all that well in their regular conference season, was dynamite in the ACC tournament and thus got invited to the NCAA. They had the much-heralded Albert King from Brooklyn, New York, and another superstar, Buck Williams, from North Carolina. The Maryland Terapins took a significant early lead of 8–0, and everyone wondered when Coach Knight was going to call a timeout. He didn't. But despite this, the Hoosiers responded to the call, and soon took the lead. Then IU began to dominate. It was showtime, as Al McGuire and Dick Vitale might say. Isiah was feeding assists to Landon Turner and Ray Tolbert as they took turns dunking the ball on the fast break. It ended up a real blowout, as IU won the game by about thirty-five points. We now knew that we would definitely be one of the four teams to play in Bloomington.

Earlier that year, we had been given the opportunity to order four tickets to the Mideast regional at Assembly Hall since we were regular season-ticket holders. Of course we did, and obtained seats in the second row. This provided us with a good, closeup view of the action. Indiana was to play the first game against the University of Alabama–Birmingham (UAB). You see, not only did DePaul get upset, so did Kentucky and Wake Forest. So here was IU, at home in the Mideast regional of the NCAA with UAB, Boston College, and St. Joseph's of Pennsylvania. That was lucky because we could have hosted DePaul, Kentucky, and Wake Forest, all ranked powerhouse teams.

I had to spend that week in New Orleans at the annual ASCPT meeting, but planned to return home on Friday, even though the meeting still continued through Saturday, and despite the fact that Friday evening was the society's banquet. At that time, I was chairman of the finance committee and was faced with some critical decisions. Earlier in the week, three of us agonized for hours about how to salvage the society and get it back onto a sound financial basis. When the "work" was over, I informed the others that I was leaving on Friday to attend the Indiana basketball game. I explained this to Ed Sellers, the society's president-elect, who jokingly implied that "You won't have a good future in the society because IU basketball and the NCAA always seem to conflict with our meetings." Well, I did leave early on Friday, anticipating the game that evening and the weekend in general with a great deal of enthusiasm and excitement.

Dressed in red, our whole family drove to Bloomington. In Assembly Hall, there were about 250 to 500 UAB fans, 250 to 500 Boston College fans, and 250 to 500 St. Joe fans. The remainder of the 17,300 seats were occupied by loyal Hoosier fans in full uniform. Essentially, Assembly Hall was filled to capacity with these fans waving red pompoms, wearing red shirts and red pull-over sweaters, and causing the arena to look like a sea of blood.

We defeated UAB, despite the fact that they had some good players who, incidentally, we would see again the following year. The day after (Sunday), we played St. Joseph's, who, you recall, had beaten DePaul and then Boston College. IU eventually took charge of this game and won, 78–46, thereby earning a berth in the final four.

The following morning I boarded a plane bound for Boston, to attend a committee meeting at Harvard University. I was a member of one of the panels for the National Academy of Science Institute of Medicine which was assessing health issues relating to marihuana usage. While in Boston, I was curious to see what their local newspaper would report about yesterday's game. The *Boston Globe*'s article covering the event was very flattering to the IU team and its coaches. In addition, they devoted a whole column to the overall atmosphere in Assembly Hall and made special note of the fan enthusiasm. They specifically gave a great deal of credit to the fans, their loyalty, the tradition, the Sea of Red, and contrasted this to the program at Boston College. Well, the reporter was right. The atmosphere in Assembly Hall and the enthusiastic, diehard fans go a long way to making Indiana University basketball a total experience.

Well, Indiana won the regional and the right to advance to the final four in Philadelphia, where the other participants would be the North Carolina Tarheels, the Virginia Cavaliers with Ralph Sampson, and the Louisiana State University (LSU) Bengal Tigers. I called the IU ticket office and was fortunate enough to get two tickets for this extravaganza. I also asked our close friends, Gus and Peg Watanabe, that if they were not planning to go, could they, if possible, please get tickets anyway so that we could take Harriet and Margo? They were also successful in their quest for tickets, and we breathed a sigh of relief. This would be our first opportunity to see the final four in person. What a treat! Fortunately, it was to be played during the children's spring break from school, and I was able to take several days of vacation myself. Coincidentally, I got a call from a friend in Philadelphia who knew I was an avid IU fan. He invited me to give a seminar on my research at Hahnemann Medical College on the Monday of the finals. I agreed, and everything seemed to be falling right into place. In addition, Myrna found us a nice hotel which offered a half-price weekend rate.

We couldn't wait for Friday to arrive at which time we packed the car, put our red and white "Go Indiana" sign in the rear window, and it was off to the City of Brotherly Love. You may recall that that city was quite good to Indiana basketball in 1976. It was difficult for me to imagine that five years ago we were watching this event on TV and now we would be an integral part of the festivities.

We arrived in Philadelphia on Saturday and spent the day sightseeing. Of course, I wore my red jacket, and we mingled with many other red-garbed IU fans, especially in the sector near the Liberty Bell and Independence Hall. Later that day, we went to the Bellview Stratford Hotel, where there was a pep rally. The pep band was there, the cheerleaders, and even the governor of Indiana, Robert Orr. We also saw several of our fellow compatriots who sit near us in Assembly Hall. Everyone left the rally excited and hopeful that we could beat LSU.

On the way to the Spectrum—the famous basketball arena where Julius Erving and the Philadelphia 76ers play—we stopped at a McDonalds to get burgers and french fries before the game. At the Golden Arches, we met, by chance, several nurses from Indianapolis. They worked at Riley Children's Hospital at the IU Medical Center, just across the street from my laboratory at Wishard Memorial Hospital. After the usual thumbs-up sign and Go Big Red salutations, we all headed for the game. We took our hamburgers with us so we would be sure not to miss any of the day's activities.

The final four—what a sight. I had seen it on TV, but television doesn't do it justice. The Spectrum was packed with about 18,000 partisan fans. The area comprising the lower stands was divided into quadrants. We were in the midst of Indiana Red. To the left of us were the Virginia fans, decked out in dark blue and orange. Then to our right were the North Carolina fans in Carolina blue—you know what they say there, "The sky is colored Carolina blue." Finally, diagonally across from us were the purple and yellow-frocked LSU fans. In front of each section were their pep bands and cheerleaders. Myrna and I had two seats together in about row ten, just opposite the IU bench and Coach Bob Knight, while Margo and Harriet sat about six or seven rows behind us.

The IU and LSU fans each cheered intensely for their respective schools, while the other fans present simply sat and observed. I guess they were saving their energy for their own games. Myrna and I rooted hard. We watched the band director's signal and stood up like good little soldiers to the strains of "Indiana Fight" or "Indiana Our Indiana" as they were being played. We responded like it was second nature when the song elicited the phrase, "Go IU, fight, fight, fight" or when the proper timing was to shout "IU!" We had been trained and programmed for years to do this. We had four to five consecutive years in Assembly Hall which served as our basic training for the real battle. The one that counted. No one usually remembers who won the Big Ten in a specific year. Or even who went to the final four, unless they were the winner.

There are several other examples demonstrating this. For example, people in general can't tell you who the vice-presidential running mate of the loser is (I'm sure you have seen the American Express ad with William Miller from upstate New York, who was Barry Goldwater's running mate), or who came in second in the Indianapolis 500, or who even ran for president and lost, or who lost the World Series two years ago. Well, the same holds true in college basketball. Only the NCAA winner gets inscribed in the minds of the majority of people and memorialized. They don't sell T-shirts or sweatshirts advertising, "We're No. 2" or "NCAA Runnerups to the Champions." No sir, it's all or nothing. That's what makes it so exciting. Unlike college football, there is no question. There is only one number one, and it is decided on the battlefield—the basketball court, the hardwood.

The Indiana–LSU game was close throughout the first half and the first part of the second half. Indiana was losing. We were getting beat on the boards. But then the team turned it around and Indiana charged forward, dominating the remainder of the game, winning 67–49. The LSU players were devastated. They had been favored to win. At times I felt bad for their players, who were crying into towels draped over their heads. However, I had no sympathy for their coach, Dale Brown. He was never one of my favorite sports figures. I am sure a lot of the fans from other schools say the same about Bob Knight. I guess "that's what makes horse racing." Well, that weekend an LSU fan demonstrated his dislike for Coach Knight and suffered the consequences. The Philly newspaper said he started up with the coach and ended up in the trash can. After Myrna, Harriet, Margo and I read that in the morning papers, we knew we were in for an interesting evening at the finals when we played North Carolina. We were sure that the University of Virginia would root for their conference sister school, both coming out of the ACC. We had hoped LSU would root for Indiana, but with the turn of events, we knew we were standing all alone. In fact, that's the way it turned out. The Indiana fans versus the remainder of the fans present at the Spectrum. We had no allies in this match.

On Sunday, which was Myrna's birthday (what a way to celebrate), we visited with friends and did some more sightseeing and culminated the day with a birthday dinner. Then on Monday, we relaxed around the hotel until it was time for me to drive into the city to give my seminar. We arrived at Hahnemann Medical College at about two o'clock. Myrna and the girls decided to wait downstairs in the doctors' lounge until I could be reunited with them later that afternoon. I gave my seminar, totally unaware of what was happening in the world. Little did I realize the grave events of the day. Just after the seminar, someone entered the lecture hall and told us the president had been shot. President Reagan had been shot in an assassination attempt. I was in shock, as was my host and the other scientists who were just leaving the lecture room. I went down to meet Myrna and the girls, and before I could say a word, she immediately told me the news. She and the girls had been watching the events of the day on the TV screen in the doctors' lounge. Everyone was praying for the president's life and for his recovery. It was alleged that before entering surgery, he said, "I would rather be in Philadelphia" and that he hoped the surgeon was a Republican. Well, we were there, and above all we were glad that he was alive and conscious. It's events like this that put everything in its proper perspective.

The message was communicated by TV and by word of mouth that the NCAA finals would be played as scheduled that evening. This was in contrast to the Academy Awards, which were also to be aired that night, but were, in fact, postponed. Some people, such as Al McGuire, one of the better known TV sports announcers, were critical of the NCAA for going on with the games. Be that as it may, they played. Although the president was alive and in surgery, the country suffered another tragedy that day. Press Secretary Jim Brady was also injured during the assassination attempt and was undergoing neurosurgery after being shot in the head. However, in retrospect, having the games played may have served to take the minds of the US citizenry off the tragedy and furthermore demonstrated the resiliency of Americans and how we can go on, even in times of adversity.

The mood at the Spectrum was somber. In the consolation game, the University of Virginia beat LSU. That evening, just before the start of the second game, that is, the NCAA final game for 1981, everyone seemed to sing the National Anthem just a little louder and clearer. I know I did. No one felt like rushing through it, as is often the case at sporting events. You know, the fans are already applauding and yelling when the vocalist reaches "the land of the free." Things were different tonight before the IU–North Carolina game for the national championship. Moreover, everyone in the arena paused for a minute of prayer for the president.

Then things seemed suddenly to be back to normalcy. The ball was tipped up, and before you could say Jack Robinson, North Carolina scored, and soon the score was North Carolina 5–Indiana 2 (on two foul shots), then 7–2. At this point, with four and a half minutes of the game played, Ted Kitchel picked up his third foul and was replaced by Steve Risley. Indiana had been beaten by the Tar Heels by nine points (65–56) earlier in the year in Chapel Hill, and so another loss to them would not be a surprise. IU finally scored a basket, after five minutes had elapsed. We cheered and tried to urge them on, and they eventually tied the score at 8–8. North Carolina then went on a spurt and led 16–8. Soon there was a TV timeout, and IU regrouped.

In time, they narrowed the score, and with this we all started to relax a little. The start of this game was basically a replay of the first game we had played in the NCAA against Maryland several weeks earlier in Dayton, where Indiana also found themselves having to fight back from an early deficit. Three quarters of the fans in attendance were rooting against Indiana, but the IU fans tried to give their team moral support. During the early part of the first half when it looked like North Carolina was going to dominate, the North Carolina and Virginia fans shouted in unison, "ACC! ACC!" At this time, Isiah Thomas was in foul trouble, and Jim Thomas entered the game, trying to fill the gap. Randy, Ray, Steve, and Landon all tried to keep us in the game. Just at the end of the first half, we were trailing by only one point when Randy Wittman hit a shot at the buzzer. Indiana went into the locker room leading 27–26.

Soon after the start of the second half, Isiah, who again entered the game, moved into the passing lane, stole the ball, and drove for an easy layup. This seemed to be the turning point. Myrna and I hugged each other. Soon thereafter Isiah stole another pass. IU went on to control the game and with several minutes left to go in the game, the IU fans had their chance for revenge. Just as previously the Virginia and North Carolina fans had shouted "ACC," the IU fans now chanted "AC Who? AC Who?" We could smell the victory as we all knew at that point that we probably had the game won. Coach Knight played very conservatively down to the end. Now we all could taste the victory for which we had waited anxiously over the past five years.

After the conclusion of the game, the IU fans (including yours truly) stormed out of their section onto the court as the team was cutting down the nets. Ray Tolbert was waving the large black and gold NCAA decal. I spotted Lee Suttner—the fellow who sits behind us in Bloomington. He was wearing a red flannel shirt and was as happy as a lark. We approached each other, our arms opened, and we embraced. We were both enjoying the outcome and moreover we enjoyed sharing it with each other. At the game, sitting a few rows away, we also saw our next-door neighbors from Indianapolis. It seemed like everyone was there and was celebrating.

After a while, our family left the Spectrum, and we returned to our car in the parking lot. We had planned to stay in Philadelphia overnight and leave for home the next morning. However, we were so "wired" and stimulated that we felt we probably wouldn't sleep anyway, so we decided to drive as far as we wanted, and then stop for the night. In the car, the conversation between the kids and us revolved around the game, reliving every play, every aspect of the victory, and of course the festivities. It was a great evening. We felt fortunate that we had been able to participate in such a great year, one which gave our family yet another event to share. Once on the highway, we stopped for gas and at the station met several Kentucky students, who congratulated us. They seemed genuinely happy that IU had won, stating that they had been rooting for us. See, this was a significant event, since it indicated that there was hope and a chance for peace in this world. If Kentucky and Indiana fans can share a common goal when basketball is concerned, then anything is possible. We drove continuously from 11 P.M. to 3 A.M.

(about 200 miles), at which time we stopped for the night at a motel in Breezewood, Pennsylvania.

Late the next morning we resumed our trip, hoping to arrive home early enough to possibly share in the festivities in Bloomington (as we had in 1976). However, the team had flown to Indy earlier that day, and the festivities in Bloomington started shortly after their arrival at Assembly Hall. Unfortunately, we didn't get home until that afternoon, and were disappointed that we were unable to participate in the celebration. Myrna felt it was unfair for the rally to begin immediately upon the team's arrival without giving fans who had gone to the game the time to return to Assembly Hall and share in the celebration. I agreed totally.

We did however have our own celebration. With the discovery of the technology of the videocassette recorder (VCR), we were able to relive the 1981 NCAA games involving Indiana over and over. I had asked a friend of mine, Chuck Matsumoto, to tape the semifinals and the finals, and I had previously taped all of the other games from the regional sites in Dayton and Bloomington. Then we called the Suttners, the Towells, the Hattins, the Claytons, and Jeff Sagarin and Wayne Winston and invited them to a celebration party in Indianapolis. Not all of our basketball family could make it, but those who did enjoyed the day as we all watched in awe as Landon, Ray, Isiah, Randy, Jim, Steve, and Ted excited us once again. The play of Landon Turner throughout the tournament was, perhaps, the most important factor in Indiana's winning the NCAA championship.

Speaking of VCR's, every time we go to the ball game in Bloomington, I also tape the game at home. You see, it's fun to sit and watch the TV, critically examining and analyzing every aspect of the game. When you see it in person, you get to see the whole general picture, but you miss some of the specifics. For example, I am sorry to admit that there have been many—well, maybe just a few—occasions when I thought the official missed the call, such as a charge versus a block or when a player allegedly stepped out of bounds. In Assembly Hall, I would voice my displeasure loudly and in no uncertain terms. However, on closer examination of the tape at home, I was forced to admit that the official was right. But then again, there were many instances when I was right and the official wrong, so I guess it's a standoff.

Well, the season was now finally over, except that we still had the basketball banquet to attend. We always order tickets to the banquet, where Coach Knight and the players make speeches, presentations, and receive the senior awards and others such as the most valuable player award. This event is sponsored by the local Kiwanis Club, and we never know in advance when we order the tickets if, in fact, it will be a time for celebration or just a time for introspection. Regardless, Coach Knight always makes it a time for the latter, no matter how the team has fared. I guess this is why he is considered to be such a good teacher. This is evidenced by his often being voted as one of the better teachers on campus. As you know, as good as he is a coach, a motivator, and a teacher, he is also very controversial and does have a few shortcomings, for which he has received criticism. Certainly the Hoosier fans would be exposed to Coach Knight's shortcomings over the next few years, as well as to his strengths as a caring, compassionate individual. Unfortuately, his shortcomings often detract from his overall good performances and from the whole basketball program, and often would take the shine and polish off an otherwise sterling program and tradition.

This time the Hoosiers were winners, and fortunately, this year's banquet was, in fact, a victory celebration. We looked forward with great anticipation to next year. What a team we would have. Isiah would be junior, Landon a senior, and Randy, Ted, and Jim Thomas would all be back in Hoosier uniforms. The future prospects looked bright, indeed. Little did we know when we left Assembly Hall for the last of the festivities of the 1980–81 season that April day in 1981 how fate would alter things, not only for the upcoming season but for life in general. Little did we know what the summer months had in store.

Chapter 10
The Sad and Troubled Years: 1981–83

Isiah Thomas had played well in his sophomore year. Everyone knew he was a blue chipper and that he would eventually play in the NBA, but we didn't think it would happen so quickly. The decision of Isiah's good friend Magic Johnson to leave college after just two years of eligibility may have influenced him. No doubt the fact that Isiah grew up in a large, relatively poor family in Chicago must also have been a contributing factor. He announced that he would leave IU and play professional basketball for the Detroit Pistons of the NBA. Seven years later he led them to the NBA finals and had he not been hampered by injuries, they might well have won the championship. Instead, his good buddy, Magic, and the Los Angeles Lakers won in a close seven-game series. However, the following year (1989), he did lead them to the promised land.

Of course, we were all personally saddened not to have the opportunity to watch such a great player perform for the next two years. He, without a doubt, would have added much to maintain IU's tradition of excellence during those years. Despite our admitted selfishness, we were still very happy for him. He was such a charmer. I remember when we first met him in the lobby of the Holiday Inn in Columbus, Ohio, during his freshman year. Harriet and Margo went to ask for his autograph, and he sheepishly spoke with them, signed the piece of paper, "Isiah Thomas No. 11," and then thanked them for asking him for his autograph. We were glad that he was representing IU and college basketball in general.

Well, we finally psyched ourselves up and prepared for the

next year's season without him. Then the tragedy occurred. It was in late July 1981, and I was traveling to scientific meetings and making presentations in Taipei, Taiwan, Tokyo, Japan, and various cities in mainland China as part of the International Congress of Pharmacology. I was in Beijing (Peking), China, when a messenger came to my room stating that I had a telephone call from the United States. I didn't know what to expect. Was it from the office? Was there an emergency or an illness in the family? I went to the phone—you see, this hotel was not like a typical hotel in the U.S. There were no phones in the rooms; they were in a central location in the reception area, quite far from the room. Myrna was on the line. She told me to brace myself and explained that on July 25, Landon Turner had been in an automobile accident. He and some friends were driving to Cincinnati to spend the day at Kings Island—an amusement park. The car turned over and he was in the hospital in Indianapolis with a spinal-cord injury. She knew I would be devastated, but wanted me to know and keep me apprised of team events. You see, our extended family, and I am sure the same thoughts apply for other IU fans as well, include the basketball team. We consider ourselves as a part of the university family and it actually is just like one big family. It was traumatic for the whole IU family.

When I returned to Indianapolis a week later, the seriousness of Landon's condition became clear from reading the newspapers. We followed his progress closely in the media and attended special events designed to generate funds to help defray his hospital expenses and to help him through this trying time. We made contributions, as so many others throughout the state did. Bob Knight was a jewel. He personally set out to make sure that Landon got the best medical care and aftercare available. He sponsored fundraisers and although he was personally involved, it was predominantly in a behind-the-scenes fashion. But everyone knew that he was instrumental in arranging these activities and played a major role.

Although Landon would never again play for IU or professionally, he would never be forgotten in the minds of the IU fans. When I replay the 1981 NCAA championship videotapes, it is clear that it never would have come to fruition had it not been for Landon. This tragic event must have been especially hard for Coach Knight. On numerous occasions he had made Landon his fall guy and scapegoat, primarily, I feel, in an attempt to get him to live up to his potential as a basketball player and as a person. Although Landon was involved in the Seawolf Classic (the Great Alaska Shootout) incident, Knight put him on probabtion and allowed him to stay on the team. Often, Knight would bench him after having just inserted him into the line-up. On one occasion it was reported that Coach Knight would not allow Landon to practice with the team because he felt Turner was not adequately committing himself to his studies. I personally think Coach Knight treated Landon, more than anyone else on the team, as if he were disciplining his own son. Then this tragedy happened. It was obvious that Knight was devastated.

When the new basketball season started in November of 1981, IU still was loaded with talent, despite the absence of Landon and Isiah. They were competitive throughout the whole season, but clearly were not the dominating team that they would have been. They had Randy Wittman, Ted Kitchel, Steve Bouchie, Tony Brown, and Jim Thomas returning, and Knight had recruited a seven foot, two inch redhead from West Germany via Effingham, Illinois, named Uwe Blab. He also had a highly touted freshman from Fort Wayne, Indiana, named John Flowers. The enthusiasm of Flowers reminded me of that generated by Ray Tolbert, the exceptional center who had just graduated.

The Hoosiers' pregame season was going well. They had beaten good teams such as Notre Dame and Kansas State and had lost only to second-ranked Kentucky at Lexington. During the Christmas vacation, they were on their way to Madison Square Garden to play in the Holiday Festival in New York City and were sporting a 6–1 record. We viewed this as a great opportunity for our family to spend Christmas in New York and to see our team return to the site of their 1979 NIT victory. It would also give us an opportunity to visit with my sister and her family in the Catskills and to show Harriet and Margo New York City, with

101

all of its excitement and glamour. This was especially true during the holiday season, when the Christmas decorations and the tree in Rockefeller Center give the city a special charm and aura. Friends in Indiana who knew that we always went to Florida to visit Myrna's mother during the Christmas vacation break suspected that this trip must have been planned solely because IU was playing in New York. You know, our friends may have been right.

We drove east, and our first destination was the Catskill Mountains. I took the girls and my niece Ellen alpine skiing at a nearby resort. The ski slope was just behind the house where my mother and father had lived. This was, in fact, the first time Harriet and Margo had ever gone downhill skiing. First they took a lesson and then they skied on the beginners' slope. By the end of the day, they were feeling a little confident and really enjoying themselves. Outside the ski lodge, a young deer was walking in the parking lot. Harriet and Margo played with the fawn, and everything was just super.

The next day, my nephew Andy took me snowmobiling through the pine forest near the place I lived as a youngster. It was of interest to note that the Catskills had returned to dense, lush forest, mainly as a result of the disappearance of many of the hotels, roominghouses, and bungalow colonies that used to populate the mountains. The hills, the ground, and the trees in the forest were all covered with fresh snow. As we snowmobiled on trails through the dense forest, a deer was "spooked" and crossed our path. What a wonderful scene and an idyllic time. This surely looked as if it was going to be the start of a great vacation.

Several days later, we journeyed down Route 17, the "Quickway," then entered the New York State Thruway at Harriman, and headed to New York City. When we arrived, we checked into the New York Statler Hotel at 34th Street, just across from Madison Square Garden. That first evening in the city, we walked around Rockefeller Center and viewed the giant Christmas tree and the wire angels which were illuminated in a celebration of the holiday season. This was just great for Myrna and me, sharing some of our own childhood memories with our girls. We really did enjoy that family vacation.

The next evening we went to the Garden to see the basketball game, and as the saying goes, "Into everyone's life a little darkness must fall." Well, that's what happened. The teams participating in this tournament were St. John's, Kansas, Villanova, and IU. In the first game, Indiana played Villanova. The Hoosiers led most of the game, but then things went astray and Indiana lost 63–59. We were not very pleased since, at one time, they had been leading by as many as a dozen points. In the second game, St. John's, the host team, beat Kansas, and thus we would face Kansas in the consolation game the following evening. The last time Indiana played in the Holiday Festival Tournament had been in December of 1975. Then, the famous undefeated 1975–76 NCAA national championship team won the tournament. We had hoped the Hoosiers could repeat in December, 1981, but that was not to be. In fact, it was even worse. They placed fourth in a field of four after losing to Kansas by a score of 71–61.

Indiana was playing in the Big Apple, the greatest city in the world, and was unable to show the local media what Hoosier basketball was all about. For me the games were somewhat depressing. When the team plays in Bloomington or Indianapolis, they play to packed arenas of about 17,000 to 18,000 people. In contrast, in Madison Square Garden, the most famous basketball court in the nation, they played to relatively small crowds, and worse, to relatively disinterested fans who, it was obvious, were simply waiting for St. John's to play Villanova. It's not easy being the "preliminary" game or playing in the consolation game. Except for the handful of Hoosier faithful, not too many people in the stands rooted for IU. Perhaps all of these factors were instrumental and played a role in Bob Knight's decision that his teams would no longer play in out-of-town Christmas-vacation tournaments. They already played in Bloomington as the host of the Indiana Classic and they were instituting a new tournament, the Hoosier Classic, to be played at Market Square Arena in Indianapolis. This latter classic would start the following year. Thus they would now play both tournaments in front of their own fans and would not have to travel during the vacation.

All in all, we were glad we made the trip back to the Catskills and to New York City. Margo, who had aspirations of being in the theater, really enjoyed our walks down Times Square and through the Broadway theater district. Likewise, we all enjoyed Rockefeller Center and the city's holiday spirit, and, I must admit, the dinner atmosphere at Mama Leone's is special at Christmastime. All of these activities certainly brought back fond memories of earlier times, when we lived in New York. The whole trip was very memorable.

The following day, we started our journey back to Indiana. We did it at a leisurely pace and tried to psyche ourselves up to get ready to return to work and school. We knew it wouldn't be easy to get back into our regular daily activities. We hoped that the IU basketball team would be able to do the same, and thus would be ready to fire up and "burn up" the Big Ten Conference.

They opened the season in early January 1982, at East Lansing against Michigan State, and so we once more donned our red uniforms, and become boob tube fans. IU looked atrocious. They made numerous turnovers and the final result was a devastating 65–58 loss. They next traveled to Northwestern University in Evanston, Illinois. Surely, the three-game losing streak would be terminated here. We hadn't lost to Northwestern since 1970, and they were usually the Big Ten's cellar team. We again faithfully dressed for play and watched the game on TV. What a disaster! The Hoosiers played poorly again, with poor execution and numerous turnovers. The final score was Northwestern 75–IU 61. IU had lost to the Wildcats by fourteen points! Not only was it a disappointment, but a humiliation. Here was IU, now with four consecutive losses, 0 and 2 in the Big Ten and an overall record of 6 and 5. This surely was a new all-time low for IU fans.

The next week, when we finally returned to Assembly Hall in Bloomington for the first home game of the Big Ten season, no one knew what to expect. Would they continue on the skids, or would they snap out of it? With great fan support, Indiana virtually destroyed Michigan by a score of 81–51. The Hoosier fans always support their team, but it seemed they respond especially well for the big games such as Purdue and Kentucky. Just one step below them in the rivalry ranking list are Michigan and Ohio State—maybe this is related to how these two schools usually manhandle IU during the football games.

The rest of the Big Ten season was generally positive, with IU winning 11 of the remaining 15 conference games and finishing the conference season with a final Big Ten record of 12 wins and 6 losses. Despite their poor start, the Hoosiers ended the season tied for second place. Fortunately, this was sufficient to get them a bid to the NCAA, and considering what had transpired in the preseason and the difficulties the team had midseason, we were all quite pleased with the outcome. Minnesota, which had won the Big Ten championship, was assigned to the Mideast Regional, which was being played in Indianapolis. I had mailed my order for seats for the Mideast Regional as soon as I saw the ad in the local newspaper. As a result, I had two seats in the second row, essentially at courtside. Some of the other teams assigned to play in Indianapolis were Virginia with superstar Ralph Sampson and Tennessee with All-American Dale Ellis. Both were fantastic ball players. Indiana had drawn the other Mid-East Regional site in Nashville, Tennessee, which was being hosted by Vanderbilt University. The games at the Vanderbilt site were to be played on Thursday and Saturday, while those at Market Square Arena were scheduled for Friday and Sunday. This way, all of the sites have the opportunity to be viewed on television.

Myrna and I were fortunate to get tickets for Indiana's Thursday evening first-round game against Robert Morris, which was being played in Nashville, about a six-hour drive from Indianapolis. Myrna was notified by phone early Thursday morning that we had seats, so I arranged to leave at about noon that day. Since I was doing clinical studies, I was unable to leave any sooner. She picked me up at the hospital and we headed south to Nashville. Margo and Harriet had school, and they stayed with friends that evening. What I am now about to tell you sounds crazy. In retrospect, even I think it's crazy. What an ex-

105

perience! What a week! Never again!

Well, Myrna and I drove to Nashville. Fortunately, it was not snowing, but there were scattered showers and fine, drizzling rain as we traveled south. Because it was a long trip, we knew we didn't have much time to spare. As we drove through the Kentucky countryside, we were impressed by the low clouds settling in and about the mountains and by the extensive degree of road construction. Little did we know what a nightmare this would be later that evening on the return trip home.

As we drove through the Bluegrass State, we found ourselves in a caravan with many Kentucky Wildcat fans. You see, the University of Kentucky was to play the second game of the evening against Middle Tennessee. As a result, everyone was talking about how valuable the tickets for this regional were because the Louisville Cardinals were also playing at this site and they could eventually wind up playing Kentucky. However, Louisville, being the seeded team in the regional, received a bye and would play the winner of the Kentucky Wildcats–Middle Tennessee game. For most fans it was a drawn conclusion that Louisville and Kentucky would finally meet at the regional in Nashville, after a long hiatus of about twenty years. It seemed these two teams, geographically located only sixty miles apart, would finally have their long-awaited match. This was to be the hottest game and the most valuable ticket of the decade. The rumors were that because of this possibility, tickets for this regional event were selling for $300 each so the fans could see the Saturday matchup between these two perennial powers from the Bluegrass State. It was said that Kentucky and its coach, Joe B. Hall, refused to schedule Louisville since it might give credibility to Denny Crum and the Cardinal program. Whatever the reason, it appeared that what the universities and their athletic directors could not, or would not, arrange would become a reality due to the NCAA pairings.

When we arrived at Vanderbilt's arena, I inquired about tickets for Saturday's game, since we wanted to take Margo along. Harriet, a senior in high school, had another commitment and could not go with us. I can assure you the scalpers were, in fact, asking for $300 a ticket for the "game of the decade." I even tried to trade one or two of my tickets to some Tennessee fans for the University of Tennessee Volunteers' game in Indianapolis, where they were playing in the NCAA, for a ticket for Saturday's Indiana game, but there were no takers. I couldn't even get a "Volunteer" to volunteer. We entered the arena and went directly to our seats in the end of the court. These were in stands which one could best describe as the balcony or mezzanine. Viewing the Vanderbilt court for the first time was something of a surprise to me. I have seen many basketball courts in my years, but this was the first time I ever saw one in which the teams sat at each end of the court, rather than along the side.

In the first ball game, Indiana handily beat Robert Morris. They played exceptionally well and led throughout. Robert Morris, a school from the east, had gotten to the NCAA by defeating my alma mater, LIU, but they were no match for IU. It was an easy win for Indiana, who defeated their opponent by thirty-two points (94–62).

Knowing that I had to be at work the next morning, Myrna and I decided to drive home right after the IU game and elected to listen to the Kentucky–Middle Tennessee game on the car radio. We were confident that it was a sure thing and that Kentucky would win by a blowout. Thus, we left the area shortly after 9:30 P.M. By the time we got onto the expressway (Route I-65 heading north) and made our way out of the city of Nashville, it was obvious that the drive home would not be a relaxing or leisurely one. The fog was as thick as soup. I felt that in order to see the road, I almost needed to keep my face right up against the windshield. I drove cautiously and quite slowly as we were keenly aware of the road construction which was underway throughout the whole Kentucky countryside.

Another thing we were becoming acutely aware of was that the Kentucky basketball team was in deep trouble, and that they were having a great deal of difficulty with Middle Tennessee. As the game progressed and as the underdogs forced more Kentucky turnovers, it was clear that there might be a major upset in the making. The final outcome was just that. In fact, Middle Ten-

107

nessee won. Myrna and I joked about the poor fans who unsuspectingly had actually paid $300 for tickets to see Louisville play Middle Tennessee on Saturday. In fact, when we drove back down to Nashville on Saturday, we decided to take Margo along with us, confident that we could get her a ticket at the listed price. We were right!

As we continued on our trek home Thursday evening, we finally drove out of the fog when we were about fifty miles south of Louisville. It was only at this point that we were able to make reasonable time the remainder of the way home. We arrived at our house at about 4:00 in the morning (now Friday) and I slept for a few hours before going to work. That evening I went to Market Square Arena to watch the other half of the Mid-East Regional. In fact, this was a piece of cake since it was in Indianapolis. After a good night's sleep, I arose on Saturday morning and it was on the road again. Didn't Willie Nelson write a song like that? Well, it was off to Nashville again. Back down Route I-65 through southern Indiana, through Kentucky, and into Tennessee. As we drove down the highway, we interacted with many Louisville fans who displayed "Go Cards" placards in their windows. We exchanged thumbs-up gestures with them, and everyone seemed to be in a festive mood.

Unfortunately, ours was premature. We were to play the University of Alabama–Birmingham (UAB), a team we had played last year in the NCAA regionals in Bloomington. I guess they really wanted revenge, because from the tipoff, they played like they were literally shot out of a cannon. They were as hot as the proverbial house on fire. UAB didn't appear to miss a shot. Mind you, IU didn't play poorly, it was just that they were no match for the highly motivated UAB team. Alabama–Birmingham had a huge lead at the half, and continued to pour it on after the intermission. Although IU played valiantly, trying desperately to get back into the game, its efforts were for naught, and the Hoosiers lost 80–70. UAB thus progressed to the second round of the Mid-East Regional, to be played the following week on its home court. It eventually lost, and thus did not progress to the final four.

After the game, we drove home at a leisurely pace and decided to spend the evening in a motel in Bowling Green, Kentucky. We called Harriet at home, and she commiserated with us about our team's loss. To be honest, I was not confident that IU could have gone all the way, but, in fact, stranger things had been known to happen, as when the North Carolina State Wolfpack team won the NCAA championship in 1983.

The next morning we returned to Indianapolis, just in time for me to rest awhile and then go back to Market Square Arena to see the remainder of the Mideast Regional that afternoon. Minnesota played the University of Tennessee–Chattanooga, and Virginia played Tennessee. I asked Dave Towell, who sits behind me in Assembly Hall, to join me, since Myrna refused to go. As she stated, "I'm all basketballed out." Well, I told you that this was a crazy week. I assure you that this is not a schedule which I intend to undertake again, or if I do, I will promptly visit a psychiatrist to talk me out of it and to have my head examined.

The summer passed quickly and in the fall of 1982, we and the other Indiana fans were very optimistic. This was for good reason, since we essentially had the complete team returning from the 1981–82 campaign. This was a team which might have progressed to the regional finals had not the UAB team played exceptionally well in what was probably their best effort of the season. Coach Knight had Wittman, Kitchel, Bouchie, Brown, and Jim Thomas returning as seniors. All were seasoned players who had contributed to the 1981 NCAA championship. He also had some good recruits, including Winston Morgan and Stew Robinson from Anderson, Indiana, and Mike Giomi, the number-one high school player from Ohio. Moreover, Uwe Blab had a year's experience under his belt. The Hoosiers looked good. We saw them play many times in the preseason, and I can assure you we liked what we saw. They finished the preseason schedule with ten wins and no losses and were highly ranked with victories over Notre Dame, Kansas State, Texas–El Paso and second-ranked Kentucky. Everything looked rosy. However, one thing had changed in our family situation. Harriet was now a freshman at the University of Michigan and thoroughly involved in the Wolverine sports scene at Ann Arbor.

During that Christmas holiday, the very first Hoosier Classic was being held in Indianapolis' Market Square Arena. I personally did not attend, but Myrna, despite not feeling well, went with Margo. We also had house guests—Jeff Sagarin and Wayne Winston—who came to Indy for the games and stayed at our house. Myrna prepared an ethnic dinner, including her famous matzo-ball soup, and they all relaxed by watching the oldtime TV shows, including "Leave It To Beaver."

Why would I miss such a festive event? Well, because I finally made it to the Rose Bowl, in Pasadena, California. Myrna and I, and our family, are not only avid basketball fans, but as I mentioned, we also follow Indiana University football. We attend all the home games and, when possible, drive to the away games, making each a mini-vacation. Harriet, who had started college in Ann Arbor in August 1982, wanted to try out for the Michigan marching band, since she had been a member of her high school band. I was somewhat skeptical about her trying out, not wanting her to be hurt if she didn't make it, but Myrna was very supportive and encouraged her. This shows you why it's good to have two parents—you can take the best of each.

Well, you guessed it—a dyed-in-the-wool IU fan, Harriet was now a member in good standing, or should I say good marching, of the University of Michigan Marching Band. That year, one of Michigan's early season home games featured IU as its opponent, or should I say, victim. Myrna and I traveled to Ann Arbor, as did the Indiana University Marching Hundred. As the red and white attired IU band marched onto and across the field during its entry procedure, and the IU fight song was being played, Harriet stood up in her blue and gold Michigan uniform. Very embarrassed, she told her fellow band members, "Old habits die hard." I told you we were programmed to this response.

This year, the Michigan football team had won the Big Ten and the team and the band were going to the Rose Bowl. Harriet came home for the holiday and then returned to Ann Arbor to make the trip to Pasadena. Myrna, who had just gotten over a hospital stay due to pneumonia, elected not to make the trip to California, and so I went to the Rose Bowl with a friend of mine from the Catskills—Red Hedman, who now lives in the San Francisco Bay Area. Myrna stayed home and she and Margo cheered IU's basketball team on to victory at the inaugural Hoosier Classic. It was an exciting time, but sad in a way—it was the first New Year's Eve in twenty-seven years Myrna and I did not spend together. She assured me it would be the last. The University of Michigan band was performing a concert at the Century Plaza Hotel in Los Angeles and Myrna's sister Helen and her family drove from Huntington Beach to share in the festivities.

Harriet returned to Ann Arbor in the beginning of January 1983, but flew back home later that semester to see the IU–Michigan game in Bloomington, where her favorite player, Randy Wittman, scored twenty-two points to lead the Hoosiers to a one-sided victory. At one point, Indiana had been leading by more than thirty-three points. That April, she again flew home for the IU basketball banquet sponsored by the Suburban Bloomington Kiwanis. This annual event honors the team, especially the seniors, one of whom was Randy. As a matter of fact, when Randy Wittman was a freshman at IU, a friend of mine who knew Randy and his coach when he was attending Ben Davis High School in Indianapolis got a picture for Harriet of Randy in his Indiana High School All-Star uniform. This evening, Harriet wore her U of M band jacket to the banquet and was approached by the director of the IU Marching Band, Wilbur England, who coincidentally was a U of M alumnus and a past member of their band. They shared their common stories about the band and Ann Arbor.

Despite having gone 10–0 in the preconference, IU started the 1983 Big Ten season on a low note. They lost their initial Big Ten game to Ohio State on the road. However, they went on to lose just two other times prior to that fateful day late in the season in Michigan when Ted Kitchel was injured. Both these loss-were at the hands of Iowa, first in Iowa City (63–48), then later in Bloomington. Even after this tough loss to Iowa by just one point at home (58–57), they were still in the hunt for the Big Ten title

111

when they traveled north of the state border to play their last two away games in Michigan. First they played in Ann Arbor on Thursday evening. As we watched the game on our television set in our family room, Indiana was doing well. Then we sat stunned and in amazement when another unexpected incident occurred. We all felt like saying, "Oh no, not again." First Scott May, next Mike Woodson, then Landon Turner and now Ted Kitchel. Kitchel had somehow injured his back when he hit the floor after taking a jump shot, and he had to be escorted from the court. From that point on, the IU players performed as if they were stunned and in a state of shock. They lost the game 69–56.

Our family left Indianapolis on Friday afternoon for our annual trek to East Lansing. Harriet met us at the Gebbers', and we all looked forward to a nice weekend of cross-country skiing with their family on Saturday, and then going on to the game that night. Unfortunately for IU's basketball fans, the news that evening was not very positive. Ted Kitchel had been diagnosed as having a herniated disk and would soon be undergoing surgery. Meanwhile, the Spartans, led by their playmaker Scott Skiles, were performing surgery on the Hoosiers. Skiles, a native of Plymouth, Indiana, who had led his team to the state's high school championship in Indianapolis, took great pleasure in playing well and in winning against IU and Purdue—I guess because neither of these schools recruited him. Skiles eventually went on to become a first-team All-American in his senior year at Michigan State. That evening, the Michigan State Spartans played well and unfortunately defeated a gallant IU team, who at times still seemed to be playing as if they were numb and in shock.

After this road trip, the Hoosiers returned home and were to finish out the season playing the next three consecutive games at home against Illinois, Purdue, and Ohio State. Three of the toughest opponents in the league and all in contention and vying for the Big Ten championship. Coach Knight did the best job of coaching and motivating that anyone could imagine. Here was the master at work. A genius by all coaching standards. From our seats in Assembly Hall we could appreciate how the defense

112

functioned as one unit. Jim Thomas and Randy Wittman were exceptional. It was as if the team consisted of one contiguous group. No passes were able to penetrate the lanes. The fans also responded to the adversity. We all drew deep down and cheered louder, stronger, and harder than I can recall in the past. During this period, and shortly thereafter, I developed a hoarse throat but it didn't prevent me from cheering hard and urging the team on to victory. The coaches and the players gave a great accounting of themselves and the team played valiantly.

The victory in the last game in March against Ohio State was especially sweet since prior to that encounter, we were in sole possession of first place in the Big Ten. But a Buckeye victory would have resulted in a tie, and thus we would have shared the title. Therefore, this was for the championship without any partners. It was even sweeter because, when the season started in January—which seemed like years ago—Ohio State had given IU its first defeat of the season. IU totally dominated this current game, and the fans cheered as they had never done before. Even with my sore throat, I am sure I contributed. What a victory! What an ending to the Big Ten season! Indiana had won all three games without Ted Kitchel, beating Purdue 64–41, Illinois 67–55, and Ohio State 81–60.

As was customary at the final game of the regular season, the seniors and the coach spoke to the fans. Coach Knight's praise of his players, and especially the fans, was magnanimous. He started out by reminding the fans that in Assembly Hall only national championship banners or banners commemorating significant events related to national level play were given recognition—the NCAA championship banners of 1940, 1953, 1976, and 1981, the NIT banner of 1979, the UPI Number One Ranking for the 1975 undefeated regular season (with a record of twenty-nine wins and zero losses), and the NCAA banner depicting IU's participation in the final four in 1973. Although the Hoosiers had won numerous Big Ten or tournament titles, none hung in Assembly Hall, unlike the policy in some other arenas. Now he would break precedent. Coach Knight promised the fans that a banner commemorating this past Big Ten season and the winning of the Big Ten championship would adorn Assembly Hall, and would thus serve as a constant reminder of the valiant efforts of that team and the tremendous support from the fans. Sure enough, next fall the banner was there. It still brings back fond memories of that remarkable finish, as it hangs near our seats in the arena.

As expected, Indiana got a bid to the NCAA and was placed in the Mideast Regional. Our first opponent was Oklahoma and the game was to be played in Evansville, Indiana. Myrna and I took the long, five-hour drive to Roberts Stadium in Evansville. We had arranged to meet Jeff Sagarin and Wayne Winston and a reporter, who was an acquaintance of theirs, for lunch in a nearby motel. We all shared a pizza before the game. The reporter, from a Cincinnati newspaper, had known of Jeff, and wanted to meet him in person. He was aware of his reputation, as Jeff was now gaining national acclaim; his computer rankings were becoming well accepted. Eventually they (both football and basketball) were published every Tuesday in *USA Today*. It's strange to be in Oslo, Norway, or Sydney, Australia, and to see Jeff's column and his name in print. It certainly always gives me a feeling of being close to home when I get homesick.

After the pizza and some interesting conversation, we drove to the arena, where IU struggled against a Wayman Tisdale-led Oklahoma team. You could sense that Indiana without Ted Kichel was not capable of going all the way. After IU got a slim lead, Coach Knight decided to freeze the ball. This, to me, was an indication that he wasn't confident this team could run with Oklahoma. In this case, Knight's masterful coaching pulled the game out of the bag. However, next it was on to the regionals in Knoxville, Tennessee, to face Kentucky, a longtime rival and a much more formidable opponent.

I called Lee Suttner and Dave Towell and asked them if they could get me a ticket, since I was unsuccessful in obtaining tickets from the IU athletic department's varsity club. They called on Wednesday morning, informing me that they had a ticket (Dave's son had been willing to give up his ticket), and they would meet me in Knoxville at a designated motel. I had planned to take va-

114

cation time and drive to Knoxville on Thursday to watch Indiana play the Kentucky Wildcats. Wednesday afternoon and evening, I blossomed into what turned out to be a fullblown case of the flu, with a temperature of 103–104°F. The next morning I felt terrible, but I was still planning to drive to Knoxville. It's not every day you get a ticket to one of the "sweet sixteen" regionals! Myrna was insistent that I stay home. We discussed it—I guess you could say we had a heated discussion, or maybe it's called an argument—and she won. (She also hid my car keys.) In retrospect, she was 100 percent right, as she usually is on these matters. I stayed home and drank lots of hot drinks, had chicken soup, and did all the other good things you're supposed to do for treating the flu.

I did, however, get out of bed long enough to put on my red shirt and watch the game. It was, to say the least, a letdown and quite disappointing, because Indiana lost to Kentucky by the score of 64–59. Myrna, not one to say "I told you so," said, "I told you so." I guess I certainly would have felt a lot sicker had I taken the long trip alone and had to drive home sick, disillusioned, and dejected because they had lost. Well, I must admit, if one has to be sick, "There's no place like home." She's right again!

This past year, Indiana had gone on to NCAA tournament play, being included by virtue of their first-place finish in the Big Ten. We all knew that our postseason could be short without Ted Kitchel. We really didn't have the complete machinery needed to go all the way, since Ted was an integral cog in the wheel. IU played totally inspired and motivated ball to win the Big Ten championship. It was not, however, enough to carry the team through the NCAA. In fact, most everyone felt that the NCAA was anticlimactic, anyway, after winning the Big Ten in such a dramatic fashion. We had really given our all—the team, the coaches, and the fans—during the final three games of the regular season. By and large, it had been an exciting and fulfilling year.

Chapter 11
A Ray of Sunshine and Then "The Roof Falls In": 1983–85

In October, the 1983–84 season looked as if it could be a no-lose situation for those rooting for the cream and crimson. Indiana had some good, young talent in Mike Giomi, Uwe Blab, Dan Dakich, Winston Morgan, Stew Robinson, and Daryl Thomas, and Coach Knight had just recruited Indiana's 1983 high school Mr. Basketball, Steve Alford. For those members of our family up north who were rooting for the maize and blue, they also had exceptional talent with Antoine Joubert Roy Tarpley, Butch Wade, and Richard Rellford among others. In most of the pre-season polls, Michigan was expected to do well in the Big Ten. Thus Harriet, who was now also a member of the University of Michigan basketball pep band, would have a super time and a great seat for all their home games. This year was interesting because we had a true family rivalry with Harriet and her boyfriend Neil on the one side and Myrna, Margo, and me on the other.

The season started with everybody motoring to Bloomington on Thanksgiving weekend. It has become a tradition that our family and our guests go to see this game at the start of the season as part of the turkey holiday festivities. You know, just like in Detroit and Dallas, where the Lions and Cowboys' football games are played before Thanksgiving dinner. We also follow a similiar tradition on the Saturday after Thanksgiving. We all go to Indiana's first home game. Fortunately, tickets for this event aren't difficult to find since many of the students are vacationing off campus and are willing to sell theirs. This year the company was great, but the game was not so hot—that is, if you were an IU fan. They lost to Miami of Ohio 63–57. This was the first time I could recall IU losing the season's opening game. In the past, they had close games, such as in 1981 when Ball State, with five foot, eleven inch Ray McCallum, made them sweat, but never in my recollection had they lost. Miami of Ohio, which is located in Oxford, Ohio, near Cincinnati, is a member of the Mid-American conference and is well known for its football program. It has been referred to as the Cradle of Coaches, having served as a training ground for such leaders as Woody Hayes, Weeb Ewbank, Ara Parseghian, Bo Schembechler, Johnny Pont, and Bill Mallory, who incidentally is the current football coach at Indiana University. Periodically Miami has good basketball teams, and that year's team, led by Ron Harper, was one of them. Harper had a good day against IU and was one of the primary reasons for our loss.

We went on to beat Notre Dame at home (80–72). This rivalry always brings back fond memories, since in 1976 Notre Dame was the first team we ever saw IU play in person. It is also enjoyable to watch the interaction between "Digger" Phelps and Bob Knight. From our seats in Assembly Hall, we can watch them perform with respect to their friendship, as well as being able to observe their coaching antics. Each pleads with or tries to intimidate the officials as well as each other. Each is a showman in his own right, but I must admit nobody can match Digger's approach. Here is this guy in a dark suit with a light green carnation prominently displayed in his lapel, always in sartorial splendor, holding the side of his head and complaining about an official's call. In contrast, there is Knight in a red plaid jacket, pleading with an official for a hometown call or kicking the scorers' table in disgust when the ball players or officials don't come up to his expectations. Each has his own way of getting the officials' attention or riling up the crowd. At times they would both meet in front of the scorers' table and commiserate about how bad the officiating was and about the referees' level of incompetence. Could you imagine the opposing coaches in agreement about anything? Well, I could assure you it's not unusual for Knight and Phelps to get together to cry on each other's shoulder.

The next two games on the road resulted in two more losses,

first to Kentucky (59–54), then to UTEP (the University of Texas–El Paso). We watched those games on TV, and in the latter game, although we lost by the score 65–61, it was clear that Mike Giomi, who basically carried the team in scoring and rebounding during that game, would be a future star for IU and a force for the rest of the Big Ten to reckon with. This was refreshing for us since we could look to the future with great optimism if Giomi could demonstrate consistency.

Following this loss to UTEP, the team went on a streak, winning the next seven games in a row. One of these victories was in the Hoosier Classic against Boston College. I especially enjoyed that game because it was interesting to watch Indiana's response to the press. In my estimation, Indiana teams coached by Bob Knight never did well against the fullcourt press. In 1976 against Michigan, the notorious photo of Coach Knight and Jim Wisman was the outcome of such a press. It was clear that they were not very proficient in this regard. Similarly, when Iowa used their trapping fullcourt press, Indiana always had difficulty. Now, here in Indianapolis was Boston College from the Big East, whose coach was Gary Williams. This team's style used a forty minute fullcourt press. On this evening, in contrast to past performances, Coach Knight and his team were especially proficient in their ability to break the press, and eventually burned Boston College. This effort resulted in an Indiana victory 72–66, winning the Hoosier Classic. Little did we realize that several years later this style of play would be an important part of the Big Ten game, since Gary Williams would become the head coach at Ohio State and Tom Davis, his mentor at Boston College, would eventually come to Iowa (via Stanford). In 1988, it was clear that at times IU still remained vulnerable to the press, losing blowouts to Louisville and Iowa on the road. The fullcourt press was also instrumental in their loss to Kentucky in Indianapolis that year.

Shortly after the start of the Big Ten Conference season, we beat Illinois in overtime at home, then lost to Purdue at home, and beat the Michigan State Spartans in overtime at East Lansing. As usual, the competition was tough, but IU was relatively lucky. Throughout that season we played four overtime games, three home and one away. We were very lucky, indeed, winning all of those overtime games, although luck is not the only thing that comes into play during those times. Overtime wins require a mature, disciplined team with coolness at a time when it counts the most. I must admit, there is nothing more exciting for a fan than to watch his or her team win an overtime game. However, there is also nothing more emotionally draining.

After the Michigan State game, the team traveled farther east to Ann Arbor, where the Wolverines defeated IU by the score of 55–50. We watched on TV and taped the game for Harriet so that she could have a permanent memento of her stint in the pep band, and of course as a later reminder of her full college experience. During this game, Knight and Bill Frieder, the Michigan coach, had some dispute: Frieder wanted the officials to give Coach Knight a technical, and he vehemently complained about their reluctance to respond to his request. Ironically, this was after Knight had allegedly gone out of his way the day before to defend Bill Frieder to the Michigan news media. Well, just as Knight and Frieder were at odds, you can imagine what it did to our family situation. Harriet defended the Mighigan coach's stand on the matter. In contrast, we thought his behavior was terrible and showed lack of class. She was happy because of their win, as she should have been, since she was taught to be a diehard fan. Understandably, we were upset with our loss.

We went on to win the next seven games, and then lost to Northwestern in Evanston, 63–51—not a close game at all. Obviously, Knight and the team were not pleased with their performance and it motivated them for the IU–Michigan game to be played in Bloomington several days later. IU was ready to a-venge their earlier loss to Michigan. Harriet and Neil came to Indiana for the game, which was played during their spring semester break. Michigan was handily defeated, and our U of M visitors tolerated the loving needling from our Bloomington family. The score at the final buzzer was 72–57. Wait, don't despair or have pity on Michigan because next year they would get their revenge. Boy, would they have their revenge.

The 1983–84 regular season ended with IU splitting its final four games and finishing in third place in the Big Ten. Michigan finished the rest of the season on a positive note, and I felt bad when they were denied an invitation to the NCAA. Harriet was upset, and I tried to console her by telling her that they probably would have been eliminated from the NCAA early, but would be very competitive and stood a good chance of winning the NIT.

A number of Big Ten teams did get NCAA bids. However, Michigan was just at the cutoff point and accepted a bid to the NIT. They did quite well and advanced to the semifinals in New York's Madison Square Garden. You may recall that while growing up in New York State, one of my dreams was to play in Madison Square Garden. Although I never made it, another Lemberger did. Harriet went to New York with the Michigan pep band and played in the Garden. She played the clarinet and cheered the team on to the finals and to a victory over Notre Dame. A friend of mine, Ronnie Kuntzman, got me two tickets, and so I took vacation time and flew to New York City. I met his son, Fred, at the Garden, and we both watched Harriet and rooted for the Wolverines. My sister, Rozy, and brother-in-law, Murray, drove down from the Catskills, and also watched her. After the semifinal game, Harriet and I spent a few hours together, talking about the game, college, and the Big Apple. It was truly a nice time that we spent, just father and daughter.

The next day I went to several Broadway ticket box offices and bought tickets for Myrna, Margo, and me for our upcoming Easter vacation trip to New York. We planned to see the musicals *Cats*, *42nd Street*, and *The Golden Age*, a show with Margo's favorite performer, Stockard Channing. I returned to Indianapolis that afternoon after having lunch with Charles and Walter Shapiro, my childhood friends from the Catskills and the now defunct Alamac Hotel, before going to the airport. Meanwhile, in the NCAA, Indiana was placed in the East regional, which was without a doubt the toughest region, containing North Carolina, the nation's top-ranked team.

In the spring of 1984 I was serving as the president of the American Society for Clinical Pharmacology and Therapeutics

(ASCPT). Our annual national meeting was in Atlanta, Georgia, and that weekend, Indiana was to play the Richmond Spiders in Charlotte, North Carolina. Unfortunately, I couldn't attend, but I rooted via the TV as the Hoosiers won 75–67.

The next week IU was going to play in the East regionals in, you guessed it, Atlanta, Georgia. Their first game was scheduled for Thursday, but once again I had a speaking engagement in Florida, to which I had already committed. Here I was again, just a few hundred miles from the site but unable to attend. Well, to be perfectly honest, I didn't even try to get a ticket, probably subconsciously thinking IU could never beat number-one North Carolina, who were loaded with talent of the caliber of Michael Jordan and Sam Perkins. I watched the TV set in amazement as Dan Dakich's super defensive effort controlled the indescribable Michael Jordan, and as Indiana's freshman star, Steve Alford, played superbly. As a result, Indiana defeated—yes, I said defeated, top-ranked North Carolina from the powerful Atlantic Coast Conference by the score of 72–68.

The following Saturday the Hoosiers played the Virginia Cavaliers, one of the weakest and the lowest ranked of the ACC teams to be included in the NCAA tournament. This was the same Virginia team who had lost Ralph Sampson to graduation, and who had struggled through their regular conference schedule. With about one minute left in the game, Indiana had a very slim lead and was in the process of freezing the ball. Ironically, Dan Dakich, the individual who had just completed an outstanding game against North Carolina, was in possession of the ball when it was stolen away. Virginia scored and took the lead. Indiana didn't score on their next possession and was forced to foul Virginia to again regain possession of the ball. IU lost 50–48. Here they were, just two points shy of going to the final four in Seattle's Kingdome. Even though Indiana had lost in their bid to win the NCAA, we still felt good since they had gone much farther than anyone had expected. As a major bonus, Harriet and Michigan had won the NIT.

What would the future hold for this team? Even the most critical individual could only be optimistic. Indeed, Indiana had a very bright future, but before even considering next year, Indiana's coach and their loyal fans were being treated to a great honor. Coach Bob Knight had been selected to coach the United States team in the 1984 Olympics, despite the opposition and criticism relating to the incident in San Juan, Puerto Rico, which surrounded the Pan Am Games in 1979.

We were excited to hear that tryouts for the 1984 Olympics, to be played in Los Angeles, would be conducted in Bloomington, Indiana, and the Coach Knight and a group of prominent coaches would hold trials by invitation. These trials would last about one week and would culminate in the selection of a team which would represent the USA. The final selection process took place through a series of scrimmages amongst the players. I got tickets for Myrna and me and for a close friend and colleague, Bob Wolen, and his wife, Marion. Bob and I worked together, but had much more in common. We both grew up in the Catskill Mountains. He came from Lake Huntington, a small village about twenty miles from the town in which I was raised. We never knew each other until I moved to Indianapolis, but we did have mutual acquaintances. As we sat in Assembly Hall, reading the program and watching the players practicing before the scrimmage, we noticed that Maurice "Moe" Martin, one of the invitees from St. Joseph's in Philadelphia had, in fact, gone to high school in Liberty, New York, a town in Sullivan County in the heart of the Catskill Mountains. Bob leaned over, looked at me and said, "How many people do you think are here from Sullivan County? I'll bet you there are only three people—you, me, and Maurice Martin." We joked about it, but it surely was a coincidence. Unfortunately, he didn't make the final cut, but he did play well. I guess there are still good ball players from the small schools in the Catskills who are succeeding at the collegiate level of sports competition today.

Several weeks later we had the distinct privilege of attending what can only be described as a true happening. It was Indiana's tribute to Bob Knight and the 1984 Olympic basketball team. This tribute consisted of an exhibition game between the NBA all-stars (including Larry Bird, Isiah Thomas, Quinn Buckner, Magic Johnson and many other superstars) and the Olympic team, including great players such as Chris Mullin, Patrick Ewing, Michael Jordan, Steve Alford, and Sam Perkins. The site was the Indianapolis Hoosier Dome. The crowd was about 70,000, the largest crowd ever to watch a basketball game. The theme for the evening was "A Knight to Remember" and portions of it were organized by former Governor Otis Bowen, a close friend of Bob Knight's, who later served as the US Secretary of Health and Human Services.

Myrna, Harriet, Margo and I participated in the celebration and, like the other fans, played an integral part in it. We waved our American flags and took part in all the activities designed for fan participation. During the actual Olympics, I was at Oxford University in England and watched the US team steamroll over their competition on the "tellie." As everyone knows, the USA won the Olympics, and Knight joined the select group of coaches who have won the Olympics, an NIT and two NCAA's. Moreover, he had also won the Pan Am gold medal. Although these were his own personal accomplishments, we all felt that they were also accomplishments that all Hoosier fans, and fans all across America, shared.

When autumn came to beautiful southern Indiana, the stands of the football games in Memorial Stadium were already buzzing with gossip. Just as nature's chemistry was working hard, causing the color changes of the trees, so were the rumor mills also working overtime. I must admit, Myrna and the other female fans were not pleased with what they were hearing. My own feeling was that someone's personal and private life should be kept private and confidential as long as it doesn't interfere with what they are supposed to be doing for the public and doesn't affect their function at a professional level.

By the time the basketball season started, the rumors were in high gear. Nancy Knight's seat across from us on the opposite side of Assembly Hall was empty. This elicited comments from those around us that perhaps the rumors about his personal life were true. To add fuel to the fires, new rumors surfaced that the coach and his star player, Steve Alford, were, in fact, burnt out after last years's long season and their participation in the Olympic efforts.

This 1984–85 season was a crazy, unusual one. It started with IU playing nationally acclaimed Louisville at the Thanksgiving weekend home season opener. This was in contrast to their usual opponent, a Mid-American conference team. The arena also had a new addition. The Olympic flag had been added to the display that includes the Indiana State flag and the American Flag on the "rafters" of Assembly Hall. The outcome of the basketball game was not what we all expected or wanted. Louisville won 75–64, and some of our optimism quickly disappeared.

However, the Hoosiers ultimately had a good preconference record (8–2), losing only to Louisville at home and Notre Dame away, and beating such schools as Kentucky and Iowa State. Thus the high level of fan enthusiasm resurfaced, and with the newfound success, most of the talk and gossip were temporarily put to rest.

Myrna and I went to San Diego to watch Harriet and the Michigan band march in the Holiday Bowl parade and perform during the game's halftime extravaganza. Michigan lost to Brigham Young, but we enjoyed ourselves despite the outcome. We returned home to Indiana for a few days and then the entire family flew to Florida for the Christmas and New Year's vacation to visit with Myrna's family. While there, I religiously followed the newspapers regarding the scores of the Hoosier Classics and tried to listen to the games on the radio when we could get good reception. Although we truly wanted to listen to these games, I felt that if we did miss them it would not be catastrophic. However, it was imperative that we get to hear the first game of the Big Ten season, which unfortunately was being played early in January, while we were all still on our vacation. IU was opening the season against Michigan in Ann Arbor.

That evening, Harriet and I walked all over Century Village—a senior citizens' community in West Palm Beach, Florida, composed of garden apartments with wide open expanses. As we walked and talked, we alternated holding the radio, which had seemingly become a permanent appendage to our ears. Indiana was having an excellent game, led by Uwe Blab. I personally had never thought Uwe would ever become the kind of dominant player one would expect from a smart, seven-foot-two guy. At least in this game, I was clearly wrong. He dominated play and scored a career-high thirty-one points. I teased Harriet just a bit, but being sensitive to her feelings, I didn't persist.

With a win like this over Michigan (87–62) at Ann Arbor, there was no limit to our expectations for the team and their coach. Then strange things started happening. We lost the next game to Michigan State in East Lansing, then we beat both Northwestern and Wisconsin at home, and lost a close game, 86–84, to Ohio State in Columbus, Ohio. This loss must have been the straw that broke the camel's back, because after this game, the coach kicked Mike Giomi off the team for not going to his classes, and he benched Winston Morgan. Winston was banished to the end of the long bench, which, as the fans know, is synonymous with being in Coach Knight's doghouse. We read all sorts of stories in the newspapers, such as: these two players were told to find their own way home, they were off the team permanently, they were just suspended temporarily, et cetera.

In the case of Giomi, it was clear that his playing days at IU were over. He eventually transferred to North Carolina State where, after one year as a red-shirt, he contributed significantly to the success of Jim Valvano's team. We fans at IU could only dream about what would have been if all had gone well that season and had there not been any turmoil associated with Morgan and Giomi. But that was not to be. We lost our next game, an easy game, to Purdue; then the team traveled to the University of Illinois' Assembly Hall in Champaign-Urbana.

Myrna, Margo, and I assembled in front of the TV set in our red garb. When the player introductions occurred we were dismayed, disappointed, and downright angry. Coach Knight had the audacity to bench Steve Alford and all of the regular starters except Uwe Blab. He started four freshman and Blab. Of one thing I am sure: every time I think about that game, my blood boils and my blood pressure and heart rate jump significantly.

As a fan who had invested a great deal of energy and emotion in IU basketball, *this* was the straw that broke this camel's back. What nerve—what an affront to the fans, not to field the best team. Well, it was a blowout. You know the old expression, "You play to the level of your opposition." Thus, considering that Indiana didn't play well, neither did Illinois. The final score was Illinois 52–Indiana 41. All of the Indiana fans were furious, yes, but also deeply hurt and puzzled.

The season continued and Indiana lost to Iowa at home and then was to play Minnesota at home on Saturday afternoon. This was also the weekend that Margo had an Ohio Valley regional meeting of her youth group in Cincinnati. Myrna and I thought this would be a good opportunity to relax and spend the weekend together in the Queen City on the Ohio River. Friday afternoon we drove Margo to Cincinnati and we checked into the newly redecorated art deco hotel, the Netherland Plaza. The next morning we had planned to drive to Bloomington for the ball game and then to return to Cincinnati. Well, our plans were slightly affected by the weather.

Saturday morning when we awoke, a snowstorm was in progress in the Cincinnati area and it extended into parts of southern Indiana. As a result, our timing was a little off. Considering that I had never made this trip before and didn't know what type of roads I would be driving on, I was angry with myself because I didn't plan for or anticipate any adverse weather conditions. We had only made it to Bedford, Indiana, by tipoff time, and so we were forced to listen to the game on the radio as we sped north on Route 37 to Bloomington. We missed what might be described as ten of Indiana basketball's most exciting minutes. Don Fischer, the radio commentator, who is one of the best in the business, was relaying all the excitement that was going on in Assembly Hall in his usual highly emotional and enthusiastic manner. IU could do no wrong, and as a result Minnesota was being plagued by IU's great defensive effort and was forced into committing a lot of turnovers.

When we arrived at the arena, I dropped Myrna in front, parked the car and we rushed to our seats. As I mentioned, we missed the first fifteen minutes, but were pleased that the onslaught continued throughout the game. IU won 89–66, despite the fact that the reserves played a good portion of the second half of the game. Was this the same team that had played last week? What was happening? The fans were all very confused, as I can imagine the players were.

Next the Hoosiers beat Wisconsin and Northwestern on the road and returned to play the Ohio State Buckeyes at home. If the Ohio State away game at Columbus, Ohio, was the precursor of the Hoosiers' problem, then the Ohio State game in Assembly Hall was the beginning of the end. The Hoosiers lost to Ohio State by nine points and then to Illinois by sixteen points in their next game. Then came the notorious Indiana–Purdue game. This game was to be forever etched in infamy, both for Coach Knight and for the fans. As is customary, I set my videocassette recorder to tape the game. We arrived early in Bloomington that afternoon, and everyone in our group was buzzing about what would happen. Here it was an IU–Purdue game with all the rivalry attached and with IU having a difficult season. I personally suspected something was going to happen when Coach Knight entered the court area. In contrast to his usual attire of a plaid jacket with a shirt and tie, he was wearing a white pullover sport shirt with a red pattern. Clearly this was not his usual attire for Assembly Hall, although he had dressed in this casual manner for the Summer Olympics. As the game progressed and he got more and more embroiled with the officials, I had the feeling he was just looking to get a technical foul assessed against him. At that point, we were trailing, and the game seemed to be getting away from the Hoosiers. To my way of thinking, the coach was going to try to motivate his team, as he had in 1974 in the final game of the Commissioners Collegiate Tournament against the University of Southern California. In that game, it appeared that Coach Knight purposely had three technical fouls assessed against him, was ejected from the game, and his team responded by overcoming a large deficit and handily beating USC.

I leaned over to Myrna and back to Lee and Dave and stated that this was déjà vu and predicted what would occur next. He did get three technical fouls and was ejected from the game, but little did I anticipate it would occur in such a manner. The coach responded to the official's call by throwing his chair across the floor. This was an act that was viewed by most basketball fans in the country, since it was a nationally televised game. In fact, it even made the regular news and thus was seen not only by basketball enthusiasts, but by Mr. and Mrs. John Q. Public as well.

The fans present at Assembly Hall that day, Myrna and I included, were in shock. We had been very supportive of our coach over the years. However, we had never been witness to an incident of this magnitude before. Most of the fans in Assembly Hall that day also shared these feelings. Unfortunately, there was a small number of fans who jeered and threw coins and debris. This further embarrassed us. This was, in fact, a sad day for IU basketball. Although they lost the game 72–63 with Knight in abstentia, after that incident, the team, the fans, the university, and Coach Knight lost much more. Coach Knight was criticized and publicly reprimanded, as well as being awarded a one-game suspension by the Big Ten conference. Ironically, the president of Indiana University, Dr. John Ryan, and athletic director Ralph Floyd did not issue any statement or reprimand, something that clearly would change.

So, after that IU–Purdue game, the diehard fans like myself would be the brunt of constant, not-so-funny, furniture jokes. Everywhere I went, I would be the fall guy for comments relating to this incident. But a Hoosier fan is understanding, supportive, and forgiving, and I learned as a youngster, you don't kick someone when he is down. It was clear that Bob Knight was dealing with more than just basketball. Coach Knight, a very private person, seemed to be dealing with other significant aspects of his life that took a toll on the man. He went from the heights of his profession, by winning the Olympics, to the depths of despair on that ill-fated Saturday afternoon. The rest of the regular season was erratic. The team won their next away game against Minnesota, lost on the road to Iowa (70–50), and again lost, at home, to Michigan State.

The last home game of the regular season was against Michigan. Again, Harriet and Neil, who were now juniors at the U of M, came to Indianapolis for the weekend so they could join us at Assembly Hall, so I needed to rustle up another ticket. I finally got one in another section, where I sat, but fortunately I moved around until I was finally able to sit near Lee and Dave, behind my family.

This game was reminiscent of when Michigan came to Bloomington in 1977, ranked number one in the country. That game, a special Sunday afternoon contest, was also played on national TV. At that time Michigan was humiliated by lowly IU by a score of 71–59. Unfortunately for Indiana, the script and the final outcome were not the same. But it was also a great game. The Hoosiers were fighting for respectability against the Big Ten's leader, but more important, they were fighting for their own self-esteem. They knew they could not get into the NCAA, but I imagine it was a matter of pride, and they were, in fact, fighting to show their fans and the college basketball world that they were not losers or quitters. The outcome of that game came down to the last second. It was tied, and Gary Grant drove the lane and took a shot, which Uwe Blab blocked. Ironically, the ball caromed right back into Grant's hands, and he put up an off-balance shot as the buzzer went off. "Swish" went the net, and Michigan won by two points. The IU fans were very disappointed because their players had risen to the occasion and looked as if they would beat nationally ranked Michigan. Even Neil and Harriet were somewhat compassionate and felt bad for Myrna and me and the other 17,200 screaming cream and crimson fans.

The postgame was also different. As Artie Johnson, from the famous *Laugh-In* show, used to say, "Very interesting, but stupid." Knight and the team were obviously devastated. They all left the floor and went into the locker room as is customary. However, shortly thereafter, they usually emerge and return to the court to have the seniors speak to the fans. The Indiana fans, as you can imagine by now, are traditional and are creatures of habit. They show up for each game in red, stand up and clap in unison when the fight song is played, and so on. One of the traditions is that after the last home game, the senior players talk to the fans, and that Coach Knight introduces them. The fans wait eagerly for this part of the program. This gives us, the fans, a final opportunity to show our appreciation to the seniors for having given us four years of pleasure and enjoyment.

This day, five minutes went by. Then ten minutes elapsed and still nothing. The fans were antsy and clearly upset. Obviously, the message got to the Indiana locker room, and Uwe Blab and Dan Dakich, the two 1985 seniors, came out of the tunnel to address the fans. Unfortunately, they were by themselves, the coach having elected not to join them. Therefore, they improvised. Uwe, being a member of Phi Beta Kappa and a double major, was comfortable and articulate under the circumstances. As I recall that afternoon, he made no mention of his coach, although he spent much of his time thanking the fans and selected university personnel for giving him an education and making his days in the state of Indiana and at IU productive.

When we drove home that afternoon, we didn't know if we would ever see that specific team play together as a group again in an organized activity. I did, however, feel confident that even with thirteen losses, Indiana would get a bid to the NIT, but I was not sure if the team members and the coaches would accept an invitation. Why prolong the agony of such a soul-destroying season, not only for the team, but for the fans.

Fortunately, Bob Knight is a man of genius and insight. He and the team elected to accept the bid. They probably saw this as an opportunity to work together toward a new beginning—a rebirth. It was, in fact, an opportunity for them to start a "new season," and moreover for them to put the unpleasant events of the past season behind them. It was a chance for them to show the world that the Indiana Hoosiers were still the epitome of what good, wholesome college basketball is all about. I can assure you that as a fan I was glad that they made that decision.

Fortunately for the loyal fans, the Hoosiers played their first three games in Assembly Hall. We easily beat the Butler Bulldogs, our instate neighbors from Indianapolis, and then went on to beat the Richmond Spiders, the team that we had played against and beaten the year before in the NCAA first round regionals. However, we had difficulty against Marquette, the independent, perennial power from Milwaukee. Difficulty is a gross understatement. This game really tested Indiana as a team, and they came through with flying colors. It was a real character builder. Since this was a tournament game, we didn't sit in our usual seats, but were assigned to the floor-level bleachers behind the basket. This was quite a different vantage point from what we were used to, and it provided us with a different perspective of the game. Uwe was effectively boxing out, and thus was making spectacular rebounding efforts. Most important, he was making his free throws down the stretch, in the closing minutes of the game. Indiana finally won, 94–82, in an emotion-packed double-overtime encounter.

I left Assembly Hall with mixed emotions. I was glad that Indiana had won and that they were going to New York and Madison Square Garden for the semifinals against Tennessee, but I was unhappy because I knew I could not follow them. Again, I had to attend a scientific meeting, the ASCPT meeting in San Antonio, Texas. However, I did follow them via the newspapers and TV newscasts and was elated when they defeated Tennessee and earned the opportunity to play for the NIT championship against UCLA, an adversary of long standing. Here it was about ten years after both UCLA and IU had been the NCAA champions in 1975 and 1976, respectively. Now neither had received invitations to the NCAA party, but had to compete for the NIT championship in what some people feel had become a diluted college basketball tournament. This fact alone speaks to the point of parity in college basketball. Who would imagine that UCLA and Indiana would not be in the top sixty-four teams in the country? In fact, this parity has made college basketball that much more exciting.

I couldn't watch the game on TV that evening because of my meeting, so Myrna was kind enough to tape it for me. I was certainly not pleased that IU lost, but was happy with the fact that this team, these individual players and their coaches, were able to regroup and make it to the point in the NIT championship game where they lost in the closing minutes, despite the tumultuous events of the past season. This, in fact, speaks well for them and supports the decision that Coach Knight made to accept the NIT bid. It gave the team an opportunity to re-establish their self-esteem and to vindicate themselves in the eyes of their supporters and their critics.

This year the roles for IU and Michigan were reversed. While IU played in the NIT, Michigan, who won the Big Ten conference, was seeded in the NCAA Mideast Regional and played in Dayton, Ohio. Harriet went to Dayton with the pep band, and they played well. However, the team had a tough time getting motivated to play unranked Fairleigh Dickinson, but managed to win. However, the next game was against Villanova from the Big East. Michigan lost, and the band members and all their fans were devastated. Little did they know at that time that their opponent would eventually go on to win the national championship, defeating powerful Georgetown. In retrospect, it gave them some solace.

When Indiana's season was finally over, we went to the annual basketball banquet in Assembly Hall, which this year was indeed an interesting experience. Usually Coach Knight asks a friend of his to be the master of ceremonies for these events, and also plays an important, active role himself, maintaining a special role in the evening's activities. He is not only the introducer of the master of ceremonies, but is usually the brunt of the emcee's jokes. The two establish a unique dialogue. He also conducts and orchestrates the evening. Finally, he gives a talk. It is always an eloquent talk about that individual team, the season and its goals and accomplishments, and what it specifically has taught the players as individuals. Most important, he philosophizes on life in general and puts basketball into its proper perspective, providing a sort of sermon to these young men who will now be leaving Assembly Hall for the last time. His orations always receive tremendous ovations from the fans and supporters. This event serves as the culmination of the seniors' past four years as Indiana basketball players and as IU students who have gained the affection and respect of the fans.

This year's banquet, as it seemed the whole year had been, was very difficult for both the fans and the players. When the team entered and took their positions in the press boxes in Assembly Hall, there were two people absent. One was Nancy Knight, but this was not unexpected since she had not been visible at any games that season. More importantly, Coach Knight was not present. I, for one, and the other fans at our table were surprised. Joby Wright, one of the assistant coaches, explained that Coach Knight was scouting a junior college championship tournament in which two players whom he hoped to recruit were playing. I was not sure this was a satisfactory reason, since it clearly was not fair to Uwe Blab and Dan Dakich to just dust them off and send them on their way. But, as in the past, they handled themselves in an exemplary fashion.

I personally rationalized the coach's absence by convincing myself that he was committed to build the team and thus was already planning toward the future. Joby Wright, in fact, stated that the fans would be pleased with Coach Knight's efforts. Well, Wright was right because the players Bob Knight was scouting and recruiting were Keith Smart and Dean Garrett. You know Keith Smart, he's the guy who made that famous last-second shot in the 1987 NCAA finals against Syracuse. That evening we left the banquet, hoping that next year would be less tumultuous. I was also optimistic that Indiana basketball would once again rise to its formerly respected and revered position and that it would regain its image as one of the premier programs in college basketball.

Chapter 12
How Sweet It Is: 1985–87

Maybe you've heard the catchy tune, "Reunited and It Feels So Good." Well, for the Hoosiers in 1985–86, one could change the words to "Reincarnated and it feels so good." As a fan I especially looked forward with much excitement and anticipation to the basketball season, which would start in the fall of 1985. As a matter of fact, when I left the basketball banquet in April 1985, I was literally sitting on the edge of my seat. I couldn't wait for the new season to start. There was only one way we could go with respect to the regular Big Ten season, and that was up. I was sure that none of the adversity associated with the 1984–85 season would carry over, especially after our rebirth and fine showing in the NIT. This feeling was fortified further in anticipation of the arrival of Coach Knight's new recruits. In particular, I was eager to see Rick Calloway and Coach Knight's two new junior college transfers, Andre Harris and Todd Jadlow.

To reiterate, there was only one direction to move, and that was upward. From the fan's standpoint, this year would also be unique since we would be given a view through the retrospect-a-scope at the Indiana University basketball program. We would get a look into the intimacies, the behind-the-scene goings-on in the locker rooms, and the players' and coaches' minds. Author John Feinstein had termed this campaign the "Season on the Brink." The book by the same name became a bestseller. In retrospect I can't believe that Coach Knight agreed to allow himself to be put in such a situation: allowing a reporter—a member of a profession for whom he says he has little regard and respect for—the privilege of sharing his, the team's, and the staff's most intimate thoughts and moments. Don't misunderstand. As an avid basketball fan, I enjoyed reading the book in its entirety and can certainly understand its widespread appeal. However, I was upset with Mr. Feinstein's total disregard for the feelings and sensitivities of the Indiana basketball players—part of my extended family. His expose of Coach Knight was fine if, in fact, the coach had no objections and was in agreement. However, his relating what might be considered confidential and personal aspects of the lives of the players, really just a bunch of teenagers and young adults, appears to me to be in poor taste. But that's another issue.

In the fall of 1985, Margo made her way to Bloomington on a "permanent" basis. She was now starting college and had decided to attend Indiana University. Of course, she was no stranger to Bloomington, having been "physically dragged" there for football and basketball games since she was about five or six years old. Margo had played the flute and piccolo in her high school marching band and her high school symphony orchestra, which incidentally was chosen as the best in the state, so she auditioned for the Marching Hundred, IU's marching band. It was great watching her march on autumn afternoons as we attended the football games. Now, in addition to watching the game, we had a personal involvement. In the past, she always picked on me for insisting that we go down to Bloomington early on football Saturdays to watch the band perform their pregame show. Now, as a band member, she was appreciative and wished more fans would do this, so the band would perform to full stands. In high school, Margo was also active in her school's swing choir, the North Central Counterpoints, of which she was president. When she went to school in Bloomington, she fulfilled a childhood dream, that of becoming a member of the Indiana University Singing Hoosiers, a swing group which had an excellent reputation and was world renowned. Thus, with the start of the fall school semester at Indiana University, we had much to look forward to—seeing Margo and the IU football and basketball games.

Over the Thanksgiving weekend, we went to the first basketball game against Kent State. It was a blowout. I must admit, I never knew Kent State to be a basketball power, so one really couldn't evaluate the play of Calloway and Harris. I remember Kent State more for its notoriety. During the period of the Vietnam War, this Ohio campus was the site of the Ohio National Guard's shooting of thirteen student "protestors." This incident, which occurred in early May of 1970, tragically resulted in the death of four young students and the wounding of nine others. This was certainly not one of the more positive moments in our country's history. Unfortunately, this is what I personally relate to Kent State—not basketball. It is probably not fair to this institution of higher education, but it's hard to erase these memories and biases.

Notre Dame was the next opponent, and the game was being played at home. As a team, we always had difficulty rebounding. However, the addition of Andre Harris, with his outstanding athletic ability, complemented that of Daryl Thomas, and hopefully the rebounding would be less of a weakness. If only Andre could keep out of foul trouble, I thought. That game, against the Irish from South Bend, also went to IU, and the positive vibes were starting to flow. Notre Dame, as you know, is a well-respected basketball power. So an 82–67 win was reason for elation and some early celebration.

Next on the agenda was Kentucky, and it was an away game. Since Steve Alford, the typical Wheaties All-American boy-next-door type, had agreed to pose for a calendar sponsored by a sorority, the proceeds of which were to go towards charitable organizations, he was given a one-game suspension by the NCAA. Do you believe that? Such inequities in the system—Alford is suspended, while Scott Skiles from Michigan State played uninterrupted after being arrested several times for such violations as possession of marihuana and drunken driving. Skiles eventually was convicted and sentenced to a disciplinary jail term, and was still allowed to continue his college basketball career without any disciplinary action from the school or the NCAA. Boy, the world is topsy-turvy. Perhaps what had the effect of pouring salt in the open wound was that Alford's suspension was to be applied to the game against Kentucky. Why not against

Louisiana Tech, or Texas Tech, our next opponents, instead of one of our archrivals? The whole state was up in arms, but to no avail. As we watched the game on TV, I let everybody around know my feelings and my disgust with the system. Well, Indiana lost, going down to defeat in the final minutes. The final score was 63–58. This could be partially construed as a positive sign, because it demonstrated how good IU really was. Even without Alford, they almost won in Lexington. This was something we all know rarely occurs.

The Hoosiers won the next three games, and then shortly thereafter Myrna and I went off to the annual neuropsychopharmacology meeting, which this time was being held in Maui, Hawaii. We stayed an extra week in Honolulu to vacation. Myrna had never been there before and, let's face it, it's a nice place to visit in December or, as a matter of fact, any time. During that week we watched Louisville and Indiana University play at what surely was an unusual time for us. The afternoon game was being televised from Louisville and because of the time difference, it was seen in the morning in Hawaii. This felt weird. The game itself went down to the wire, IU losing in the final seconds (65–63). Again we came close, but no cigar. Here I was in Honolulu, Hawaii, watching TV in a purposefully darkened hotel room rather than being sprawled out on a blanket on the beautiful, sandy beach under the constantly sunny sky. Well, first things first. I could always go out in the sun, but it's not every day we play the Louisville Cardinals.

When we returned home, we psyched ourselves up for the start of conference play. The Big Ten season opened with a loss to Michigan (74–69) in Bloomington. Next we lost another game, a close one, to Michigan State (77–74) at Assembly Hall. It almost appeared as if we might be headed into a year like the previous season. I hoped that was not going to be our fate. Fortunately, things changed. We triumphed in our next five games, including victories over Illinois (71–69), Purdue (71–70 in overtime), and Ohio State (69–66) at home. All were close, but we survived and got to the bottom line, emerging victorious. No doubt about it, things began looking up. Except for a loss to Iowa in Iowa City, the Hoosiers again won their next five games, then went on to beat Illinois on the road 61–60, but lost handily to Purdue (85–68) in West Lafayette.

The Hoosiers then beat Iowa and were again rolling in high gear after a 97–79 victory over Michigan State in East Lansing. They were coming into the final game of the 1985–86 regular season. At this point, IU was tied for first place in the Big Ten with Michigan, and as fate would have it, the next stop was Ann Arbor.

Unfortunately I couldn't go, even if I had been able to obtain tickets. As a matter of fact, Harriet, who was now a senior, called and said that she had an extra ticket for me if I wanted it. She and Neil reveled as the Wolverines decimated, demolished, destroyed, and downright embarrassed Indiana. As I watched the massacre on TV, I was becoming more and more infuriated. The Michigan players were acting like "hot dogs" and were purposely rubbing it in during their 80–52 surgical dismemberment of the Indiana Hoosiers. I looked forward to the time when we could get our revenge. Tarpley, Wade, and Rellford were playing their last college home game. Joubert and Grant were also at their best. They all rubbed it in, high-fiving, slam-dunking—the works. We were all demoralized—the fans, the team, but especially Coach Knight. Harriet and Neil were ecstatic since Michigan had just won the Big Ten championship and would go on to the NCAA as the top seed, thus staying in the Mideast regional. Indiana, on the other hand, was sent to the East regional in the Syracuse Orangemen's Carrier Dome to play Cleveland State, not a well-known team and clearly not one of the top teams selected in the tournament. Cleveland who? Well, the sports world would soon find out who they were.

I couldn't go to Syracuse because of an earlier commitment to attend a business retreat organized by the Indiana University School of Medicine's department of pharmacology. Having no choice, I took my portable TV and periodically watched segments of the game. Near the end of the game, everyone present crowded around the TV and we all were in shock when IU went down to defeat. I had planned to go to the regionals had Indiana beaten Cleveland State. I knew Cleveland State wouldn't be an easy team to play, but I didn't expect us to be out of it so early in the game, and to have to claw our way back from a significant deficit. Well, that was all she wrote. No next game. No tomorrow. Just back to Bloomington to prepare for next year. Since Knight is so prominent and at times controversial, and since I am an ardent fan and supporter of him and Indiana basketball, my friends and colleagues in the ACC and Big East had more ammunition with which to give me a hard time.

Sure Myrna, I, and the other IU fans were disappointed by the Hoosiers' short stay in the NCAA tournament, having been eliminated in the first round, but we were happy with the considerable turnaround from the 1985 season. Now IU's final record for the 1986 season was twenty-one wins and eight losses, not too bad.

During the offseason, Ohio State's Coach Eldon Miller "resigned," and the rumors ran rampant that Bob Knight would leave Indiana to return to his alma mater. The Hoosier fans were somewhat squeamish since this seemed like a logical scenario. Fortunately for us and the other IU fans, Knight declined and quickly dismissed these rumors and alleviated our anxiety. Not being able to attract Coach Knight, the Buckeyes selected Boston College's Coach Gary Williams. We all breathed a sigh of relief and eagerly awaited the start of the next season.

Do you remember when I talked about the basketball banquet where Coach Knight didn't show up in order to allegedly scout some junior college players? Well, October 1986, the time they were scheduled to arrive in Bloomington for the 1986–87 season, had arrived. The local and national newspapers played up their potential and most important their possible immediate impact on the team. As George Allen, the former Washington Redskin and Los Angeles Ram's coach said regarding his philosophy on drafting players, "The future is now." He always went after the immediate-impact player. Well, this time so did Coach Knight. He had recruited Keith Smart and Dean Garrett, two junior college transfers (JUCO), and in retrospect, I'm glad he did, in spite of having to give up hosting the banquet. I know, this is completely opposite to my thoughts at that time, but that surely is an advantage of the retrospectoscopic view.

Indeed, the fall of 1986 signaled the start of an interesting year. Andre Harris was gone due to difficulties with his grades, Winston Morgan had graduated, and Stew Robinson, who had used up his eligibility, was finishing his studies toward his degree. However, Rick Calloway, last year's Big Ten freshman of the year, Steve Alford, an All-American, and Daryl Thomas were now to be joined by Garrett and Smart. The addition of the two JUCOs was like getting an instant infusion of talent. Both quickly worked into the system and Coach Knight could effectively use them with his returning stars.

Since we had heard so much about the talents of Smart and Garrett, we were anxious to see them play in person. IU opened the season against Montana State in the turkey weekend special, and won by thirty-five points. I virtually was on the edge of my seat waiting to see if they would mesh. I was hoping they could function like a well-oiled machine. The presence of Dean Garrett clearly freed up Daryl Thomas to play forward, his natural position, rather than playing under the basket with much taller players. In this game, Dean Garrett had ten points and a phenomenal fourteen rebounds, something not seen by the fans in Bloomington in quite a while. He also was an exceptional shot blocker and an intimidator on defense. Keith Smart and Joe Hillman both played and each did well.

Early in that game, the fans already had visions of a great season. The returning stars were also doing well. Steve Alford was shooting consistently and running the team well, while Daryl Thomas was mobile and contributed by scoring and helping Garrett rebound. Well, with a victory such as this and with the two new players looking so good, what's the problem? One of the brightest stars of the game was Ricky Calloway, who in a short period of time had scored seven points, had five rebounds, and looked like he was on his way to a super season. Then it happened. Going for a loose ball, he and a Montana State player got their feet tangled and they both went down together. Ricky's leg was twisted as the two players were tied up in a knot. Silence filled Assembly Hall with its over 17,000 fans in shock. Was this

140

to be a repeat of the 1975 or the 1980 season when the team would not reach its full potential due to injuries.

Ricky was taken off the court and everyone anxiously awaited that prognosis. In the papers and on the evening news it was reported that he was to be taken to Indianapolis's Methodist Hospital, where the sports medicine department would do arthroscopic surgery on his knee to determine the extent of the injury. His physician was Dr. Steve Ahlfeld, an orthopedic surgeon who incidentally was also a former Indiana University basketball player under Coach Knight. Steve played on the 1973 team that went to the NCAA final four and graduated in 1975, having played on what some have termed the best basketball team in IU history, despite having never won the national championship.

Unfortunately, I got to meet him later that season (in February of 1987), also under adverse conditions. This was after I ruptured an Achilles tendon while taking time off during a business trip in Palo Alto, California, to play some racquetball. Dr. Ahlfeld saw me a week later in the emergency room at St. Vincent's Hospital in Indianapolis, after I had been hobbling around with a cane for a week. He confirmed my worst fears and then subsequently operated to repair the condition. When he treated Rick Calloway, his diagnosis and prognosis were also right on the mark, however he decided no surgery was needed because Ricky had only stretched ligaments, with no major damage. The paper stated that Calloway would probably be capable of playing in three or four weeks. During that time, he sat on the bench and walked with crutches. In mid-December, he would return to the starting lineup against Morehead State.

Even during Ricky Calloway's actual absence from the court, the fans were treated to some very exciting basketball, whether we saw it in person or watched it on TV. During this period, IU played Notre Dame away, Kentucky at home, Vanderbilt away in Nashville, Tennessee, and then hosted the Indiana Classic, where they played the University of North Carolina–Wilmington and East Carolina. Beating Notre Dame in South Bend is a worthy feat for any team, and the win was very satisfying. However, beating Kentucky, especially after last year's close loss, was really gratifying. Last year Steve Alford hadn't played in that game because of the calendar incident, but now he played well and scored twenty-six points. The Hoosiers lost to their next opponent, the Vanderbilt Commodores, also from the Southeastern Conference (SEC). I was in San Juan, Puerto Rico, at the neuropsychopharmacology meeting, but when Myrna and I talked on the phone, she gave me a blow-by-blow description of the game. Although the loss was a surprise, it was not a fluke. Vanderbilt was developing into a perennial power in a very tough and competitive conference. This fact would be substantiated the following year, when they defeated the number one ranked Tarheels of the University of North Carolina, and a highly ranked Kentucky team, with many of the same players as they had this year. We also received a scare in the first game of the Indiana Classic, beating the University of North Carolina–Wilmington by just one point. This was the closest IU had come to getting beaten in their own tournament since its inception. However, the next evening they defeated East Carolina to win the Classic.

Next on the schedule was the home game against Morehead State. This was a significant event since it marked the return of Ricky Calloway, who came on to the floor to thunderous applause, his thin leg supported by a huge metal knee brace. Although he played well, scoring nine points in a limited appearance, it was apparent that, because of his injury, he was a little hesitant and tentative in his moves. This was also evident in IU's next game against Louisville. Hopefully, this would change for the better as his confidence returned. Again the fans were hungry for a victory against Louisville, wanting to avenge and to temper the memories of last year's game when IU lost in the last few seconds. This time, Rick Calloway contributed significantly to the effort with nineteen points—he was clearly on track, and our hopes of a great season were revitalized.

After winning the Hoosier Classic, IU entered the Big Ten season with a record of 9 and 1. Not too shabby, huh? Well, now for the real test! The first three games—against Ohio State, Michigan State, and finally Michigan—were on the road. We watched them diligently on TV. The first two went well. In the opener against Ohio State, Steve Alford was not playing up to his usual capabilities, possibly because of a great defensive effort by Ohio State, but Keith Smart was phenomenal and showed everyone why Coach Knight recruited him. In the third game of that series in Ann Arbor, IU did very well for the first half, then the roof fell in as the Hoosiers blew a substantial lead. It was in the closing seconds of that game that Steve Alford demonstrated why he was truly an All-American. After Gary Grant, Michigan's premier guard, missed a free throw, Alford got the tip from a teammate, dribbled the length of the court, and made a shot. *Swish*. All in two to three seconds. IU won 85–84. Now it was home to friendly Assembly Hall, where the Hoosiers annihilated Wisconsin 103–65 and Northwestern 95–43. Their conference record was now 5 and 0, and I and all the other fans were tickled pink, as their overall record was fourteen wins and one loss.

The Iowa game, played in Iowa City, was a difficult game for me to watch on TV. Both teams were scoring freely, and IU, who had come back from a deficit, was closing the gap near the end of the regulation time. At that point, Steve Alford made a long shot, a three pointer, but he was allegedly in violation for standing on the out-of-bounds line, thus negating the basket. This single officiating call seemed to have a demoralizing effect on the team, as Iowa ran off a string of baskets in the last two minutes to ultimately win, 101–88. It was as if IU gave up after Alford's score was erased.

After the Iowa game, IU traveled to Minnesota and won handily 77–53. They returned to Bloomington and beat a tough Illinois team 69–66 in front of about 17,200 fans. Three days later they beat Purdue 88–77, again in front of a maximum Assembly Hall crowd of 17,310 partisan fans. Although Indiana was ahead by only one point at the half, the team, led by Steve Alford with thirty-one points, put it all together in the second half. Garrett, Eyl, Smart, Thomas, and Calloway all played well in the victory, and the home town fans all left Assembly Hall elated.

On Wednesday evening, February 4, we played Michigan State at Bloomington. Myrna and I drove down early that eve-

143

ning and met Margo. It was another tight Big Ten game. Steve Alford was hot, hitting everything in sight. He scored a total of forty-two points and Coach Knight took him out with some time remaining so that he could get a standing ovation from the fans. He had just set a record for the most points scored by an individual in Assembly Hall. Although we had a comfortable thirteen-point lead at halftime, it still ended up in a close game with us winning by only four points, 84–80. I couldn't wait to get home that night since I had to get up early the next morning to catch a flight to California to attend an editorial board meeting. We arrived home at about 12:00 midnight, and at 5:00 A.M. I arose and started to get ready to catch my flight, which departed at 7:45 A.M.

I arrived in San Jose at about 12:00 noon. My friend Red picked me up and took me to lunch and then to the hotel to check in and drop off my bags. There I met my other friends and colleagues who were also attending the editorial board meeting of the *Annual Reviews of Pharmacology*, a scientific publication the offices of which are in Palo Alto. We had a group dinner scheduled for that evening, so several of the guys were going to take in a game of golf that afternoon. Since golf is not my forte, Red and I had arranged to play racquetball at the Palo Alto Elks Club. When I left, Myrna pleaded with me not to take my sports gear and just to relax and reminisce with Red. I guess I should have listened. She is usually right. We played doubles, and after one game I was getting back into the swing of it. However, the second game ended prematurely when one of our opponents, as I mentioned earlier, stepped across the back of my leg on my Achilles tendon. Such pain! I stood up five times and immediately fell down five times. After the excruciating pain subsided, I showered and dressed. We then went to the drugstore, where I bought a cane and some Ace bandages. I wasn't sure if it was a severe sprain, since I was wearing hightop basketball sneakers, or a ruptured Achilles tendon. I found out a week later.

The group met late that afternoon and evening, and we had a cocktail hour and dinner. The following day, Friday, was taken up with the editorial board meeting, which takes a full day. I usually fly directly home on the red-eye after these meetings, to get back in time to see the Hoosiers play on Saturday. Fortunately, this year the next game, against Michigan, was being televised nationally and was scheduled to be played in Assembly Hall on Sunday. This allowed me to leave Saturday, like a normal traveler not intent on rushing to a basketball game. Fortunately, it also gave me sufficient time to hobble home, limping along with my cane. When I arrived home Saturday night, Myrna let me have it with both barrels with the "I told you so's." Boy, if I had only listened. As a friend of mine said, a ruptured Achilles tendon can be a career-ending injury. Fortunately, that does not hold true for a pharmacologist.

Sunday morning we all drove to Bloomington. Now the family roles were reversed. Normally I drive and let Myrna off at the front entrance of the arena so she won't have to walk in the cold due to her asthma. Now she would have to leave me off, park the car, and walk to the arena. As you could imagine, the thought of this didn't make her happy, nor did it put me in her good graces. Boy, had I only taken her advice and not played racquetball. I hobbled into Assembly Hall and finally made it to my seat. Well, Indiana beat Michigan 83–67, and, as you would expect, when we returned home, we phoned Ann Arbor and chided the Michigan fans in our family, stopping short of being obnoxious.

IU next traveled to Evanston, Illinois, to play Northwestern. At home we won by a margin of fifty-two points, which everyone would admit was quite sizable. But life in the Big Ten is interesting, to say the least. At Evanston, IU was lucky to just eke out a win. The final score was a close 77–75. But let's face it. A win is a win. In 1988 IU wouldn't even be that lucky in Evanston and would be on the short end of the stick, losing to the Wildcats by the score 66–64.

That weekend I went to the local hospital's emergency room and asked to see an orthopedic surgeon. Interestingly, Dr. Steve Ahlfeld was on call and he examined me, confirmed my worst case scenario that, in fact, I did have a ruptured Achilles tendon, and scheduled me for surgery on February 17—Harriet's birthday.

The day before, February 16, IU traveled to Madison, Wisconsin, for the second part of an ESPN television doubleheader. These are great for the avid basketball fan, enabling us to see a Big East game followed by a Big Ten game. Speaking about the Big East, I was working on this chapter of this book while sitting in Washington's National Airport on Friday, February 5, 1988, waiting for a flight back to Indianapolis. Anyone who has been in the US Air's terminal there undoubtedly noticed that the ceiling is quite low. Thus it was not difficult to recognize John Thompson and his Georgetown Hoyas as they checked in to board a flight for Hartford, Connecticut, where, I imagined, they would play the University of Connecticut. In fact, they did play the next day and lost.

I have to admit that I recognized John Thompson quicker than I was able to recall Senator Christoper Dodd from Connecticut, who, in fact, was sitting just one seat away from me. It was not until someone came up to him to say hello that I even paid any attention. I had seen both of these gentlemen on TV on many occasions, but I guess because I am a basketball fan, Thompson came to mind sooner—even without his usual towel draped over his shoulder. This is not meant to be anything negative toward public servants and politicians, but if Bob Knight and Senator Dan Quayle from Indiana were in a room, I am sure 98 percent would recognize Knight. I am not a betting man, but I would go out on a limb to say maybe 50 percent, at best, would recognize the senator. (Maybe things are different now that he is the vice president.)

Well, back to basketball. The Big Ten game in Wisconsin started about 9:30 or 10:00 Indianapolis time. Remember the scoring differential depending on whether IU played Northwestern at home or away? Well, it was no different against Wisconsin. In Bloomington we beat them by thirty-eight points, and in Madison we were required to go past regulation time into a triple overtime situation before we could beat them, and then only by one point. The final score was 86–85 after the three overtimes. What a game! I have to admit that Myrna and I felt bad that Wisconsin lost—it was not to say that we weren't happy that IU won, but it was the kind of game you hated to see anyone lose. The players on both teams gave their all and clearly Wisconsin, the underdog, was, I am sure, the favorite of most of the TV audience, and I must admit even our own family felt like rooting for them at times.

The next morning when I showed up at the hospital for my surgery, I teased Dr. Ahlfeld, telling him that I hoped he had had a good night's sleep, since I knew that he, like I, stayed up past midnight watching the game. He never responded to my comment, but be that as it may, he did a good job on my foot. I stayed in the hospital for two days, where I was made reasonably comfortable with the help of analgesics (painkillers) and hypnotics. I then returned home to my own bed, just in time to watch the IU–Minnesota game on TV.

Indiana had just returned to the hospitable, nurturing confines of Assembly Hall, and I am sad to say I was not there to cheer them on and to give them moral support. Although Bob Knight has stated on numerous occasions that it doesn't matter where you play—the court is ninety-four feet long and the baskets are ten feet high—I am sure he is much happier coaching and having his team play at home in Assembly Hall than on the road. At home you have the advantage of the friendly environs and the sixth man—the hometown fans. If the recent Northwestern and Wisconsin experiences are meaningful, and I think they are, then it is clearly much more beneficial to play at home than on the road.

However, in this evening's game, Indiana beat Minnesota in a squeaker 72–70. Again, as a fan you often have ambivalent feelings. You want your own team to win, but you feel for the underdogs and at times like this wish that no one had to lose. Minnesota, a young team with a new coach, had struggled all season long, and here they were in IU's arena playing IU, who had an overall record of twenty wins and only two losses. Well, IU was being taken to the wire by the Golden Gophers. How could you not feel ambivalent and subconsciously root—at least a little bit—for the underdog. Myrna and I faced reality and continued

147

to yell and cheer for the cream and crimson. Here I was, sitting in bed with my leg in a cast, at times yelling at the official when I thought their calls were inconsistent, as if I were in Assembly Hall. Indiana pulled it out and won, as I mentioned, 72–70. You really never know what to expect. This is a good example of the level of excitement that college basketball generates and why it is so popular. We did, however, feel bad for the Minnesota coach and their players.

As a result of my surgery, I was in a cast and on crutches. Sadly, I would also have to miss the IU–Iowa home game. What a bummer! For me, a few days after my surgery it was back to work, and for the IU players after they did well in their home stand, it was on the road again!

Although it is only about a hundred miles from Bloomington to West Lafayette, and although these cities are located in the same state, it's like going to a foreign country if you wear cream and crimson. The reverse is true in the opposite direction if you wear black and gold. So when IU plays in Mackey Arena, Purdue's home court, it is like going into a lion's den or an alligator pit. The natives are hostile and so is the team. This was certainly evidenced when IU traveled to Purdue. They were both fighting for the Big Ten championship title and for the right to represent the Big Ten in the NCAA as the first seed in the Mideast regional. Incidentally, this NCAA game was to be played in the friendly surroundings of the Hoosier Dome in Indianapolis. Because of all these factors, this was not just any ordinary IU–Purdue game; it had much greater significance. Purdue was up for the occasion and won 75–64.

As the expression goes, there is no rest for the weary because next IU traveled to Champaign–Urbana, the home of the University of Illinois Fighting Illini, to play in their arena, also known as Assembly Hall. At this point, Purdue and IU were tied for the Big Ten championship, so this game at Illinois was critical. We gathered around the TV set, hoping we could win and stay in the race with Purdue. With seconds left in the game, Indiana was trailing 69–67 with the ball in Steve Alford's hands, which anyone who knows IU basketball would tell you is exactly where you want it to be. He tried to get off a good shot at the buzzer, but was unsuccessful. IU went down to defeat. Meanwhile, Purdue remained in first place, now all by themselves.

With Purdue playing its last conference game at Ann Arbor and with them having sole possession of first place, the general consensus was that they would win the Big Ten outright. Moreover, this logic was fortified by the fact that Purdue had handily beaten Michigan earlier in the season, and Michigan had been playing poorly down the stretch. However, eternal optimists like myself felt we still had a chance. Our last game at home was against Ohio State, a team which we had beaten at the start of the season at Columbus. However, they were now clearly a different team than they were in our first encounter, because Dennis Hopson, the leading scorer in the Big Ten, had not played much in the first game, due to a stomach virus. In addition, the Buckeyes were playing consistently well of late. Despite these facts, I still honestly felt we had a chance of winning the conference championship.

The season's final home game is always a special treat for me. There was no way I would miss it, so I got on my crutches and tried to manipulate the ramps and steps in Assembly Hall. Not an easy task, but one certainly worth the effort. IU always plays well at home for the last game of the season. The final home game in front of the fans who have cheered loyally for them for the past four years is the ultimate motivation for the seniors to finish their season in style. This year with Steve Alford, Daryl Thomas, and Todd Meier as graduating seniors, this wouldn't be hard, because they are all overachievers and normally highly motivated individuals. In all the years we have personally followed Indiana University basketball, except for the 1985 campaign where we sustained a last-second loss to Michigan (73–71), I can't recall Indiana University losing the final home game. (My memory is pretty good. The time before that was in 1971 against Illinois, 103–87, as I found out after checking the record books.) Meanwhile, up in Ann Arbor where Purdue was playing, it was the Michigan seniors' last home game, including their never-to-reach-his-potential star, Antoine

Joubert, who played erratically during his entire college career. I took my five-inch portable TV, which uses a cigar lighter adapter, to the game so that we could follow the Michigan–Purdue game during the drive home.

In Bloomington, the Indiana Hoosiers struggled against Ohio State. The score at halftime was Ohio State 40–Indiana 39. Indiana eventually took control of the game and won by a final score of 90–81. It was a classic affair between two good teams, each possessing great players. The competition between Hopson and Alford was electrifying, each contributing heroics to keep his team in the hunt. Steve Alford ended the game with twenty-two points, whereas Hopson had twenty-five. (In the earlier game Hopson scored only four points on two field goals.) Both played superbly, as did their teammates. After the game, Coach Knight introduced the seniors and each had an opportunity to thank the fans, as well as his teammates, coaches, teachers and parents for their support. Since the Michigan–Purdue game was a late afternoon event, it was just getting started as the Indiana seniors spoke. Therefore, all the players referred to the fact that the Purdue game was on, intimating they would love to be watching it. After Alford spoke for about ten minutes, he again thanked everyone and received a standing ovation. During his four years, we watched him break almost every IU scoring record, and, as fans, we were proud and honored to have had the privilege to see him, Daryl Thomas, and Todd Meier reach this point. It must have been especially gratifying for the latter two, who overcame numerous injuries in their college careers. Steve honestly begged the crowd's forgiveness as he and his teammates left to watch the Purdue–Michigan game on TV.

After the festivities, we rushed back—as best as you can on crutches—to the car to watch the Wolverines and the Boilermakers. Myrna drove and I tried to get some decent reception on the TV. I didn't get a good picture, but was able to hear the sound commentary. When the halftime score was announced, Michigan was blowing Purdue out of Crisler Arena. We were estatic. I was, however, furious and frustrated that we couldn't get any reasonable reception in the car. I listened to the game and periodically did get a distorted picture. Michigan was awesome, and Antoine Joubert (the Judge) was phenomenal. Purdue lost, and as a result, IU and Purdue were cochampions of the Big Ten. What a fantastic finish for Indiana University and for the Big Ten conference in general. What a lucky break. Michigan defeating Purdue on the final day of the regular season, 104–68. Wow!

We knew IU and Purdue would both get bids to the NCAA, but where would we go, and how would we be seeded? Well, the seedings were to be announced the next day. When that moment arrived, I parked myself in front of the TV, watching the pairings and simultaneously taping them on my VCR so that I could study them later. As the suspense built up, all at once our most optimistic scenario came to fruition. Hooray! IU was being sent to play in Indianapolis, in the Hoosier Dome, and was to be the first seed in the Mideast region. Considering that I still had to wear the cast for more than a month, this also turned out to be a big break for me since I would have had difficulty traveling to some other site. Moreover, I already had four tickets to the games at the Hoosier Dome, having ordered them earlier in the year after seeing, through an advertisement in the newspapers, that they were being put on sale. I was able to get really good seats on the court level. See, it always pays to plan ahead! Or, as the proverb goes, "The early bird catches the worm."

The day of the game rapidly approached and then it finally arrived. That morning I went to work on my crutches, carrying a bag that contained my red sweater and sweatpants. After attending a regularly scheduled 8:00–10:00 meeting, I changed into my casual clothes and called a cab to take me to the Hoosier Dome. You see, although I went to my 8:00–10:00 meeting, I was actually taking the day off as a vacation day. The first game started at 11:00 A.M. and I needed time to get from the handicapped elevator to the proper section and then down the steps—about twenty rows—to my seat. Myrna said she would meet me there for the IU–Fairfield game to be played in the evening. On that Thursday, the first day of the Mideast regional, there were two sessions (a total of four games): the daytime session, with games at 11:00 A.M. and 2:00 P.M., and an evening session. I got comfortably (as best as possible) situated in my seat and watched some very exciting basketball. In the first game, Missouri, from the Big Eight Conference, the overwhelming favorite, played much smaller Xavier of Cincinnati, representing the MCC (Midwestern Collegiate Conference). If you like basketball, there was nothing more exciting than watching Xavier pull out the victory. The other games included Duke versus Texas A & M, Auburn versus San Diego State, and Indiana versus Fairfield.

After the completion of the second game, I made my way with great difficulty to one of my favorite restaurants in Indianapolis, St. Elmo's Steak House. It's about one and a half blocks from the Hoosier Dome, and is fashioned after an old-time New York City restaurant, with the waiters in tuxedos, and with pictures of prominent sports figures, such as Indy 500 race car drivers, basketball players, et cetera, adorning the walls. Each picture was autographed with best regards to the owners. There is even one of Bob Knight. The steak, as usual, was sumptuous and was well received, especially after my exhausting trip—hobbling on crutches from the Dome. Just the thought of going back for the evening session made me tired. I made it and again got situated in my seat for the Indiana–Fairfield game. Myrna, Harriet, and Margo arrived and we all settled in to watch Indiana demolish the Stags (92–58). This was no surprise, since IU was expected to dominate the team from Connecticut.

Indiana's next opponent, to be played on Saturday at the Dome, would be powerful Auburn from the SEC. They were strong, fast, and talented. Auburn started out like a house on fire, but IU caught up and started to dominate. The noise level in the Hoosier Dome was thunderous. The majority of fans wore red, and it was obvious for which team they were rooting. I would stand up on my crutches and clap and cheer as the Hoosiers surged ahead and as the Indiana pep band played the fight song. An added attraction this evening was watching the sideline interactions between Sonny Smith, the Auburn coach, and Bob Knight. This was very humorous and was almost like watching a comedy act. Their charades were precipitated by aggressive team play on both sides and were magnified by some ineptness by the officials in their failure to call fouls against both teams. At times, the two coaches commiserated at midcourt to "cry" on each other's shoulder. The final score was Indiana 107–Auburn 90. Indiana's dominance near the end of the game, as exemplified by their ability to achieve such a high score against an excellent Auburn team, was reminiscent of the way IU played in the 1981 NCAA games.

Well, it was time for the Hoosiers to leave the friendly confines of Indianapolis and its womblike atmosphere. Next week the quest to the final four and the NCAA championship was to be continued in Cincinnati's Riverfront Coliseum. Cincinnati, the home of Rick Calloway and sort of a "border town" to Indiana.

I made every effort to get tickets, but to no avail. I pulled out all the stops, starting with the varsity club, then asking friends in Cincinnati. I was even tempted to call the chancellor of Duke University, Dr. Keith Brodie. You see, the previous week, as I was reading the game program during the twelve hours I spent at the Hoosier Dome, I came across Dr. Brodie's name listed as Duke's highest official. Keith and I were at the National Institutes of Health together and had been good friends during our stay in the Washington area. Unlike the Hoosier Dome, which seats about 40,000 people for a basketball game, the arena in Cincinnati, Riverfront Coliseum, seats only about 17,000. Despite the lack of tickets, I made a hotel reservation for Myrna and me. We had every intention of going there and trying to obtain tickets from a scalper outside the arena, if necessary. I was really determined to see IU make their drive to the Final Four. It's amazing how irrational one can be. Here I was on crutches, thinking of going to a strange city, standing outside an arena I never saw before, not having the faintest idea where I even would stand to get a scalper's ticket, and I was planning to do it anyway. Well, enter Myrna. She really knows how to get her point across as to what's rational behavior and what's irrational behavior. "How are you going to manage to get around on crutches, try to get a ticket, and then if you are lucky, get to your seat?" she repeatedly reminded me. Well, as usual, her logic sank in, and we watched the game at home on TV.

First there was the Indiana–Duke game. It was especially tough for Coach Knight and IU to have to play against the Blue Devils and Coach K (Mike Krzyzewski)! Coach K was first a player for Bob Knight when he was at Army and subsequently trained under his tutelege as his graduate assistant at Indiana. In time, Coach K became the coach at Army, and eventually moved on to his present position as head coach at Duke University. Last year at the final four in Dallas, Knight was an outspoken Duke fan, going so far as to wear a Duke booster button.

Several years ago I had the opportunity to present a seminar and to lecture at Duke University Medical School. My host and a good friend, Dr. Saul Schanberg, is also an avid basketball fan. He took me to watch the Duke team practice when the blue-chippers Mark Allary, Tommy Amaker, and Johnny Dawkins were playing. After watching the practice, Saul and I went over and spoke with Coach K about his Duke team, and he and I exchanged some conversation regarding IU and Bob Knight. It was an enjoyable five or ten minute discussion. He is quite personable, intelligent, and a real gentleman. Thus it wasn't easy for me to be rooting against Duke, but let's face it—they were playing my team, the cream and crimson. Indiana led by ten points at the half, but then it became a close game, with IU finally being victorious (88–82).

Next up on the agenda was LSU and its controversial coach Dale Brown. What a matchup! Coach Bob Knight versus Coach Dale Brown. Two really benign and withdrawn individuals. Just kidding. Actually, they are two very, very controversial coaches, especially when they have the opportunity to play against or to confront one another. As I said earlier, Dale Brown was never my favorite coach and so it was easy for me to get psyched up for the game. As expected, the game and the coaches didn't let anyone down. The LSU team was very physical, as was Indiana. I can recall a picture in the newspaper showing Steve Alford taking a jump shot with a fist—yes, I said a fist—deep into his abdomen. Coach Knight wasn't especially happy with the officiating, and this prompted his banging his fist against the scorer's table. In the act, he hit the telephone in front of Gene Corrigan, the Notre

Dame athletic director and also a member of the NCAA committee. This incident also made the front page of the papers and cost Knight a fine, imposed by the NCAA. This incited Dale Brown, who later alluded to this act in numerous press conferences and newspaper articles and interviews during the next few months.

Personalities aside, it was a game befitting an NCAA regional final. The final score was as close as you can get, Indiana winning 77–76 on a basket by Rick Calloway at the buzzer. He was in the right place at the right time and grabbed an errant last-second shot, an airball. He put it back up and into the hoop—in his home town of Cincinnati, Ohio. What a homecoming! What a celebration we had in our house, screaming and yelling and hugging each other! We had made it to the final four! Next in store was a homecoming for another Hurryin' Hoosier—Keith Smart from Baton Rouge, Louisiana, who was now on his way to New Orleans. On to the NCAA final four in his first year as a Hoosier. What a thrill. The four participating teams were Syracuse and Providence from the Big East, Indiana from the Big Ten, and UNLV, the team that was ranked number one most of the season and which was the most favored participant. Just our luck. We had to play UNLV our first game.

Well, as for me, I had ambivalent feelings. The final four was being held in the Louisiana Super Dome, which seats almost 65,000 people for basketball games. Unlike the regionals in Cincinnati, I knew I could surely get a good seat. Fortunately, or unfortunately, I was the president-elect of ASPET and, due to circumstances beyond my control, was responsible for running our society's annual meeting in Washington, D.C. Moreover, I had to attend our council and finance committee meetings, which are held several days prior to the actual meeting. It is in this forum that all the society's business is discussed and policies are established. I had a major conflict! I could get away from the meetings on Saturday afternoon and fly to New Orleans to see the Indiana–UNLV game. However, there was an even more important event that evening. The Indiana University Singing Hoosiers, of which Margo was a member, was having its annual spring concert in Bloomington. Let me tell you—there was no conflict and no question as to where I would be. Bloomington had the decided edge. Let's face it. First things first, and everything has to be put into its proper perspective. Basketball is one thing, but a family event is something else.

I left the ASPET meeting at 2:00 P.M. Saturday and took a cab to Dulles Airport. Here I was, on crutches, hobbling through the airport to catch a 3:00 or 3:30 flight to Indianapolis. We had arranged that Myrna and Harriet would meet me at the airport with the portable TV. I knew I would miss the start of the IU–UNLV game, but felt confident that I could see most of it. When I hopped and skipped out of the airport, Myrna was waiting and I immediately got into the car and got an update on the game. It was close; the game had just started and only a few minutes had elapsed. We drove to Bloomington; Myrna did the driving and I gave the commentary as I kept struggling with the TV reception. We arrived at Margo's dormitory room at just about the end of halftime. The campus and the dormitories were quiet. You could almost hear a church mouse. Everybody was obviously in their rooms sweating it out while watching the game.

We watched the second half of the game in Margo's room with a group of her friends. It was a close game most of the way. If UNLV's Banks was not hitting from the outside (he had thirty-eight points), Gilliam was hitting from the inside (he scored thirty-two points). However, Coach Knight's strategy was successful in that one of the UNLV's stars, Wade, only scored four points. We were also quite lucky in that we played super defense, thus limited their other superstar sharpshooter, Paddio, who normally is a deadly shooter from the three-point range, to only six points. He made only two baskets in thirteen attempts. In contrast, Indiana had good balanced scoring with Alford scoring thirty-three points, Garrett eighteen, Smart fourteen, and Calloway fourteen. Daryl Thomas, Joe Hillman, and Steve Eyl also contributed, scoring a total of twenty points. The final score was 97–93, but this was deceiving since the score was really not that close. IU let the Running Rebels have one or two easy baskets at the end to avoid fouls and to let the clock continue to run down. What a win for the underdog Hoosiers.

From our vantage point via television, everyone in New Orleans appeared to be ecstatic, but that was nothing compared to what was about to happen on the campus in Bloomington. The second the game ended, the silence in the dorms and on the streets ended. The students poured out of their rooms, screaming and cheering. I looked out the window and students were exiting all the dormitories. It was like rats leaving a sinking ship, or ants in a frenzy when someone steps on their anthill. The streets filled up with students and cars with horns blasting. It was obvious that everyone was heading towards the fountain—Showalter Fountain in the center of the campus. The school's officials must have anticipated this and were prepared, since they made sure that the water in the fountain had been drained. Unfortunately for us, the fountain is located just in front of the IU auditorium where we needed to be for the Singing Hoosiers concert.

The program for the evening's concert did not have an official starting time. Can you imagine a concert in a theatre— IU's 2,000-seat auditorium—with no definite starting time? This is of interest, and probably only in Indiana could one find a similar situation. Well, I stand corrected. There was a time—it said: "Concert starts forty minutes after the conclusion of the IU–UNLV basketball game." This was, in fact, a very smart move because it certainly would have been hard to compete with the game for an audience.

As expected, we got caught up in all the traffic and eventually had to let Margo out of the car so that she could walk across the campus green to get to the auditorium before curtain time. A while later, Myrna let Harriet and me off as close as she could, and I, still manipulating on crutches, made my way through the crowds. By this time I was pretty proficient. The circle where the fountain is situated was jammed with happy students and adults. What a celebration. Some students, who must have excelled in gymnastics, climbed on top of an overhang in front of the auditorium, waving a Big Red flag. Other students made their way into nooks and crannies of the auditorium's edifice, also waving flags and leading cheers.

Eventually the overhang that the students were on started to break through from the weight of the dancing and cheering students.

Fortunately, the concert started late, allowing people to enter the building and find their seats. I am sure they hadn't anticipated the students' reaction and how difficult it would be for the audience to get through the rambunctious, overzealous crowd. Professor Robert Stoll, the director of the world-renowed Singing Hoosiers, a season ticket holder himself and an ardent supporter of the basketball team, started the concert with the IU fight song, leading the Singing Hoosiers and the audience in the celebration. The concert was excellent. The Singing Hoosiers are the premier swing choir in the number one music school in the country, so it's no surprise. They have been featured on national TV, toured all over the country and the world. (In 1988, Margo traveled with the group to Australia.) That evening their performance was superb, as usual, and included a medley of songs from the new Broadway show, *Les Miserables*. I was really glad I made the trip from Washington to see them perform. As the saying goes, I wouldn't have missed it for all the world, or even for a ticket to the NCAA. After the concert we took Margo out for a snack and then we drove back to Indianapolis. You see, the next morning I had to catch an early flight back to Washington, D.C. to continue presiding over the ASPET Council meeting.

I arrived at Washington's National Airport Sunday morning at 8:30 A.M., just in time for my meeting. Fortunately, things were falling right into place and everything was happening as I hoped they would. There were no delays and I had no problems getting through the airports, even though I was still on crutches and had a large cast on my foot. Myrna and Harriet, who was on spring break, arrived in Washington later that day, since it was necessary for Myrna to help with the special aspects of the meeting. Margo still had classes in Bloomington and remained behind for what would prove to be one of the most exciting days in her whole college experience. That day was also Myrna's birthday, and in the evening we celebrated with a cake and candles in Washington.

Indiana was to play Syracuse in the championship game on Monday evening. This evening is traditionally the time that ASPET has a special dinner for the editorial boards of all the society's scientific journals. It is a gala event, including a cocktail party, followed by a dinner. This is the society's way of thanking all of the reviewers who spend many hours, with no monetary compensation, critically looking over scientific manuscripts. I must admit that I was a real clock watcher at the dinner. We stationed ourselves at a table close to the exit. The salad was being served when it was about ten minutes to the tipoff. I asked the waiter to let me take my main course, a nice prime rib, up to our suite—the society president gets a complimentary suite for entertaining, and fortunately it had a great, large screen TV. I excused myself from the table and got some encouragement from some of my colleagues to root hard for an Indiana victory. Myrna, lending a little class to the act, stayed for a while longer. I made it on the crutches to the elevator, then up to the room. Shortly thereafter, they sent my dinner via room service. Harriet, who didn't go to the society dinner, was already in the room with some of her friends from medical school, who just happened to be in the Washington area. She quickly brought me up to date regarding the details of the starting lineups, Billy Packer's gossip, and a variety of related issues. I then settled in to do what I think I do best, that is, root for my Hoosiers.

Indiana's opponent was Syracuse, a team which was playing well and which appeared to be peaking at the right time. This turned out to be a very tough game. Although Indiana led at the half, 34–33, IU was behind most of the second half and had to scrap and struggle to keep the game from getting away from them. Just as Calloway had excelled when they played in Cincinnati, now it was Keith Smart's turn. He took control near the end of the game and made the crucial steals and converted them into critical plays. The Hoosiers were trailing 76–75 as time was expiring. The plan was to get the basketball into Steve Alford's hands for the last shot; however, Syracuse denied him the ball. Keith got a pass from Daryl Thomas, and let go with his now famous shot from the corner with five seconds left in the game.

This will long be remembered as one of the most exciting events in NCAA final four basketball, and especially in IU basketball history. Indiana won 77–76. By this time, I now had more company in the suite. All of my friends who were basketball fans joined us for the second half of the game. Everyone congratulated me—as if I had made the last shot. Well, that's what being a fan is all about. You share in the happiness of the victory and in the despair of the defeat. I called room service and got a few bottles of champagne and we all celebrated—especially Myrna, Harriet, and me. We were on top of the world and having a great time.

Meanwhile, back in Bloomington, Margo and thousands of other IU students and Bloomington residents were also celebrating. Once again they descended upon Showalter Fountain. Since the basketball pep band was in New Orleans, Margo and a few of her friends from the IU marching band, known officially as the Marching Hundred, organized a makeshift pep band that played at the fountain that night. Margo played her flute. There was also a tuba, a trombone, a clarinet, and drums. As she related it, this makeshift pep band played the fight songs and the Indiana classics, to which the students responded accordingly. In time, Margo ended up cheering, while sitting on one of the mermaids on the fountain. The streets of Bloomington were jammed with cars and throngs of happy residents, all in a celebrating mood. The following day the team returned to Bloomington to a hero's welcome in Assembly Hall. Margo and other students jammed the basketball arena, and the celebration continued. She had the distinction of attending the festivities in 1976 as an eight-year-old, and again in 1987, now as an IU student.

That next evening in Washington, I was the master of ceremonies and the host of the ASPET society banquet. Our guest speaker was Dr. James Wyngaarden, the director of the National Institutes of Health, who incidentally reports to Dr. Otis Bowen, the Secretary of HHS, and as I mentioned earlier, the former governor of Indiana. Of course, Dr. Bowen is a staunch supporter of IU's basketball program. I gave Dr. Wyngaarden an Indiana University tie to thank him for coming that evening and for being our speaker. Then I jokingly said that if he wore the tie at his next business meeting with Dr. Bowen, it might get him in good with his boss, who I knew was an avid IU fan. Later that week, President Reagan invited Coach Bob Knight and the Hurryin' Hoosiers to visit the White House. This was followed by a reception and party hosted for them by "Doc" Bowen in the nation's capital.

Although I could not personally be in New Orleans, my friend Dr. Arthur Hayes was there for a medical convention a few days after the NCAA final four extravaganza. Knowing of my interest in the Indiana Hoosiers, he bought me some buttons and a T-shirt attesting to Indiana's winning the NCAA championship in New Orleans. See, that's what good friendships are all about.

About two weeks later, the annual Kiwanis Banquet to honor the Indiana basketball team took place in Assembly Hall to a record crowd of about 3,000 adoring fans. When we arrived, it was clear that this was to be an eventful evening. Normally, if they won the NCAA, the banner would not be unveiled until the first game the following fall. In contrast, this year there was a brand-new red banner with white lettering reading "1987 NCAA Champions Indiana University." That evening the banner was displayed above the players' and the coaches' seats. What a fitting end to a great season. The Hoosiers finished with a record of twenty-six wins and only four losses. What a year!

Steve Alford, Daryl Thomas and Todd Meier said their last good-byes to the rest of the team and to the fans. We already knew who the new recruits would be: Jay Edwards and Lyndon Jones were coming to IU. They had played together since the eighth grade and were the leaders of their high school team, the Marion Giants, who had won three consecutive state championships. They were selected as co-Mr. Basketball for Indiana. This is the most coveted individual award in high school sports in Indiana. They hopefully would contribute to IU's efforts over the next couple of years.

What a season this was. As Bob Hammel, the sports editor for the Bloomington *Herald Telephone* wrote, it was the season "Beyond the Brink" in answer to John Feinstein's book on the

and it helped ease the tensions and anxieties associated with school and with her mother's being away.

Margo was now in her third year at Indiana University and was an old pro in the Marching Hundred. I must say that she was very fortunate. IU hadn't gone to a bowl game since 1979, the Holiday Bowl in San Diego. The band did not make that trip, so last year's trip to the All American Bowl in Birmingham, Alabama, was indeed a treat. The football team, the fans, of course, and the marching band were hoping Coach Bill Mallory could produce a repeat performance. In fact, he and the team did. They were fantastic! They were legitimate contenders for the Big Ten championship, having beaten Ohio State and Michigan in the same season. This, in fact, was a feat they never accomplished in their ninety- to one hundred-year history. Unfortunately, the team lost to Michigan State, the eventual champs, who even won the Rose Bowl for the Big Ten—a feat and prize long overdue, and one which had eluded other Big Ten teams such as Michigan, Iowa, Illinois, and Ohio State for numerous years. It appeared as though IU was embarking on a new football tradition and was becoming a team to be reckoned with—a university that would no longer say, "Wait 'till basketball season."

As a result of Margo's school interests, the band and the football team's successes, we spent many pleasant Saturdays together. I would go to Bloomington to visit her, watch her march, and see the football game. Myrna got right into step with band and football season when she returned at the end of September. We traveled to Kentucky and saw the Hoosiers lose for the first time that season. The atmosphere in Lexington was interesting. I was pleased and pleasantly surprised, but above all, delighted, with the hospitality, friendliness, and magnanimous attitude given to us by the Kentucky football fans. Well, I guess it isn't the same as the basketball rivalry. In fact, the only argument I got into that day was with a fellow Hoosier fan who insisted on standing up in the aisle in front of Myrna, who, at five feet, two inches tall, normally has difficulty seeing the game anyway.

The last game of the football season was being played against Purdue in Bloomington. It was of great interest that this was the front end of the football/basketball day/night double-header because usually the combination event occurs earlier in November. I guess it was scheduled that way because it best coincided with the travel schedule of IU's basketball opponent that evening, the Union of Soviet Socialist Republics, better known as the Russians. You may recall that the USA boycotted the Olympics in Moscow in 1980, and the USSR boycotted the Olympics in Los Angeles in 1984, when Bob Knight was the Olympic coach. This would be the first encounter between Coach Knight and the Russian team in quite a while, that is, since Indiana lost to the Soviet national team in Japan in the summer of 1985.

The weather forecast for that day called for very low temperatures and considerable winds. Myrna, who was not feeling well due to her asthma, elected not to subject herself to the elements, since she was still recuperating from the flu. That day, I had invited a friend, Greg Brickler, and his wife to attend the game. Greg is a Purdue graduate and was a member of their baseball team during his undergraduate years. As expected, he is an avid Purdue fan. He and his wife didn't particularly enjoy the football game since IU won handily. I guess it's hard for a Purdue fan, who is used to seeing IU's football team go down to defeat, witness the Hoosiers play well and win. That's life. It's a new era for Indiana University football and the tides may have turned. Since I knew Greg was a basketball fan as well, I had also invited him to attend the IU–USSR game that evening. Unfortunately, or is it fortunately, for him, he had to decline because of another commitment. I assured him he would be missing a special event.

Little did I know how "special." Indeed, this was an exceptional evening. In my wildest imagination I could not have predicted what would take place at Assembly Hall. After the football game, Margo and I went out for Chinese food, and then she drove up to Indianapolis to keep her mother company and to watch the game on TV. I stayed in Bloomington by myself, wanting to see the game "live and in person."

Everything started as expected. The pep band played the Russian and the US's national anthems, and the vocalist sang

165

them to perfection. The usual exchange of gifts by the players and coaches also went off without a hitch. Then, unfortunately for all concerned, the game started. The Russians must have been waiting for this occasion for many years, i.e., playing against Bobby Knight. In addition to playing against the Olympic coach, they were, of course, playing the NCAA national championship basketball team of 1987, obviously another incentive to show up Coach Knight and the Hoosiers, and the US. The Russians were leading at the half. They were high as a kite, as is always the case when teams play against IU. Our opponents always seem to "get up for the game" and play above their potential.

In this case, the officiating didn't help IU's situation either. In fact, it was downright atrocious. This circumstance with the officials came to a head early in the second half. There were times when the Russians had six men playing on the court simultaneously, and no penalties were imposed. As you must realize by now, Coach Knight is a perfectionist. Not only must the players play up to their own potential, the fans must perform as is expected, he and his staff do their jobs well, but oddly enough he expects the referees to do their job with proficiency. Well, clearly, that was not the case this evening. As a Russian player was taking a foul shot, one of his colleagues backed out of the lane—a clear violation. Coach Knight protested when the officials didn't call it, and, in fact, he got testy when the official let them line up again.

Well, you can imagine what transpired. It became a matter of principle. Jim Burr, the official—incidentally a Big Ten official that Knight and the Hoosiers would be meeting several times during the season—would not relinquish his authority. *Technical foul number one.* Knight persisted and Burr motioned with his hands again. *Technical foul number two.* Play resumed temporarily and Coach Knight wouldn't give up. Then *technical foul number three* was assessed, and by US rules, Coach Knight was to be automatically ejected from the game.

This is where it all gets muddy, as I saw it from my vantage point. Knight argued with the referee and then discussed it with

166

one of the officials of the Olympic organizing group who is responsible for setting up and sanctioning these international games. Coach Knight had his team on the sidelines, by the bench, and I guess the official warned the coach that the game would be forfeited. Knight did not take his team off the basketball floor, as the newspapers implied. At that point, Jim Burr, probably feeling he was losing control because Coach Knight would not leave voluntarily, must have felt he was forced to call a forfeit. He signalled this to the official scorer's desk, then signed the scorer's book and left the arena. You can imagine the amazement and consternation of the fans. Earlier, I, and everyone around, had loudly booed the officials, not only as the technicals were being assessed, but for their ineptness throughout the abbreviated game. Now the fans just stood quietly and were stunned. I had never seen this happen before, especially not in a game of this magnitude. Even though it was only an exhibition game, it was the US against the Russians. What a setting for an international incident.

As I mentioned, the officials left the court, and Coach Knight stood there dazed and amazed. Then Knight and the team left the court. The Russian players and their coaches were also in shock. They eventually picked up basketballs and started practicing. However, this activity was shortlived, as the balls were confiscated from them. Unfortunately, at this point, a group of fans started booing the Russians, who, in my opinion, were perfectly innocent in the whole incident. True, they had committed a lane violation, and at times had six men on the court, but this type of behavior and treatment from the fans was not warranted. I will have to tell you—at that point I was embarrassed to be a part of the crowd and, in fact, to be a part of the activities that had occurred that evening.

Despite this unfortunate incident, the majority of the fans still present in Assembly Hall responded positively and broke out in a round of applause for the Russian players and their coaches who, as they left the floor, waved their hands in a goodwill gesture. This, in some way, made me feel a little better.

The next morning, I flew to Washington to attend a ASPET-related meeting at the Federation of the American Societies of Experimental Biologists (FASEB) to be held on Sunday evening and Monday. Here I was with the top biologists in the United States, all wanting to know what had transpired. Were the papers, TV, and radio correct? Did Bob Knight take his team off the floor during the game? I tried to explain what had happened. The point I want to make is that no matter where you are, there is a cross section of every segment of the population who are fans of college basketball. It is probably our national sport since, I think, more people relate to it than to professional baseball or professional football. Nothing draws more enthusiasm than the NCAA's ascension to the final four and then on to the crowning of the national champion.

Well, it became clear that things had changed at IU during this past year. There was now a new president, whom my sources tell me "read Coach Knight the riot act." As a result, he was given a public reprimand, resulting in the coach's making a public apology to the fans and the university. I must tell you, the expression that you either love him or you hate him is apropos. I personally like him most of the time. As I said earlier, as in a family you're not always happy with the behavior of your spouse and children—and, vice versa, they are not always happy with you—but you will always love them. This, in fact, is the relationship I think I have in my mind with Coach Knight. I am clearly not always happy with what he does, especially the Purdue chair incident and now the Russian incident, but I think when one weighs the good points and the bad, the balance is clearly towards the good. This is not to say that it isn't a dynamic state and if it swings too far towards the bad—such as a future similar incident—I might not be very upset. So much for that.

The 1988 team without Steve Alford and Daryl Thomas was not the same as the 1987 national championship Hoosiers, but I personally felt they could have been a better, more versatile team. They beat Miami of Ohio on Thanksgiving weekend and then beat a good Notre Dame team led by senior David Rivers, everyone's preseason choice for All-American. The next scheduled game was indeed a treat. Several years earlier, Indiana,

Kentucky, Louisville, and Notre Dame had agreed to participate annually in a one-day basketball affair in Indianapolis's Hoosier Dome. This was the inaugural year. A crowd of 44,000 people jammed the Hoosier Dome to view Indiana playing Kentucky and also to see Notre Dame take on Louisville.

What an event. Having been to the final four in 1981, Myrna and I got the same feeling at this event. The Dome was divided up into quadrants. One quarter was Kentucky blue, another Indiana red, a third was a mixture of the Irish's green and yellow, and the fourth was the Cardinal's red. Each school had its band and cheerleaders, and thus with this milleu, it was reminiscent of the atmosphere at the final four. As was often to be the case during this year, Indiana had a comfortable lead over Kentucky in the beginning, then squandered it. The result was that it became a nip-and-tuck game. Indiana tied the game in regulation time on a last-second shot by freshman Jay Edwards. Throughout the game, Steve Eyl and Keith Smart both appeared to have mental lapses, as they were pushing too hard. Unfortunately, Indiana lost in overtime. Although we left the arena disappointed, we still felt positive that the team could be very competitive during the season.

That week I went to the neuropsychopharmacology (ACNP) meeting in San Juan, but conferred with Myrna on the telephone regarding the outcome of the game with Vanderbilt, our next opponent. Before leaving, I gave my tickets to my secretary, Patricia Newman, and she and her daughter went to see that game. Everyone in Indiana loves to watch them play, so tickets are difficult to acquire. A few nights earlier, Vanderbilt had beaten North Carolina, the then number-one-ranked team in the country. This evening, Indiana beat Vanderbilt in a close game, and then went on to win their own Indiana Classic. I had returned home from San Juan so that I could attend these games with Myrna and Margo. IU beat James Madison handily and then went on to beat Washington State. Ricky Calloway had played well in both games and was presented with the most valuable player award in the classic. Ironically, this was probably to be one of the only high points of this season for Calloway. The team next traveled to Louisville where they again played well for the first half. Then it seemed as if this was the point in the season when things were starting to turn sour, at least for a while. The team's defensive effort collapsed, and their offensive production was lacking. In the second half the Hoosiers were outscored by Louisville, who tallied an excess of fifty points.

The Hoosiers returned to Indianapolis for the Hoosier Classic at Market Square Arena. Our whole family went on the first evening, but I attended the final game against Stanford alone. You see, the next morning Margo and the IU Marching Hundred were leaving for Atlanta, Georgia, where IU's football team was to play Tennessee in the Peach Bowl. Myrna and I would be driving down later that day. Indiana defeated Stanford to win the Hoosier Classic. At that time, some newspaper reporters were critical of IU's choice in inviting the competition for the Classic, suggesting that they were simply patsies. To the contrary, UC–Santa Barbara was a team who would eventually beat the perennial basketball power, the University of Nevada–Las Vegas, twice during the regular season, and Stanford would go on to beat Arizona, one of the best teams in the country in 1988 and a final four participant. Indiana University's basketball team had now finished a tough nonconference season with a record of 8 and 2, not counting the forfeit to the Russians. The two losses were to Kentucky in overtime and to Louisville. Although on paper this record looked impressive, and most of the fans were optimistic, little did we know what was in store when the Big Ten season got underway.

The few days in Atlanta were exciting for Myrna and me. The city of Atlanta and their Peach Bowl committee did a superb job. We went to the pep rallies, where the band participated, then to the Peach Bowl New Year's Eve party at the Exposition Center, and on New Year's Day we watched the other bowl games on TV at the Omni Theater on full-size movie theater screens. Our fellow theatergoers turned out to be Coach Bill Mallory and the IU football team. I casually spoke with some of the team members; however, Myrna went back to get some coffee at the restaurant where the team was also snacking, and she spent over an hour talking to Eric Hickerson and Brian Dewitz, two of the defensive players. "What nice, wholesome kids," she related to me. In general, it has always been our impression that the student athletes at Indiana University, male or female, in basketball, football, soccer, track, baseball, swimming, et cetera, are first-class, well spoken individuals. They are individuals who represent the university well and likewise people in whom the fans can take pride. This, of course, holds true in general for most of the young people involved in university activities on all levels of participation.

The following day, the Peach Bowl game was played at Atlanta's football stadium. The pregame entertainment included the playing of "Georgia on My Mind." Little did the soldout crowd know, or realize, that this song was written in Bloomington, Indiana, by none other than Hoagy Carmichael, not for the state of Georgia, but as a tribute to Georgia Carmichael Maxwell, the youngest of his sisters. The pregame and halftime shows performed by both the University of Tennessee marching band and IU's Marching Hundred were stimulating and enjoyable. This was expected since both bands are well respected and have great tradition. Moreover, the football game was very exciting, but unfortunately Indiana lost in the closing minutes. Well, we will continue to improve and hopefully next year we will be more successful and possibly be Rose Bowl-bound. You never know, some day Indiana may be respected as both a basketball and a football power. In any event, win or lose, one thing is for sure. We will continue to cheer them on.

Incidentally, during the month of December, all was not so peaceful and quiet with the basketball team. Jay Edwards, the super freshman who demonstrated his early abilities in the Kentucky game, was declared ineligible to play basketball for at least one month. This sanction was not imposed by the NCAA or by Indiana University, but actually was Bob Knight's disciplinary action. It appeared that Jay was not getting his assignments done for a specific class, and this came to Coach Knight's attention. Rather than let Jay get into a rut and develop poor habits, and eventually be declared ineligible, the coach said he needed to commit time to his studies and could not play or practice with the team. The rumors spread that Edwards was unhappy at IU and that he and Lyndon Jones were going to transfer, but in actuality they were just rumors. Edwards's mother supported Coach Knight's decision and Jay completed his assignments and then returned to the team in mid-January as his period of suspension was met. Shortly thereafter he was reinserted into the starting lineup, and he played exceptionally well—so well that he eventually became the Big Ten's freshman of the year.

Coach Knight is an interesting person. Here he took one of his most promising prospects, basically kicked him off the team for one month, and took the chance of causing this young, impressionable athlete to transfer to another institution. Obviously, Knight felt his studies and his academic future were most important. Can you imagine many other coaches in the country doing something similar? I suspect you could count them on the fingers of a one-handed man who already had several fingers amputated. This certainly was not the first time Coach Knight had done something like this. The year before, he temporarily suspended Daryl Thomas from the team for not attending certain classes, and several seasons earlier he did a similar thing to Landon Turner. One must agree that he is a man of principle and that the student-athlete's education is one of his primary concerns.

We returned home after the holiday and waited in anticipation for Wednesday evening to roll around so that we could watch IU play their first Big Ten game against Iowa in Iowa City. This was the inaugural game of the Big Ten season and pitted two very highly touted teams. Again, IU went ahead early in the game, leading by ten to fifteen points. Part of this was due to a technical foul assessed to Tom Davis, the Iowa coach. During this period, Coach Knight looked like an angel, standing back watching Davis argue with the referees. Indiana still led at the half, but like the Louisville game, Indiana again self-destructed and Iowa came back to score fifty-eight points in the second half. Not surprisingly, IU went down to defeat.

Next it was on to Evanston, Illinois, to play Northwestern,

the perennial doormat of the Big Ten. Here were the highly touted national champions, coming to play in a game where they thought they wouldn't even need to break a sweat. Well, the Northwestern Wildcats, who incidentally had their ranks decimated by injuries, came to play. They out hustled the Hoosiers and obviously they wanted to win more than Indiana did. We watched on TV in disbelief as Indiana was defeated, 66–64. Now they had a sterling record of 0 and 2 in the Big Ten. Meanwhile, Purdue and Michigan were winning all their games. Three days later, Indiana returned to the friendly confines of Assembly Hall and again didn't play well, this time against Wisconsin, who in fact tried harder, but lost. Indiana eked out the win at home, 55–53. Next it was back on the road again, this time to East Lansing. Again, the TV set received all of our attention that evening. Indiana didn't look sharp, but hung in during regulation time, and the game went into overtime. In the extra period, Michigan State, with the home crowd advantage, was able to win in the final seconds, 75–74.

Indiana was now 1 and 3 and had to face Michigan, one of the top-ranked teams in the nation, at home, and on national television. Neil had come in for the weekend, and he and Harriet joined us in what has become a nice family event. As the game progressed, Neil was getting a lot of ribbing from Lee Suttner. Neil gave it back in spades, as Michigan went on to win 72–60. The score, however, was not indicative of how superior Michigan's play was that day. With IU's record in the Big Ten now at 1 and 4, obviously Coach Knight felt some drastic changes were in order, and drastic changes they were. To the consternation of many of the fans, including, I must admit, myself, he benched Keith Smart, Steve Eyl, and Ricky Calloway, some of the heroes of last year's national championship team. My personal feelings were that he, in fact, was writing off the season and investing in the future by preparing the underclassmen. I arrived at this conclusion when he started freshmen Lyndon Jones and Jay Edwards and junior Joe Hillman. A three-guard offense, plus Magnus Pelkowski and Dean Garrett, represented Indiana on the floor when they tipped off against Ohio State, who incidentally

173

had just defeated excellent and highly ranked Michigan and Iowa teams at home. Well, Knight the genius did it again as Indiana beat Ohio State 75–71 in Columbus. He showed up all of his critics and, I must admit, even I was impressed with the play of the team. I also must admit that I would have liked to have seen Keith and Ricky get some playing time.

The Hoosiers' next game was at home against Purdue, the best team in the Big Ten and at the time recognized as a national power, ranking second in the nation. A victory against Indiana could give them the opportunity to be ranked number one by the end of that day. Indiana, with their three-guard offense consisting of their freshman guards, went at the Boilermakers with a vengeance. Dean Garrett had a spectacular first half, and Indiana led at one time by as many as twenty-one points. As usual, the second half was a different story. Purdue took it to Indiana and eventually led in the game, but Garrett responded under pressure and was almost singlehandedly responsible for Indiana's victory (82–79), as he scored thirty-one points. Unfortunately, the situation would be reversed later in the season when IU played in West Lafayette.

The same lineup played against Minnesota and won again. Coach Knight had successfully turned the tide. They next traveled to Illinois where they escaped with a narrow victory, 75–74, as we cheered them on from our family room. Knight was now starting to give Rick Calloway, Steve Eyl, and Keith Smart more playing time. The team returned to Assembly Hall to try to avenge their earlier road loss to Northwestern. It soon became evident that the results would be different this time, as they won by the score of 74–45 (a twenty-nine-point spread). It was still possible, although quite a long shot, that Indiana could repeat as Big Ten champions.

I must admit, being the eternal optimist, I felt IU had the capabilities of winning the Big Ten. I sat down with paper and pencil and a lot of wishful thinking, saying, "If we win the rest of our games and so and so beats so and so, and Iowa and Illinois and Ohio State beat Purdue and Michigan, et cetera, et cetera, et cetera, then we can win." Well, that's what being an optimist is all about. For me, and for the Hoosiers, reality surfaced again as they traveled to Ann Arbor to play the Michigan Wolverines.

Watching this game on TV was not at all pleasant for me since I personally didn't appreciate the antics and shenanigans of the Michigan players. Gary Grant and Glen Rice were rubbing it in to the Indiana players and the coaches by their actions—high-fiving it in front of the Hoosiers' bench and clearly trying to torment them. I can assure you in all the years I have watched Indiana basketball I have never seen an IU player perform in such a manner. Well, I guess a lot has to do with the values that the coach instills into his players and what level of control he can exert, or most of all, what he will tolerate in the area of good sportsmanship. The game was a blowout, and even though I have a great love for Harriet and Neil and an allegiance to them, it didn't bother me in the least that Michigan was defeated in the NCAA by North Carolina and that Glen Rice, and especially Gary Grant, went out of the tournament with poor showings.

When Michigan State came to Bloomington, it was again clear that the Hoosiers wanted to avenge their earlier loss, as they beat State by thirty-seven points (95–58), while shooting with greater than 70 percent accuracy. Imagine if IU had won those games in East Lansing and Evanston. They lost those two games by a total of three points, and the second time around beat these teams by a total of sixty-six points. Well, that's what college basketball is all about. This was very reminiscent of the 1981 season.

The next game was Purdue, away at Mackey Arena. Purdue was now ranked number two in the country and was still leading the Big Ten. Myrna had returned to California a few weeks earlier since her sister had to undergo additional surgery and was recuperating from her operation. However, Myrna was, of course, still very much interested in the game and was planning to watch it on TV, as it was being nationally televised. Margo and I were also planning to spread out in front of the TV and watch it that weekend. That was until I got a telephone message on Thursday stating that Dr. Charles "Chip" Rutledge, the new dean of the Purdue Pharmacy School, was going to be out of town, and did I want to use his tickets for the game? Well, Chip and I have been friends for years, having first met when we became members of ASPET, the national pharmacology society. Later we served together on the ASPET council. He knew of my enthusiasm and allegiance to basketball, especially IU basketball. Before coming to Purdue, he was chairman of the pharmacology department at the University of Kansas at Lawrence, a school whose basketball program—as you will agree—is not too shabby either. Once I got his message, it didn't take me more than a few milliseconds to call his secretary and affirm that I would love to go to the game and, of course, I told her to thank him.

Margo and I drove to West Lafayette dressed in our red garb. Outside the arena they were distributing "Boilermaker Power" signs attesting to the strength of Purdue. We were in the minority, to say the least. In fact, it was nice to know that the two people in front of us were actually Hoosier fans, but they were traveling incognito. They were dressed in nonrevealing colors, neither black and gold nor red and white, because they said, "they didn't want to stand out." In contrast, Margo and I, in bright red, cheered loudly for the Hoosiers—when there was something to cheer about.

Before the game I walked down to say hello to Dr. Steve Beering and his wife Jane. Steve is now the president of Purdue University, but was formerly the dean of the Indiana University School of Medicine. I recall many occasions when we would meet at IU's Assembly Hall or would see the Beerings driving back on Route 37 to Indianapolis after a Saturday afternoon game in Bloomington. He and Mrs. Beering are still avid IU fans—as long as they're not playing Purdue. It was very exciting to watch them basking in the light of Purdue's success, and I must admit it was nice to see Purdue and their coach Gene Keady getting the national recognition that they certainly deserved and which they had had coming to them for a long time. We spoke for a few minutes and exchanged pleasantries, then I wished them luck for the game and returned to our seats.

In contrast to the great effort that Dean Garrett had expended in the earlier game at Bloomington, this time he didn't get much opportunity to demonstrate his talents. He was called for his third personal foul within the first five minutes and thus, for all intents and purposes, was essentially out of the game, since, when he did go in in the second half, he was tentative on defense and fearful of getting additional fouls. He eventually did get two more and fouled out. The Hoosiers played valiantly and kept the score close, but without Garrett they were no match for the strong Purdue front line. Well, I must admit, this year Purdue was the best team in the Big Ten going away. However, it's nice to remember that one of their few losses did come at the hands of IU.

When the team returned to Bloomington for a Monday night, 9:00, ESPN-nationally televised game against Illinois, they were essentially in a battle for the third or fourth place in the Big Ten with Illinois and Iowa. Dr. Sid Spector, a longtime friend from New Jersey, gave a seminar on his exciting research that day at the Lilly research labs, and I took him to the game that evening. On the way to Bloomington we stopped in Martinsville, a small town about halfway between Indianapolis and Bloomington. This was the hometown of another famous basketball coach, John Wooden, who graduated from Martinsville High School in 1928 and went on to become an All-American basketball player at Purdue University in 1930, 1931, and 1932. However, he is best known as the renowned coach of the UCLA Bruins, who under his rein and tutelage won ten NCAA national championships between 1964 and 1975. He was inducted into the Basketball Hall of Fame as a player in 1960 and again as a coach in 1972. We stopped at Poe's Cafeteria for a quick dinner, and I showed Sid all the pictures and memorabilia relating to famous Martinsville sports figures. Of course, Coach Wooden, who played for the Martinsville High School's Artesians, was prominently displayed.

During that whole day, and during the drive down to Bloomington, I optimistically touted Indiana's basketball team to Sid, stating how we were "in good shape" since even though Illinois was playing well, we had beaten them 75–74 in Champaign-Urbana and now this important game was at home with

177

such an important prize at stake. I assured him that Coach Knight would have them ready and they would be highly motivated. Boy, was I wrong. It was just the opposite. Lou Henson's team came out of the box like a house on fire. They dominated every aspect of the game, diving for loose balls, crashing the boards, and hustling on defense. In contrast, IU looked like they were ready to go to sleep. Maybe, because of the game's late starting time, they thought it was past their bedtime. To give you an idea of the total dominance of Illinois, they outrebounded Indiana about 48–22 and won by a score of 75–65 to ensure Coach Henson his 500th career victory.

That evening was interesting from another standpoint. The stands were buzzing. A lady in a long orange dress with a blue pattern and a press pass hanging from her garments was walking around the court before the game. She had an entourage of men with TV cameras following her every move. She first stood behind the basket, then she walked over to Coach Knight and gave him a kiss on the cheek and then took a seat near the court. It was obvious she was not just any run-of-the-mill, ordinary spectator. In fact, she was TV reporter Connie Chung. We had heard she was doing a TV special on stress and was including a segment with the coach. It all seemed so cut and dried and uneventful. Of course, coaching is a stressful profession and one could anticipate this segment would come across on TV as a good example of stress, and that would be all. Little did we know when we left the arena what the repercussions of that evening's interview would be for Indiana University basketball.

I personally didn't see Connie Chung's TV show, but had several opportunities to read about it in the newspapers. It caused a nationwide furor. As I read and interpreted it, Coach Knight made a statement regarding women and rape which was taken out of context. It allegedly caused a rift between the coach and the new university president, as well as among women's rights groups. This whole incident probably could have been avoided if efforts at fair reporting were adhered to, but be that as it may, Coach Knight was again thrust into the limelight, and portrayed in a negative manner. These events didn't surface until the show was aired, after the completion of the 1987–88 basketball season and the NCAA final four. This controversial incident continued to produce negative publicity for the coach and the university, even in the off-season.

Following that Monday night loss to Illinois, we psyched up for the next home game, which was being played that weekend against Ohio State. For me, this was going to be a very special game since I had been invited to watch the Hoosiers practice on Friday afternoon. Since his arrival in Bloomington, Coach Knight has been a prime supporter of the library program at Indiana University. In fact, he helped establish an endowment for the Indiana University library, which was initially started by his request for contributions from his former players and from supporters of the basketball program. At one of the tipoff luncheons, he asked the fans to consider contributing to this ongoing project of the IU basketball team. I must admit, his argument was quite convincing. As you may know, or may have read, he is quite an intellectual and a scholar. But at times his other side emerges and people get turned off. I must tell you that he is one of the most articulate individuals I have ever heard speak publicly. He is never redundant, and has a facility for getting his point across without following any circuitous routes. As a matter of fact, I am sure he could teach any one of numerous courses, including English or history, at any university.

Well, as a result of contributing to the library endowment, I was invited to attend an afternoon reception and then the basketball practice which was scheduled for that Friday before the Ohio State game. Since Myrna was in California and unable to attend, I invited a friend's son, Eric, who was visiting Indianapolis. I took a day's vacation and we drove to Bloomington. We first stopped by the music school to see Margo, and then went to the reception. A group of forty or fifty of the top supporters was present. We met with some of the library staff. What a coincidence. One of the women in attendance was the IU library system's major purchaser of books. In fact, this was Julie Nilson, who sits right next to me at the basketball game in what was Dr. Meinshein's seat. As we snacked, we talked about basketball,

179

libraries, Coach Knight, and a number of other issues. During the times we sat in Assembly Hall, I never knew she was associated with the library. She had mentioned that after the practice, it was the library's intention to present the coach with an inscribed plaque. Unfortunately, he was busy with other matters and didn't get a chance to visit with the group, but they assured us he would be presented the plaque at some appropriate time in the future. I must admit, many of the people in attendance were a little disappointed.

However, there was certainly no disappointment with what I had learned at the practice that afternoon. I wish I could go to all the practices before every home game. It would surely make watching the game so much more enjoyable from a technical standpoint. During the practice session, the team went through their preparations for Ohio State. One special play they designed was an out-of-bounds play. If too much pressure were being exerted by Ohio State, then the outlet man would be Lyndon Jones. Another specific play they were perfecting revolved around Dean Garrett. He was to move up toward the foul line and draw the back end of the two/three zone up towards the foul line, thus creating a free lane for Keith Smart to come down the base line and receive an Alley-Oop pass just above the rim. In general, it was a very nice day. We met Margo after her Singing Hoosiers rehearsal and went to dinner and we all drove back to Indianapolis together.

The following morning Margo, Eric, and I ventured back to Bloomington. By game time we were all psyched up to watch the Hoosiers, and of course, we were hoping they would be much more motivated then they were against Illinois. They were and they performed well. It especially was a good game for me, because, throughout the game, I would lean over to Wayne Winston and back to Lee and Dave and predict what was going to happen. For example, when IU was being pressured on a halfcourt inbounds pass, I predicted that Lyndon would come out into the back of the formation and get the pass. I was right! Likewise, when Ohio State was in a two/three zone, I told them Garrett would move forward, draw the zone with him, and that Keith would go run down the baseline for an Alley-Oop pass. Right again! Let me tell you, watching a practice the day before certainly made the game more enjoyable.

Indiana won 85–77, and despite the fact that Eric is an Illinois alumnus, we all had an enjoyable day. The next morning I left for San Diego for the annual clinical pharmacology (ASCPT) meeting and to be reunited with Myrna. This was the first time we had seen each other in the last month. I visited with her sister and mother for a few hours, then Myrna and I drove to the meeting. We were very busy during the week with the various society activities and left on Friday after the meeting to fly back home to Indiana to see the Iowa game. Some of my friends thought I was crazy. As a matter of fact, so did Myrna when I told her my plan. Could you imagine someone wanting to leave sunny southern California on Friday when they could spend the weekend there? Well, it was not just any old basketball game that we were going home for, but a special game. It was the last home game of the season. Senior day. It was the day Steve, Keith, and Dean would be addressing the fans. In addition, we were playing Iowa, the team that defeated us at the start of the Big Ten season.

Early the next day, Myrna and I drove to Bloomington to a pregame luncheon hosted by Wayne and his fiancé, Vivian. Margo joined us there, as well as Marge Clayton (Bernie had to attend a meeting out of town) and Jeff Sagarin. They served Mexican cuisine and it was great. Jeff arrived late, having had some important business which he needed to finish. He had just completed sending his computer rankings to the NCAA in Kansas City for their use by the selection committee. He shared them with us on Vivian's computer. Despite its overall record, he still had IU ranked pretty high, so I felt we would certainly get a bid to the NCAA, even though we had to beat Iowa just for pride's sake.

After lunch we all headed for the game—that is, all of us except Jeff. We had offered him Harriet's seat (she couldn't attend because she was studying for exams), but he convinced us that he could not accept because he had to follow the other games being played that day in order to assemble his final rankings for submission to the NCAA. This was dedication, since I know Jeff has a warm spot in his heart for the Iowa Hawkeyes. That day the Hoosiers were fantastic. They literally destroyed Iowa's fullcourt press. Keith Smart, who scored thirty-two points, was exceptional in the one-on-one role that Iowa afforded to him. Dean Garrett had twenty-six points, nine rebounds and eight blocked shots. Jay Edwards contributed twenty-four points. Indiana totally dominated all aspects of the game, winning by a landslide, 116–89. Unfortunately, Rick Calloway got very little playing time. He was inserted into the game with only one minute remaining, and he quickly made a turnover. It was clear that his self-confidence had been shattered. All the fans were pulling for him to break out of his slump and to play with his usual confidence and abilities, but this was not to occur on that day.

At the conclusion of the Big Ten season, Purdue had won the Big Ten championship outright, Iowa and Michigan tied for second, then came Illinois, and next Indiana. We had finished in fifth place. It was ironic because we had had only two losses at home, Michigan and Illinois, and had beaten every other team at least once. Despite this, our final Big Ten record was 11 and 7. Had we not had the poor start at Northwestern and Michigan State, it might have been 13 and 5. Regardless, we still would not have won the Big Ten since Purdue, with their senior leadership, played well throughout the season.

All season long Coach Knight had said the team was struggling because it was looking for a leader and no one was emerging. It was his feeling that this was one of the major shortcomings of this team, and a reason why this team was having difficulty. This is of interest, since in John Wooden's book on *Practical Modern Basketball*, he states, "The coach must never forget that he is a leader and not merely a person with authority." He also stated that "A team without leadership is like a ship without a rudder that is certain to wander aimlessly and will probably end up going around in circles and getting nowhere." It appears to me that to be successful, a team must have both coaching leadership and player leadership, and above all, they must have compatibility. However, in some systems, if leadership cannot emerge *de novo*, then it must be trained, nurtured, and given a chance to develop. As in the business world, potential leaders must first be identified. Next year, hopefully, a player leader will be groomed to assume this role, with its awesome responsibility.

The following day we watched the NCAA pairings. Indiana, who finished fifth in the Big Ten with a record of 19–9, and was ranked number nineteen in the nation by UPI, was slated to go to Hartford, Connecticut, as the number three seed in the East. They were scheduled to play Richmond. In fact, Indiana was seeded higher than Iowa, who finished in a tie for third place in the Big Ten. Purdue, deservedly, was the number-one seed in the Mideast. Richmond, whom the Hoosiers had met in postseason play on several previous occasions, was no pushover, since they had earlier defeated a tough, highly ranked Georgia Tech team in Atlanta.

When Neil heard that Indiana was going to Hartford, he contacted his sister and brother-in-law, who live there. They said they would get us two tickets if we wanted them, but I could not go because it was imperative that I attend an important company meeting that morning. I assure you, I made every effort to change my schedule so as to accommodate both the meeting and the game, but to no avail. Had the game been scheduled for late Friday afternoon or evening, it would have been no problem. Unfortunately, the Hoosiers were to play at 2:30 P.M. and even with the best connections, the plane would get me into Hartford at about 2:20 P.M. Considering landing, getting my luggage, obtaining a cab, getting to the Civic Center, and getting to my seat, I would surely have missed much of the first half. Even I was rational enough to realize that it would not be a smart move for me to travel all that distance, considering the possibility that I might not even get to see the game.

When it comes to IU basketball, my optimism usually surpasses my realism. Thus, I called Ronnie Kuntzman, my close friend and mentor in New Jersey, and asked him if he could get me tickets to the regionals at East Rutherford, New Jersey, where I was sure IU would play in the next round. He said he would try, and so I started to make my travel plans. Speaking of optimism, I also picked Indiana to win the NCAA in the office pool. Look,

183

after the way we played against Iowa and the potential that resided in that team, I didn't think that was too farfetched.

Well, the bubble finally burst, and all of the IU fans came down to earth with a big thud. We now had to face reality. The Richmond Spiders defeated IU by the score of 72–69, and therefore, this was the end of the line for the Hoosiers of 1987–88. The Richmond team beat Indiana at their own game, demonstrating patience on offense and an excellent defensive effort. During the action, I was hoping Coach Knight would insert Ricky Calloway into the game, and that like a knight (not a pun) in shining armor, he would spark the team on to victory.

You see, in his first year he was chosen as the Big Ten's freshman of the year. As a sophomore, he was instrumental in their winning the national championship. Thus, it was not inconceivable that he could be our savior. During the latter part of the season the fans were all pulling for him to return to his former level, that is, as a superstar. Unfortunately, this was not to be. In fact, he didn't even play in the Richmond game, and this prompted me to tell Myrna and a few close friends that I felt sure Calloway would transfer from IU, even though he was entering his senior year. Lo and behold, several days later, the newspapers affirmed that he would leave, and that he was considering such places as Xavier in Cincinnati, his hometown, and also Kansas and Maryland. We were saddened at his announcement to leave, but realized that what might be best for the team might not necessarily be best for an individual player and vice versa.

The year before we had attended the Singing Hoosiers' spring concert just after watching the Indiana–UNLV game televised from New Orleans. This year we also attended their concert. This evening, someone else was present, who was easily identifiable, and who I am sure would have preferred to be still participating in the NCAA tournament. As I was waiting in the foyer of the auditorium, lo and behold, in walks Dean Garrett, very relaxed and wearing a casual outfit consisting of a sport shirt and white cotton pants. I am sure he enjoyed the evening but I would venture to say he would rather have been on the basketball court. Well, you can't win them all, and he certainly was fortunate to have had his day in the sun last season. It's not everyone who realizes their dream of playing in the NCAA final four, let alone being on the winning team. The NCAA champions!

Another difference between that evening and the year before relates to Showalter Fountain. This year the water was splashing and spouting out of the dolphins' mouths. There was no need to shut off the water, since the students would have no reason to celebrate. However, a celebration was occurring indoors in the IU Auditorium. The Singing Hoosiers were giving a spectacular concert to a full house on the occasion of Professor Robert Stoll's twenty-fifth anniversary as the director of this illustrious group. Befitting the occasion, President Thomas Ehrlich presented him with a plaque to commemorate this special milestone. You see, IU not only excels in basketball, but in the cultural arena as well.

In 1988, Kansas won the NCAA for coach Larry Brown, another transplanted New Yorker who found a home in the Midwest. His Jayhawk team, a consensus underdog, won every game in which they were predicted to go down to defeat. All the highly touted and ranked teams, including Arizona, Duke, North Carolina, Oklahoma, Purdue, Michigan, Pittsburgh and Syracuse, went down the tubes at various stages in the tournament, just as Indiana had to Richmond. Kansas outlasted all of them and was victorious in surpassing sixty-three other potential champions on the road to the NCAA championship.

In trying to analyze the extravaganza known as the NCAA tournament, it is evident that many factors play a role, one being determination and desire. Clearly, Kansas had these more than some of the other teams. One thing I realized was that we Indiana fans surely are fortunate to be part of a unique group and tradition: five NCAA Championship banners. Three of these were acquired under the leadership and direction of Bob Knight and during my time as a devoted fan. What a feat. I guess as a fan I should be pleased to have the opportunity to see my team win just one NCAA championship, let alone three. Well, that's true, but we shouldn't just rest on our laurels. We all looked forward with much anticipation and a great deal of anxiety to the next year. The 1988–89 team would be not only without Keith Smart, Steve Eyl, and Dean Garrett, but also without Ricky Calloway.

This latter fact was brought home loud and clear when Myrna and I attended the 1988 basketball banquet. Although the official program had Ricky listed, he was not in attendance. Speaking about IU fans and their support for their team, the banquet tickets specified that the doors would open at 6:30 P.M. However, the line started forming at 5:30 P.M., assuring those fans who wanted to, that they could get seats close to the activities.

This year the mood and atmosphere were much more subdued and quiet than that of last year's. Moreover, the crowd of about 1,100 was much smaller than at last year's gathering. As usual, the seniors all had an opportunity to address the fans for their last time as an IU basketball player. All, of course, thanked their coaches, teachers, academic advisors and especially the fans. However, Keith Smart, who in my opinion is mature beyond his years, really summed up his feelings when he especially thanked those fans in attendance. To paraphrase him, he stated that there was no doubt that last year's banquet, with the NCAA banner, the large overflow crowd and the immense enthusiasm associated with the championship, was great. But he really appreciated this specific group of fans present this evening, though considerably smaller than the year before, who thought enough of him, Steve, Dean and the team in general to make their senior banquet a success, even though this year there was no banner. At this year's banquet, there was, however, a great deal of enthusiasm, respect and love expressed by the fans for the whole team, and especially for the seniors. Win or lose, the players represented the university and more importantly, themselves and their families, and yes their fans, in a credible manner.

In all the Indiana game programs is a page containing the "definition of an Indiana player," which I understand is also posted on the locker room wall. Excerpts from that poster state, "An Indiana basketball player can come in any size, shape or color. . . . He is first of all concerned with the good of the team and knows the individual recognition will come through team excellence. . . . He appreciates the support of thousands of fans, but he is much more aware of the example he is setting for some small boy watching from the sidelines. . . . He is what a small boy wants to become and what an old man can remember with great pride that he once was."

It was evident that evening at the banquet that the three seniors had indeed met the criteria and, in fact, they were leaving Indiana University and its basketball program with degrees from one of the most "complete" universities in the country and with a great personal pride in their accomplishments. They had gained everyone's respect both on and off the court by setting an example, not only for the small boy, but for fans everywhere.

When we left the banquet, we were already anticipating the start of next season. For the 1988–89 basketball season, IU would be without Ricky Calloway, the Big Ten freshman of the year in 1986 and a key member of the 1987 national championship team. Also gone, via graduation, would be Keith Smart, Dean Garrett, and Steve Eyl, all prominent members of the 1987 championship team. They were now all IU alumni, having successfully earned their degrees. On the questionable side was Jay Edwards, the 1988 Big Ten freshman of the year. As for playing in his sophomore year, Coach Knight stated that would depend upon whether Jay was willing to pay his own tuition until "he demonstrates his maturity." This development arose in early July, when Knight took away his scholarship, stating that, "At this point he has shown no understanding whatsoever of what it means to represent the basketball program at Indiana." Edwards was involved with substance abuse and had agreed to enter a treatment program.

On the positive side, Edwards' high school teammate Lyndon Jones, Indiana's high school co-Mr. Basketball for 1987, was returning. Other returning ball players were Joe Hillman, Todd Jadlow, Magnus Pelkowski and Mark Robinson, who was coming off his red-shirt year. In addition, they were to be joined in Bloomington by the new recruits, one of whom was one of the top blue-chip players in the country, Eric Anderson from Chicago. Anderson, a 6'9", 220 pound freshman, was Mr. Basketball from Illinois and an honor student in high school, possessing an A average. He would fit right into Coach Knight's plans for the coming season. Other new recruits joining Anderson included 6'8" Matt Nover of Chestertown, Indiana (who was later red-shirted), 6'0" Jamal Meeks of Freeport, Illinois, and 6'7" Chuckie White of Dodge City, Kansas, a junior college transfer.

Although we knew the Big Ten would be very strong, particularly Illinois, Iowa and Michigan, I was confident that Indiana would be competitive. Being an eternal optimist, what else would one expect me to say? However, little did I know how good the Hoosiers would actually be in 1989. As Coach Knight summed up at the 1988 basketball banquet, "For those returning, next year will hopefully find us a team hard to play against, and highly competitive." It was clear that with his new recruits, his returning ball players, and most of all, his coaching ability, this would be a truism.

With regard to Ricky Calloway's transfer to Kansas, I feel sure that all the Indiana fans wished Ricky well and would continue to follow his career and accomplishments, even though he wouldn't be wearing an Indiana uniform. You have probably realized by now that Indiana fans tend to develop an attachment to the players, past and present, as we watch them change from young boys to young men, and then to mature adults, each hopefully making contributions to society.

The 1988–89 basketball season officially started practice on October 15, but many Hoosier fans were still caught up in the excitement of the football season. The Hoosiers of Indiana were in high gear with a record of 4–0–1, having just defeated Ohio State by the score of 41–7 in front of a friendly Bloomington crowd. They next beat Minnesota on homecoming and were ranked No. 14 in the CNN poll. The following week we trekked north to Ann Arbor, where the football Hoosiers faced Michigan. They were humiliated in front of the Michigan homecoming crowd, including Harriet, who marched in the alumni band that day. She and the band sat in chairs on the sideline about ten rows in front of the Indiana section and she sort of tormented her mother and me every time Michigan scored a touchdown (which was often). Is this the respect you get for paying all that tuition to a rival school? I can assure you it was not fun for us, but we did enjoy watching her beaming face as she and her friends relived their earlier band days.

On October 20, it was announced in the local paper that Jay Edwards would be practicing with the basketball team, and we all hoped he would be allowed to play and contribute to the team. He obviously got his act together because Coach Knight did allow him to play. You know that probably never would have happened if the coach hadn't been firm and taken a stand. I am not sure many other coaches would have kicked their star player off the team.

The first game of the season was an exhibition game against Athletes in Action. Freshman Eric Anderson started and made the team's first basket, and his first as a Hoosier and hopefully an omen for the start of an illustrious career at Indiana. The team looked good, winning by the score 116–90. This game had originally been scheduled as a Saturday evening game to follow the Indiana-Michigan State football game (which we incidentally watched by sitting in the rain as IU was virtually slaughtered by State), but was moved to Sunday. Myrna wasn't up to taking the ride down from Indianapolis to Bloomington two days in a row, so I went alone. She did enjoy going to the next few games. Indiana was one of the teams participating in the Big Apple NIT. Their first opponent was Illinois State, coached by Bob Knight's friend Bob Donewald, and the game was played in Assembly Hall. At this Friday night game we watched an enthusiastic Indiana team win 83–48. Everyone was excited about the defensive effort of the Hoosiers, who held the visitors to only 32 percent shooting, while themselves ripping the nets for a 57 percent shooting effort. Todd Jadlow was high man with twenty-one points, and Jay Edwards contributed fourteen points.

Two days later Indiana hosted Stanford, starring Todd Lichti, who *Inside Sport Magazine* selected as a first-team All-

American in the preseason issue. To me, watching the game was like viewing a football game next door in Memorial Stadium. I hadn't seen a game this physical in years. The Stanford team was like a group of thugs and bullies. Five of their team, including Lichti, fouled out, and fortunately IU survived without any injuries and went on to win 84–73. We were all excited about the win and the team's advancing to New York's Madison Square Garden for the semifinals. Unfortunately, we couldn't go along because we were hosting family for the Thanksgiving holiday. I admit that I was not happy that this event was this weekend. This was a departure from our typical Thanksgiving weekend, where we would look forward to going to Bloomington as a family outing and adventure; however, I can assure you we did watch the games on TV. What a rude awakening we were to have.

We first played Syracuse, our 1987 NCAA final four opponent. They were awesome and clearly got some revenge for their 1987 NCAA loss. It was as if the matchup was between a professional team and a high school team. I reiterate—they were awesome, beating our pants off 102–78. Well, let me tell you—I would trade them 100 regular season game victories for just that one NCAA championship. As I said before, no one will remember this loss for very long, but no one will ever forget Keith Smart's shot in New Orleans in 1987. Before the game, I had predicted we would lose, but I never imagined it would be that bad (i.e., twenty-four points at the half). Deep down I was hoping for a repeat upset as the one that had occurred in the first game that day in Madison Square Garden, when Missouri defeated Dean Smith's North Carolina team. Well, here we were, forced for the second game in a row to play against an opponent that we had beaten in an NCAA championship game—back in 1981. Well, déjà vu; we lost to the North Carolina Tarheels 106–92, just as we had to Syracuse. Again, our defense was like a sieve. This was an unprecedented event in Coach Knight's seventeen years at Indiana University, i.e., to be defeated by an opponent scoring over 100 points two games in succession. Although I was frustrated, as were other Hoosier fans, we all knew this was a building year. You don't loose players such as Calloway, Smart, Garret and

Eyl—four of your five starters—and expect to be competitive overnight, especially against highly ranked, seasoned teams such as Syracuse and North Carolina. During this despair, I felt that there were some positives in these games and I was confident Coach Knight would build on these. For example, in the North Carolina game, Jay Edwards, who did not start, scored thirty-one points, while Todd Jadlow, netted twenty-seven points and was named to the Big Apple NIT All-Tournament Team.

After a road win at Miami of Ohio, the Hoosiers were to meet Louisville in the Big Four Classic at the Hoosier Dome. Myrna and I attended, and it was interesting to see the role reversal. Here were the two perenial powerhouses, Indiana and Kentucky, suffering humiliating loses to Louisville and Notre Dame, respectively. The Louisville Cardinals thumped Indiana 101–79. It was reminiscent of the earlier Syracuse and North Carolina games. They were awesome, again almost like a pro team, and again we looked terrible. I am not so sure they were that good or that we were that bad. Up to this point, Coach Knight had gone with a traditional line-up: a center, two forwards and two guards. Knight's genius then came to the forefront as he realized that he needed players who could handle the ball and bring it up court against sustained pressure, and thus he went to a three-guard starting lineup. Lyndon Jones, Jay Edwards and Joe Hillman were the guards, Eric Anderson the forward, and Todd Jadlow at center. What a difference this made in the team's chemistry. It took one game for the Hoosiers to acclimate to this new lineup. This was their game in South Bend, Indiana, (a site where the Hoosiers have always had to struggle) and of course it was against Notre Dame. The Hoosiers lost 84–71. Following this game, the Hoosiers would embark on a thirteen-game winning streak which carried them well into the Big-Ten season. After the Notre Dame loss, the Hoosiers played their next four games in Assembly Hall, and won the Indiana Classic.

Coach Knight and his troops traveled to Lexington next, where they beat Kentucky 75–52. This was a first for Bob Knight since he had never beaten Kentucky in Rupp Arena. It was a milestone, but we all realized that this was not the same Kentucky basketball program that we were familiar with from the past. They were under a veil of criticism and undergoing an NCAA investigation resulting in all sorts of allegations being leveled against them. Later in the season they would be penalized and Coach Eddie Sutton would be forced to resign. This series of events was highlighted on the cover of *Sports Illustrated* with the title "Kentucky Shame." Incidentally, the day after the Louisville game, I drove to Bloomington to see Indiana's soccer team, coached by Jerry Yeagley, win their *third* NCAA Championship of the decade (1982, 1983 and 1988) by defeating Howard University 1–0.

While the basketball team was going through its transition period, the football Hoosiers received an invitation to the Liberty Bowl to play South Carolina in Memphis, Tennessee. Myrna and I drove to Memphis. We vacationed there for several days and found ourselves, at one point, in the lobby of the famous Peabody Hotel with hundreds of other Hoosier fans and visitors, watching a group of ducks walk to and from the fountain on plush carpeting. In retrospect, this seems a bit strange, even to me. Well, we enjoyed all of our activities while awaiting game day. The evening of the game was, to say the least, unseasonable. The temperature in the stands was about 20°F. (Minus 10°F. accounting for the wind chill factor.) Myrna and I and about twelve to fifteen thousand Hoosier fans bundled up and settled back to watch the Hoosiers defeat the South Carolina Gamecocks 34–10. The only regret I had was having to see Carolina's coach Joe Morrison lose. I had rooted for him when he was a member of the New York Giants pro football team. (Later in the year, I was saddened to read that Joe Morrison died of a heart attack.) The football game in Memphis was occurring simultaneously with the Indiana basketball game in which the Hoosiers defeated St. Bonaventure.

Early the following morning, Myrna and I checked out of the hotel and started our trek back to Indianapolis. It was imperative that I make good time and get an early start because I planned to be home in time to attend the championship game of the Hoosier

Classic with Indiana meeting Utah State that evening. Fortunately, I did get back in time to see the Hoosiers win 93–61. Myrna, who clearly is the smarter of us, said she was exhausted and preferred to watch it on the TV. This game ended our pre-conference schedule. Our record, which was four wins, 3 losses after the first seven games, was now 10–4 after the first 14 games (not including the exhibition game versus Athletes in Action). Coach Knight's decision to alter the lineup, although criticized by some, proved to be effective to date, albeit against limited competition.

We spent the remainder of the Christmas vacation at home anticipating the start of the Big Ten season. Since Michigan was representing the Big Ten in the Rose Bowl, Harriet and Neil went to Los Angeles to root Bo Schembechler and the Wolverines to victory. At home, Myrna, her mother and I donned Maize and Blue, got out Harriet's Michigan paraphanalia and cheered for Michigan. I can recall numerous times when we joined into a chorus of Hail to the Victors and yelled "Go Blue" as Michigan won. We shared in Harriet's and Neil's excitement and happiness, of course.

On January 4, Indiana hosted Ohio State at Bloomington and won 75–65. They then traveled to West Lafayette for a late-night ESPN game where they defeated Purdue 74–73. Jay Edwards, who was chided by the Purdue crowd because of his previous substance-abuse problem, sank his last five of six free throws in the last fifty-one seconds of the game, providing the Hoosiers with a rare win in Mackey Arena. This victory gave Coach Knight the undisputed title as the all-time winningest coach in the Big Ten (a total of 214 Big Ten victories). The leading scorers in this game for Indiana were Edwards (twenty-two points), Hillman (eighteen points), and Anderson (fourteen points), and the victory was a total team effort. Perhaps this is what characterized this year's team. They, in fact, were a team, each knowing and performing his role to perfection.

The following Saturday afternoon, only five days after Coach Knight defeated Purdue to become the uncontested all-time Big Ten's winningest Coach, he and the Hoosiers entertained the Northwestern Wildcats in Bloomington. If the Hoosiers were to win, it would mark another significant milestone for Coach Knight. It would make him the second youngest individual (forty-eight years old) to win 500 games as a college basketball coach. (His close friend Henry Iba was the first to achieve this level of distinction.) However, Bob Knight was the youngest college coach to win 200, 300 and 400 games. That day, the Hoosiers beat Northwestern 92–76. The final score is very deceiving because at the start of the second half it was, in fact, 47–46, IU's favor. Everyone in Assembly Hall was elated to see our coach achieve this highlight in his career and to see the exciting freshman Jamal Meeks come of age with a stellar performance. Although the coach did not make much fuss over his own accomplishment, you have to know he was happy for himself, for Meeks and for the team. The Hoosiers' record was now 13–4, and they were tied for first place in the conference with undefeated Illinois (15–0), each with a 3–0 Big Ten record.

After just eking out a win at Wisconsin (71–68), the Hoosiers returned to Assembly Hall to meet Michigan State. The first half was close, but the cream and crimson went on to handily defeat the Spartans, giving Coach Knight his 400th win at Indiana University and thereby becoming the first Big Ten coach to achieve this milestone. Moreover, they had just won their twelveth game in a row. Not too shabby for a team that started out as they had in New York in November. But, to coin an expression from the late Gilda Radner, "It's always something." During the initial period of this game, we all sat in the stands expressing disgust with the officiating. Coach Knight was also unhappy and expressed his displeasure. For this he received two technical fouls (ironically, his first of the year) for protesting what was clearly an official's error when the man in the striped shirt called a regular foul against a Michigan State player rather than calling it an intentional foul. This poor call was obvious to almost all the 17,285 fans in attendance. To demonstrate his point to the official, Coach Knight grabbed "little" Jamal Meeks and tried to show the officials what had transpired, but to no avail.

Shortly thereafter, a melee occured on the court when some

of the players went for a loose ball as though they were trying to recover a fumble at a football game, and no foul was called. Unfortunately, some of the fans began throwing coins as the officials lost control of the game. To this regrettable action of the handful of fans, Knight responded in his usual admirable fashion. He went directly to the scorers table, grabbed the microphone and told the fans, to just keep in mind that, "We don't do that here in Indiana. I don't care what the quality of the officiating is, you don't throw anything in here." To this the fans responded with a loud and tumultuous round of applause. You must admit that the coach says just the right thing at the right time. As a result of the two technicals, he was restricted to coaching without much dramatics for the remainder of the game for fear he might be ejected with a third technical. However, his team (and the fans) did respond and Indiana went on to beat the Spartans.

The next two games were on the road against teams selected in the preseason polls to dominate the Big Ten (Michigan and Illinois). In fact, in numerous polls Michigan was picked as the number-one team in the nation. Unfortunately for the Hoosiers, Michigan was coming back to Ann Arbor after a 71–68 stinging defeat to the Wisconsin Badgers in Madison. As I sat in front of the TV ready for the late-night ESPN game, I knew Michigan would be psyched up for the Hoosiers and would do their best to avoid two losses in a row. To this point, Michigan had lost only one preseason game (to Alaska Anchorage) and two Big Ten games (one to Illinois and one to Wisconsin), all of which were on the road. Their overall record was 15–3. The game was a typical Indiana–Michigan game; down to the wire. Indiana won 71–70, but like so many other games in this class college basketball rivalry, Michigan could have pulled it out at the end, however, they missed their last two shots with only a few seconds left to play. What a victory for the Hoosiers! Coach Knight's strategy of making Michigan play his game worked well. When Rumeal Robinson fouled out with about seven and a half minutes left in the game, Jay Edwards then went to work and led the Hoosiers with his superb play and leadership. As a result, Indiana captured their thirteenth straight victory. The national media were talking in glowing terms and showering praise on Knight, stating that this was his best coaching effort because, unlike 1976 or 1981, he didn't have the depth of talent and, as is his forte, he was getting the most of his players. With respect to our household and the rest of the die-hard Hoosier fans, we were all quite excited to see the season progressing so well.

Well, all good things must come to an end—well, at least temporarily. Indiana went to Champaign-Urbana to play number-one nationally ranked Illinois, and again Myrna and I settled in and became glued to our TV sets for yet another Saturday afternoon. We were really upbeat and in all our glory as the Hoosiers were leading at the half by ten points. Then the bottom fell out. The Illini, who were emotionally charged up, played with a vengeance that destroyed Indiana in the second half. Illinois ultimately won by a 75–65 score, a twenty-point turnaround from the half time score. I can assure you, I was devastated and not fit to live with for the rest of the weekend. It was clear that even though we were in first place in the Big Ten, we had continuing difficulty with fast, physical teams such as Syracuse, Louisville, North Carolina, and now Illinois.

After the loss, the Hoosiers returned home to host Iowa in a late starting Monday night game to be televised nationally on ESPN. Myrna and I drove to Bloomington for the game, touted all week on TV as the battle between number seventeen-ranked Indiana and number nine-ranked Iowa. The game was all we could have hoped for. The Hoosiers took an early lead, and then Iowa narrowed it and then tied the score. IU led at the half 58–49. Iowa came back to within two points (77–75), but then the Hoosiers, led by the fine play of Todd Jadlow, went on to win 104–89. It was an old-fashioned blow out. I must admit I had not been one of Jadlow's main supporters, being quite vocal and critical of his play, but this evening he was dynamite. If only he could be consistent, we would be ranked number one. The drive home was delightful even though we didn't arrive at our doorstop until about 1:30 A.M. on Tuesday morning. As we drove home, we would drive through Martinsville. The past weekend the city of

Martinsville had honored its prodigal son John Wooden, the famous coach of UCLA, by naming their gymnasium after him. As I mentioned earlier, Wooden played for the Martinsville Artesians in 1927.

The next week we again returned to Bloomington to watch the Hoosiers play the Minnesota Golden Gophers. Let me tell you, just when you think you've seen it all, you realize there is always something new. Well, today was one of those days. The house was packed and the natives were restless for a big win. Unfortunately, the Hoosiers of Coach Knight did not respond—at least in the first half of the game. They were uninspired and their play was much less than ideal as exemplified by their being behind by the score 28–22. Obviously Coach Knight was not happy with them because he locked them out of their own locker room. Joe Hillman, their senior leader, held a "seance" on the court under the basket in full view of over 17,250 fans who gave them a standing ovation—even though at that point they probably didn't deserve it. Perhaps it was designed to urge them on and give them encouragement and support. Knight did eventually meet with them in the locker room and they did respond positively in the second half, overcoming what would become a 14–point deficit. They were led by Joe Hillman's sharp shooting and play-making. He finished with twenty points for the evening, while Jay Edwards contributed fifteen points as the Hoosiers triumphed 66–62 to lead the Big Ten with a conference record of eight wins and only one loss at the season's midway mark. One week later the Hurryin' Hoosiers beat Northwestern in Evanston, led by their fantastic freshman Eric Anderson (twenty-four points) and super sophomore Jay Edwards (twenty-four points).

The next game, a Sunday afternoon, nationally televised home event, was played in front of a sell-out, standing-room-only Assembly Hall crowd. Indiana's opponent was none other than cross state rival Purdue. It was a classic game in this exciting rivalry. The Hoosiers trailed by eleven points with about nine minutes left in the game. The game ended with Jay Edwards sinking a sixteen-foot shot with four seconds left, as the Hoosiers were victorious over the Purdue Boilermakers 64–62. Edwards was fantastic, finishing with twenty-seven points. There are not enough superlatives to explain his play. Myrna and I left the arena convinced we had seen one of the most exciting finishes to a basketball game (at least in this season). Little did we know what was in store for us the next week.

The following week we played our second straight Sunday afternoon nationally televised game. Myrna and I were joined by my sister and brother-in-law who were visiting us from the Catskills. Rozy and Murry were knowledgeable fans, but this was their first encounter with basketball in the Big Ten, and particularly with Hoosier Hysteria. What a game for them to get for their introduction to this phenomenon! In addition we were joined by those avid Michigan stalwarts Harriet and Neil. The Hoosiers played well and led at the half 42–37. However, during the second half the Hoosiers, who had maintained their lead until late in the game, started to lose ground. The Wolverines took a 75–71 lead with less than one minute to play. Jay Edwards cut the lead to 75–73, converting on two foul shots, and then when Michigan missed a shot with about ten seconds left, the Hoosiers got the rebound and started to move the ball upcourt. With about one second left, Lyndon Jones passed to his high school teammate Edwards, who let go a three-pointer from about twenty-five feet from the basket. *Swish*!! The ball went through the net with the clock reading 00:00 and the Hoosiers won 76–75. Two weeks in a row we had come from behind and won with last-second shots. Both times Jay Edwards responded as if he were Mr. Cool with ice water in his veins. My heart still beats faster just thinking about those two exciting games. Unfortunately, we had to console Harriet and Neil on the way home. They were sure the shot went off after the buzzer. I assured them that Michigan was a good team and they shouldn't be dismayed. In fact, many others and I felt that Michigan could be the best team in the Big Ten if only they would play up to their potential. I reassured them that Michigan stood a good chance of being the NCAA champions if they got their act together. I am not convinced this made them feel better, but it was my honest assessment and a sincere effort to console them.

The Hoosiers next went on the road for three games, winning them all. I was fortunte to see one of these—the Hoosiers' game against Minnesota. My friends Drs. Horace Loh and Shelly Sparber invited me to give a seminar to the students and faculty of the University of Minnesota on the Friday before the game and suggested I spend the whole weekend. I stayed with Shelly and his wife Claire, and we reminisced about our college days at Brooklyn College of Pharmacy where we had all been classmates. On Saturday we went to the game in Williams Arena. It's interesting to note the false impression you get from TV. On the tube all you see is a new, shiny court, having no concept that, in fact, it's located in an old arena with two levels of bleacher-like stands surrounding the court. This game was played in front of a sellout crowd, their largest crowd of the season (16,661). However, there appeared to be only a handful of Hoosier fans, and as usual I tried to yell loud enough so that the team on the court would know they had some following and so Myrna could hear me back in Indianapolis. This was just not any old game. Here were the Hoosiers, playing against a team which had not lost a home game in the Big Ten all season long. They had already defeated Michigan, Illinois, Iowa and Purdue just to name a few. Once it started, the score went back and forth until the last six minutes. To this point the Hoosiers had played good defense and were very patient on offense. Then with six minutes to play, Indiana let it all out, burying the Gophers by outscoring them 17–4 to win the game 75–62, and ending the Golden Gophers twelve-game home winning streak.

After defeating Ohio State next and assuring themselves of a share of the Big Ten title, the Hoosiers then returned to Assembly Hall. They had won eight games in a row and twenty-one of their last twenty-two games, with their last loss being to Illinois, who incidentally was to be their next opponent. They were to play on a Sunday afternoon on national television. If the Hoosiers won, they would be the undisputed Big Ten champions. Indiana came into this game with a 14–1 Big Ten record, while Illinois was 10–4. Myrna and I were excited about the game and again joined the capacity crowd in what was almost becoming a Sunday routine.

The game was a typical Illini–Hoosier classic. At the half, IU led 27–25 and built the lead to twelve points with about ten minutes to play. Then Indiana self-destructed, missing their foul shots and some easy layups. Eventually Illinois took the lead with about 1 1/2 minutes to play. The Hoosiers were trailing by only two points with just a few seconds left and the ball in Jay Edwards hands.

He was unable to get off a high-percentage shot from the court and was forced to launch an unbelievable shot from behind the baseline and the basket. The shot had a high trajectory and went over the backboard, and for the third Sunday game in a row, Jay Edwards' shot went through the basket and produced a *swish*—or as Marty Glickman, an old-time announcer for the New York Knicks, used to say—it is good like *Nedicks*, (a New York hot dog outlet). The clock now read 00:00. However, the officials put two seconds back on the clock. I can assure you, I have replayed that shot 20 times if I didn't replay it once on the VCR, and when the ball passed through the rim, the clock already read 00:00. Thus, the game should go into overtime and Illinois couldn't call time out, since no time was left. Unfortunately, the referee disagreed. When Edwards made his shot I went bananas as did everyone in the arena. We all jumped for joy and were elated. Across from us the IU bench was also celebrating, especially Coach Knight who was jumping up and down like a young kid. It was a rare moment to see such an enthusiastic response. Unfortunately, this jubilation on the part of the Hoosier fans and their coach was short lived. With two seconds to go, Illinois inbounded the ball to Nick Anderson, who then threw up a bomb at the buzzer and made a three-pointer from about thirty feet from the basket. The Illini won 70–67 and we were devastated. We now knew how Harriet and Neil felt just two short weeks earlier when Indiana beat Michigan on a similar last second shot. Incidentally, Harriet and Neil were quick to remind us that what goes around comes around. Well, IU's fans would have to wait a few more nights before they could clinch the title.

The next morning Myrna and I drove to Nashville, Tennessee, to attend the annual meeting of the American Society for

Clinical Pharmacology and Therapeutics at Opryland. I participated in the meeting, and after the past presidents' luncheon on Thursday, Myrna and I dashed off and drove north to Bloomington, Indiana. Well, you didn't really think I would miss the opportunity to see the Hoosiers—this fantastic team—capture the Big Ten championship, and to hear the seniors say their good-byes to the fans, did you? The Hoosiers won 75–64, led by Eric Anderson, Todd Jadlow, Joe Hillman and Jay Edwards, who scored 19, 18, 17 and 15 points, respectively. With this win, the Hoosiers became the 1988–89 Big Ten champions and Coach Knight was named Big Ten Coach of the Year and National Coach of the Year (his third time); Eric Anderson Big Ten Freshman of the Year; and Jay Edwards Big Ten Player of the Year and Associated Press First Team All-American. Beyond a shadow of a doubt, this had to be one of Coach Knight's greatest years. He directed his troops to an outright championship, after Indiana was picked to be an also-ran in the Big Ten, something that many in the media never imagined. I was optimistic about the season, even before it began, but I must admit even I didn't anticipate we would have only two losses (15–2) when we clinched the title.

The following weekend IU was to play Iowa in Iowa City to end the regular conference season. Having won the championship, and having a few of his starters suffering injuries after a hard-fought season, Coach Knight elected to rest many of these starters. As a result, IU lost 87–70 and thus ended the conference 15–3, with an overall record of 25–7.

The next day we watched the television to see what the NCAA's selection committee would do about placing Indiana. Since I already had tickets for the first and second rounds of the Mideast Regional at the Hoosier Dome, I was hoping we would be placed there. Unfortunately, or fortunately, however you look at it, Indiana was sent to the West Regional in Tucson, Arizona. Just as a matter of principle, I was angry because Indiana, the Big Ten champions, should have been placed in Indianapolis rather than the Illinois team. You know, what's fair is fair. In addition, I had good seats. However, after seeing the pairings, I felt Indiana would be facing less tough competition in the West Regional.

201

During the week, Lee Suttner called to tell me where he and Ginny would be staying in Tucson in case Myrna and I were going. He said his calling had become a tradition, and thus we would win. Well, we're all superstitious. Unfortunately, we could not attend because I had to go to New Orleans for a scientific meeting at the end of that week. On Thursday, I took a day's vacation and went to see all the games at the Hoosier Dome and Friday I departed for the Crescent City. On Friday, in Tucson, the Hoosiers played George Mason University as their first opponent. We won 99–85, although this final score is deceiving since Indiana led at halftime 57–29. Also at the West Regional site, the University of Texas, El Paso (UTEP) was playing LSU. Here I was in New Orleans, Louisiana, tied up at a meeting, while my team was playing in the NCAA. If they could win and get into the regionals, I had big plans to go to Denver to watch them hopefully proceed up the ladder to the Final Four.

Meanwhile, at the meeting I would periodically take a "break," or as we in Indianapolis call it, a pit stop. To be perfectly honest, I would really go to the bar area to catch bits of the UTEP–LSU game to see who Indiana's next opponent would be. I should have realized what was happening when I approached the bar and saw all those long faces, and an atmosphere of doom, despair and depression. It was apparent that UTEP was beating the tar out of Dale Brown's LSU team. In fact, the game was so lopsided that the national network decided to switch to another game. UTEP was the winner and got the distinct pleasure of playing the Hoosiers that Sunday. This was to be the second meeting between Don Haskins and his Miners and Bob Knight and his Hurryin' Hoosiers. Indiana had won the first encounter earlier in the season in Bloomington and was again victorious in Tucson. They won by an impressive 92–69 score and thus advanced to the West Regional at McNichols Sports Arena in Denver, Colorado. As an aside, it was of interest to note that the Louisiana papers (e.g., Baton Rouge's *Sunday Advocate*) appeared to have given more coverage to Coach Knight than to Coach Brown during the weekend.

Well, what do you think is the best way to go from New Orleans to Indianapolis? Of course you guessed right! It's via Denver, Colorado. Myrna called the Varsity Club and got me a ticket for the game and also made reservations for me to stay at the Holiday Inn right next to Denver's Mile High Stadium and McNichols Arena. So, early Thursday after the pharmacology meeting, I caught a plane to Denver. When I arrived, I checked into the hotel and then went downtown to the pep rally. This consisted of the four pep bands and their cheerleaders—Seton Hall, Arizona, UNLV and, of course, Indiana. There I saw a lot of familiar faces, all people dressed in red outfits. After the rally I went to the Hoosiers' Alumni Association headquarters hotel where I had arranged to meet my buddy, Lee Suttner, who as you know sits behind me in Assembly Hall, and Dan Sullivan, another avid IU fan. We went for a quick meal and then it was off to the game to watch Indiana play Seton Hall.

We sat in the upper deck in a section filled with Hoosier fans ready to see Indiana, who was on a roll, do its best. Unfortunately, we were all very disappointed. It was as if the teams were reversed. The Hoosiers did not play patiently and looked awful on defense. In contrast, Seton Hall was very patient on offense. They worked the ball inside for easy shots or dished it outside for long three-pointers, while always playing strong defense. At times, Indiana's players looked rattled and lost. There were moments when IU did look as though they might be able to turn the corner. With about eight minutes left in the game, Indiana was trailing by only three points (54–51), but they made a mistake, missing an opportunity to close the gap. Even at two minutes, Indiana only trailed by five points (68–63), but Seton Hall took charge and buried the Hoosiers, out-scoring them 10–2 in the final minutes. Seton Hall won 78–65, providing Indiana with its worst NCAA loss in tournament play. I don't want this to sound like sour grapes—sure the Hoosiers played poorly—but I have big problems with a team recruiting a "professional" player from a foreign country, who has no intention of attending school to earn a college degree, just so he can play basketball for a year or two and gain experience and exposure in the United States.

After the game I immediately went into the corridor to

watch the completion of the Michigan–North Carolina game on TV. Michigan, who was sent to the Southeast Regional, had earlier defeated Xavier and South Alabama to advance to the regionals in Lexington, Kentucky's Rupp Arena. They now beat North Carolina. We were all excited when that following Saturday afternoon Michigan defeated Virginia to earn a berth in the final four. Harriet and Neil had gone to Lexington to see this game, and they were ecstatic. Well, at least one of our family's teams made it there. I stayed on in Denver for the UNLV–Arizona game, and then flew back to Indianapolis. In contrast, Lee and Dan got in their car on Friday morning and started the long drive back to Bloomington. I can assure you, they were not happy campers. I felt sorry for Dan, who would have to spend all that time in the car with a despondent traveling partner.

I returned to Indianapolis Saturday evening. During the next week, the air was filled with all sorts of rumors. Allegedly, Jay Edwards had been ill on the plane trip to Denver and people had all sorts of speculations. Late in the week Edwards reportedly was going to forgo his last two years of eligibility and turn professional. Coach Knight immediately gave Edwards' scholarship to Todd Leary, a guard from Indianapolis Lawrence North, who led his team to the Indiana State High School Championship and who incidentally resembles and plays like Steve Alford. We hoped his high school teammate, Eric Montross (seven-feet tall and a natural) who is one year behind Todd, might also come to IU to play for Coach Knight. Well, our loss is Dean Smith's gain as after a long period of suspense he chose North Carolina. What a dream team that would have been—with Damon Bailey and Eric Montross and the recruits who have already committed to the Indiana program. What possibilities for keeping the tradition alive and for building what is termed in sports a dynasty, Well, we will do without him!

The upcoming weekend was to be the NCAA's big show and the two participants who progressed to the final game were Michigan and Seton Hall. At this time Myrna and I took a vacation and drove to Myrtle Beach, S.C. and beautiful Brookgreen Gardens. The azaleas and dogwoods were in full bloom and it was delightful. That Monday evening in the hotel we donned our maize and blue hats and Michigan sweatshirts and sat in front of the TV and cheered for the Wolverines. Back in Indianapolis, Harriet was doing the same. Michigan beat Seton Hall in overtime to win the NCAA championship—their first one. This, of course, made us all feel great. If Indiana couldn't win, then it was great to have Michigan—a Big Ten team—win. Besides, didn't we beat them twice during the regular season? Michigan's victory over Seton Hall also vindicated Indiana and the Big Ten conference in their ongoing rivalry with the Big East conference. All in all, we were very happy with the outcome and, of course, we were happy for Harriet and Neil, who put up with a lot of chiding by me and the other Indiana fans. Surely now they had good reason to be exceptionally proud of their team. The Rose Bowl and an NCAA championship in the same year. What an accomplishment.

Several weeks later Myrna and I went to Bloomington for the annual banquet. Although it was televised, nothing can equal attending this event in person. It was a truism this year. As I drove up to the entrance of Assembly Hall to drop Myrna off, she commented "Isn't that Jay Edwards over there talking to someone in the car?" Indeed it was Edwards. He was in shorts and a teeshirt. He obviously was going to attend the banquet. I wondered what Bob Knight would say, since Jay was no longer a member of the team. Myrna felt he should be a part of the banquet's festivities since he contributed so much during the year. I must admit I was ambivalent. The evening's emcee was Bob Hammel. As the team marched in to the music of Indiana, Our Indiana, Jay was with them, now dressed in a suit. He took his seat with the rest of the team in the stands. About halfway through the meal, in walked Coach Knight, who went directly to his seat. When he noticed Jay Edwards, he must have been upset. He showed displeasure by leaving the gym, but soon returned and he, Hammel, Dan Dakich and the other coaches engaged in numerous conversations. The coach, being a gentleman, decided to proceed with the evening's activities and, in fact, ignored Jay. Edwards was not introduced nor mentioned by name and he was not called up to participate in the festivities like the other players. When I spoke about the events of that evening to a friend who had watched it on TV, she had no idea that the atmosphere in Assembly Hall had been so electric and had no knowledge that all of this was transpiring. This underscores the fact that there is nothing like being at an event in the flesh.

During the past year, from early November to April, high school senior ball players made their commitment to the schools they wanted to attend. Indiana was considered by many to have the best recruiting class in the country. It included Indiana's Mr. Basketball Pat Graham, Greg Graham, Todd Leary, Chris Reynolds, Calbert Cheaney, Chris Lawson, and last but not least Lawrence Funderburke, one of the three top blue chippers in the nation that year, and who eventually had a short stay in Bloomington. In the summer of 1989 these individuals, plus Damon Bailey (probably the most famous high school ballplayer since he was featured in *Season on the Brink* and in *Sports Illustrated*), Eric Montross, and Pat Knight, the coach's son, formed an AAU team which was coached by Scott May. This team excelled against good competition and thus represented the State of Indiana with distinction. We should have many exciting years of basketball to look forward to in the future with Coach Knight and the Hoosiers.

What a year for the Hurryin' Hoosiers and their coach! The team won the Big Ten championship outright with a 15–3 record, and a 27–8 overall season record. What a feat, considering they were picked in the preseason to finish seventh, especially in this conference which was awesome this year, having two of the Final Four teams. They twice defeated the eventual national champion and made it to the NCAA Sweet Sixteen. For Coach Knight, this was a remarkable year filled with many individual honors. He won his 500th career game in midseason, he won more Big Ten games (225) than any other Big Ten coach (either past or present), and he was the first Big Ten coach to win over 400 games while at a Big Ten school. For all of these accomplishments he was chosen National Coach of the Year in several polls.

What a year for the fans! What a year for the team! What a year for Coach Knight! Moreover, Coach Knight was selected as the College Coach of the Decade.

Chapter 14

Epilogue

The Catskill Mountains north of New York City are still there, although the area has changed tremendously. Many of the hotels which were once the center of activity have deteriorated with the toll of time, or have become the victim of fire. When I was growing up, there was a joke about "Catskill Mountain lightning." It goes something like this: One hotel owner says to his friend, "I am sorry. I heard your hotel burned down last night." The other responds with his index finger over his lips "Shush, it's tonight." This was thought to be the way hotel owners survived the bad season, collecting the insurance and then starting again the following season. As the hotels went, so did the bungalow colonies and rooming houses, also meeting a similar fate. With the loss of many of these hotels and tourist accommodations, which had been on large tracts of land, the mountains eventually went back to "seed." In time, the fields and empty areas where buildings stood were soon replaced by forests, and the woods got more lush, and now the Catskills are almost like virgin forest territory.

After the scandals of 1951, the Alamac Hotel gave up its basketball-hosting reputation and went from a place where the elite of basketball went for the summer vacation season, to just a regular hotel. The hotel was eventually sold by the Shapiro family to an orthodox religious sect, and within a few years it also became run down and dilapidated and eventually parts of it disappeared, being replaced by woods. The once famous basketball court became overrun with weeds. Although the weed covered blacktop playing surface still remains, as do the posts which once secured the backboards, it is totally nonfunctional. The village of Woodridge still has about 500 people in the winter, but summers in my home town, and the Catskills in general, are not the same and the area is not as heavily populated as it was thirty to forty years ago. The children of the previous zealots of the Catskill Mountain lifestyle, i.e., the summer residents from New York City, were now vacationing in the Caribbean, Europe, taking Alaskan cruises, going to Las Vegas or traveling to sunny California. Obviously, the Catskills are no longer their number-one priority. In contrast, many orthodox religious sects have taken over what remains of the bungalow colonies, and thus the Catskills have taken on the image of Mea Shearim, the orthodox section of Jerusalem. Moreover, as the Catskills have gone back to wilderness, some professionals from New York City have decided to build town houses and single family vacation homes in the area. A friend of mine tells me that these are quite nice. There are now only a few of the original hotels still in business in the Catskills. They are those that had reputations of being the higher-caliber hotels such as the Concord, Nevele, Tamarac Lodge, Raleigh and Kutsher's Country Club.

The Shapiro twins left Woodridge and went to school in New York City to become court stenographers. They now own a court stenography business, and are both very successful. Ironically, today, neither is much of a basketball fan or fanatic. I still visit with them when I have an opportunity to go back to New York.

College basketball in the Catskills is a legacy of a bygone era. There is, however, still a yearly event at Kutsher's Country Club in Monticello, New York. At first it was to benefit Maurice Stokes; then, after his death, it has been used to benefit other important charities. In contrast to the Catskills, college basketball in New York City and along the East Coast did have a resurgence during the past decade. Occasionally, teams like LIU, Marist, Farleigh Dickinson, Robert Morris, and Fairfield get into the NCAA Tournament solely because they win their own conference tournament and are "guaranteed" a spot. However, they quickly exit, usually after the first round, not serving as sufficient competition fo the more proficient programs. In contrast, St. John's, Georgetown, Providence, Boston College and Villanova of the Big East have done exceptionally well. Another significant change taking place in New York City has been that Madison Square Garden has been moved from Eighth Avenue and Forty-ninth Street to a new home in the Pennsylvania Railroad Station at Thirty-third Street and Eighth Avenue. The NIT now has both a preseason series, called the Big Apple Tournament, and the usual postseason NIT.

Prior to my arrival in Indianapolis, the Hoosiers of Indiana University had won two national championships (in 1940 and 1953) under the leadership of Coach Branch McCracken. When Bob Knight came to Indiana, he quickly won the hearts and souls of many of the Hoosier fans, and he rewarded them as his teams won championships in 1976, 1981 and 1987. When he came, controversy was not a major problem, but with time he became a very controversial subject. As is often stated, people either love him or hate him. Even those like myself, who admire him as an intellectual and respect his basketball-coaching ability and the attendant successes, at times have ambivalent feelings. At times I find it difficult to defend some of his actions, but I always admire his honesty and integrity and, of course, his coaching skills.

The Puerto Rican incident was, in my mind, a set-up, but the chair-throwing incident in 1985 and the Russian forfeit in 1987 were considerable negative aspects. However, his commitment to the Indiana University library fund, the fine representation of the U.S. in the 1984 Olympics, his vigilance against drugs and his stressing the importance that college athletes are students first and basketball players second are very positive aspects that I have admired during the past eighteen years, as Bob Knight has represented Indiana as their coach.

In 1987, Dr. John Ryan stepped down from the presidency of Indiana University. He was a great supporter of Coach Knight and the basketball program and athletics in general. During those years he sustained personal criticism for his treatment, or lack thereof, of any disciplinary action against Coach Knight. However, in the fall of 1987, things seemed to change at Indiana

210

University. Dr. Thomas Ehrlich became the new president. His past experience as provost of the University of Pennsylvania and Dean of the Stanford Law School clearly made him an ideal candidate for the presidency of Indiana University. It was clear that he was not one who would stand by and not comment, when he perceived a situation as being inappropriate. In fact, this is what transpired during the Indiana forfeit against the Russians. Perhaps these actions may not have been perceived as being supportive of the coach and the basketball program, but the reputation of the University and that of the image of the state are clearly at a level above, and one must put things in their proper perspective. However, it is clear that the new president and Bob Knight share the common goal, that academics at the Indiana University are paramount.

In the nineteen years that we have lived in Indiana and given our total allegiance to Indiana University (except for the few lapses when we rooted for Michigan), Coach Knight and the Hoosiers have won three NCAA basketball championships, eight Big Ten championships, the CCA trophy in 1974, and the NIT in 1979. Moreover, Coach Knight has also won the 1979 Pan American Games and the 1984 Olympics. Quite an admirable record especially considering that over 94 percent of his players have earned or are in the process of completing their degrees. During this time, no other college coach has surpassed these accomplishments. In the past two decades, there is no doubt that we have been privileged to watch the *best* college basketball played anywhere in the country. As of 1988, the coach with the winningest percentage of all-time NCAA coaches is none other than Clair Bee, from Long Island University, who had a winning percentage of .827. He is slightly ahead of Jerry Tarkanian, "Tark the Shark," of the University of Nevada/Las Vegas, who has an .825 percentage, Adoph Rupp at .822 percent, Dean Smith at .777, and Lou Carnesecca at .745. Not too far behind in sixth place is Coach Bob Knight, with a percentage of .735. As of the start of the 1989–90 season, he had an all-time career record of 514 wins and 187 losses. It is of interest that Knight joins a select group of coaches led by one of his mentors, Clair Bee from LIU.

During his tenure at Indiana University (1971 to the present), only one other Big Ten coach had won a national championship, that being Jud Heathcote at Michigan State in 1979. However, in 1989 Bob and Jud were joined by "Interim" Coach Steve Fisher, who led the "abandoned" Michigan team to the NCAA championship. Neither Iowa, Illinois, Ohio State, Wisconsin, Minnesota, Northwestern, nor Purdue has accomplished this feat. In fact, except for John Wooden's impressive record at UCLA, in the 1960s and mid-1970s, no other basketball coach has achieved Coach Knight's level of excellence.

Indiana high school basketball continues to flourish, and so do its traditions. In the recent past, Bob Jewell was elected to the Indiana Basketball Hall of Fame and honored at a special banquet. Bob, who graduated from Indianapolis Crispus Attucks High School in 1951, was a Trester Award winner. That same evening, several other prominent Indiana figures were also inducted into the Hall of Fame. These include Bill Green, the coach of Marion High School, who coached this school to three straight state championships, with the help of his superstars Jay Edwards and Lyndon Jones. Also inducted that evening were the Van Arsdale twins, Tom and Dick, who are both graduates of Manual High School in Indianapolis and Indiana University. They subsequently went on to play professional basketball, where they achieved prominence.

One of the sad things that has occurred during the past years has been the transferring of players, who have been recruited to play at Indiana, to other schools. Some of these players who have transferred have gone on to do well and represent their new universities with distinction. These individuals have earned the respect of the Indiana fans as well as the fans in their new schools. Some of these individuals who have transferred during the past seventeen years include Rich Valavicius (Auburn), Bobby Bender (Duke), Tracy Foster (University of Alabama/Birmingham), Marty Simmons (Evansville), Mike Giomi (North Carolina State), Derrick Holcomb (Illinois), and Ricky Calloway (Kansas). Calloway had hoped to play under Larry Brown, the coach who had led Kansas to the NCAA championship in 1988. Unfortunately for Ricky, Larry Brown is no longer at Kansas, having signed a lucrative contract to return to the NBA as the coach of the San Antonio Spurs. Brown left Kansas with a legacy—NCAA probation. I guess it must be hard for some coaches to compete in the NCAA while abiding by the rules. Fortunately for Indiana fans, Coach Knight has been put up as the model that others should emulate in running a "clean" program.

It is traditional for the former ball players to come back to Bloomington to watch and root for the current team from their seats behind the Indiana bench. We often watch them from our own seats in Assembly Hall, as they and their wives and children periodically return and socialize with each other, the coaches and the present players. In fact, they are like "fraternity brothers" who give their all to their alma mater. Moreover, they now join our ranks, that of the enthusiastic, always supportive fan. It is a pleasure to watch such fine young men as Wayne Radford, Stew Robinson, Tom Abernethy, who occasionally brings his children, Steve Ahlfeld, Ted Kitchel, Quinn Buckner, Phil Isenbarger, Steve Risley, Scott Eells, John Laskowski and Steve Green, to name a few. The latter two serve as TV color commentators for IU. This is just another prime example illustrating that basketball is just a game and a passing stage of life, and is one that gives up the spotlight to other more important roles. These individuals have all gone on to achieve other successes. At times, former IU players who were in the professional ranks would return to Bloomington or join the team when they were in a nearby city for a road game. These included Scott May, Kent Benson, Quinn Buckner, Mike Woodson and Randy Wittman, to name a few. Other former IU players in the pros include Steve Alford, Uwe Blab, and last but not least, Isiah Thomas. In 1988, Isiah showed what a "gutsy" player he was in leading the Detroit Pistons to the finals of the NBA championships. Had Isiah been in top physical condition, there is no question in my mind that Detroit would have beaten the Lakers. In 1989, a healthy Isiah did lead Detroit to an NBA championship, this time beating the Lakers in four games. Although I don't go to see professional basketball games, I still watch the playoffs and the all-star game on television. How could one not want to follow ball players of the caliber of Isiah Thomas, Larry Bird and Magic Johnson. In addition to his players participating in many activities, two of Knight's alumni have followed him into the coaching ranks: Butch Carter, now an assistant coach at California State-Long Beach, and Jim Crews, the head coach at Evansville.

In addition to watching the players grow up, one of the pleasant aspects regarding following Indiana basketball has been watching the coach's children grow up. Coach Knight has two boys, Tim, who is approximately the same age as Harriet, and Patrick, who is a few years younger than Margo. We had the opportunity to see both of these boys grow up over the years, as they sat on the Indiana bench. When Pat was a senior at Bloomington North High School he led his local high school basketball team and played on the AAU (Amateur Athletic Union) team. Tim graduated from Stanford University and appears to be closely associated with his father's business enterprises. In July of 1988, Tim Knight was coaching an all-star team at the Bloomington Firecracker classic and also was doing the analysis and commentary with Chuck Marlowe. In the summer of 1989 he helped organize the Bloomington, Indiana, AAU team which played exceptionally well, winning many honors and accolades.

As Coach Knight's basketball players speak to the fans on seniors' day or at the annual basketball banquet, they always leave expressing the sentiment that he teaches them that basketball, or athletics in general, is just a game. They sincerely state that they are being prepared for the real world—life in general. Some go on to the NBA and have reasonably long careers. Others stay on for just a short stint, or play overseas. However, the majority of players go out in the real world just like the vast majority of the other university students and join the ranks of the masses contributing to society in many ways. They represent most every profession: physicians, dentists, lawyers, teachers, coaches, and businessmen. They now have the opportunity to return to society some of what was given to them. Coach Knight and his staff, as well as the faculty and staff of Indiana University, have done a creditable job, turning out such a group of fine young men in whose accomplishments everyone can take a great deal of pride and pleasure.

Over the course of my nineteen years in Indianapolis, I have received many offers from pharmaceutical firms and universities to change positions. It is common for executive search firms, more commonly known as "head hunters" to try to relocate individuals. When I first arrived in Indiana, I used to joke and state that I wouldn't move from Indiana as long as Bobby Knight stayed and coached basketball at Indiana University. If he left, then that might be the time for me to consider leaving. This statement, of course, is no longer true. My family and I have made a home in the heartland. Indianapolis itself offers us significant participation in the arts—the symphony, theater, ballet and museums. Our children have grown up nicely, my work has been fun and rewarding, and I have been given the opportunity to grow professionally. Myrna and I enjoy the lifestyle here, and embrace particularly those aspects of Indiana University already discussed.

With regard to the subject of Coach Knight leaving Indiana, it is reasonable to assume that sooner or later, this is inevitable, and the fans must be prepared to face this eventuality. The more successful he is, the more offers he will attract. In 1979, when "Red" Auerbach, the general manager of the Boston Celtics, was looking for a coach, he approached his friend, Bob Knight, who was high on the list for consideration. At that time, Knight declined, saying he could not see himself coaching players who were making considerably more money that their coach. Again, in 1986, after Coach Eldon Miller "resigned" and was relieved of his job at Ohio State, the rumor mill was rampant that Coach Knight had been approached, and that he would be taking the position at his alma mater. Fortunately, he again declined, and Gary Williams was selected to coach in Columbus. At the end of the 1987–88 season, the Indiana basketball fans probably had their biggest scare yet with regards to Coach Knight. The University of New Mexico had been trying to recruit a coach, and Coach Knight did take a trip to Albuquerque. The rumors were rampant that he was going to leave because of alleged difficulties and differences with the new university president. At that time, supporters of the University of New Mexico bought a full-page ad in the Bloomington Sunday paper which read, "The perfect place for basketball, brown trout and Bob Knight." Fortunately, Coach Knight decided that his home really is in the heartland and stated that President Ehrlich was, in fact, not the reason he might have considered relocating, and that they shared mutual goals; goals dedicated to seeing that Indiana University achieves and maintains the academic respect that it deserves, as well as maintaining its already recognized basketball program and tradition.

The Indiana fans must be prepared for Coach Knight to eventually throw in the towel (either leave IU or leave coaching). However, these same fans would be the first to reassure you that the tradition of Indiana basketball will continue when the next coach takes the reins of the program. This has been the case at many other universities which have solid basketball traditions such as Kentucky, St. John's, Purdue, Kansas, UCLA and North Carolina, and, in fact, at Indiana, as exemplified by Coach Knight eventually becoming a successor to Branch McCracken. One thing can be stated most affirmatively. When Coach Knight does decide to call it quits, all of the fans will be thankful for the memorable times he gave them as it related to Indiana basketball, and that he will be sorely missed, and always fondly remembered.

Now, let me tell you, being a basketball fan is like suffering from a mental disease known as bipolar depression—the type of depression characterized by periods of depression cyclically followed by periods of mania. During some seasons you are flying high, whereas during others you feel like you are in the pits. Sometimes this cyclical event is markedly compressed and occurs within a period of weeks or days, occasionally even during the course of one game. Your team plays well one game and wins, and then loses a sure thing, and it appears as if they are only present in body, but not in mind. Regardless, being a basketball fan is not an easy occupation. I would suspect being a basketball coach is even worse. Why would anyone put his life and his fortunes on the line and be dependent on the group of teenagers and youngsters aged eighteen to twenty-two? You would need to be a masochist. But, in fact, it must be rewarding to be teaching, developing and molding these youngsters into superstars, or molding them into a team that functions as a single unit. In a recent survey published in *USA Today*, there was a discussion relevant to jobs. Jobs and professions were ranked with regard to stress factors, salaries, and a variety of other factors. NCAA coaches were rated No. 159 out of a possible 250 with regard to the desirability of having such a job. One sometimes wonders why college basketball coaches continue on in this hyper environment, but fortunately for us fans, they do, and they are very productive, demonstrate their skills well, and bring tremendous enjoyment and excitement to the fans.

Finally, I would like to close by making one point. In my lifetime, I was fortunate to have seen many significant sporting events, including the NFL playoff game between the New York Giants versus the Baltimore Colts in 1958 in Yankee Stadium, when Alan "The Horse" Ameche crossed the goal line with the winning touchdown, the last two Brooklyn Dodgers Games in Ebbets Field in the fall of 1956, the first Mets game in the Polo Grounds with such superstars as Choo-Choo Coleman and Marv Thornberry, and numerous Indianapolis 500 races. I used to revel at watching the New York Yankees and the Boston Red Sox battle in their perennial Labor Day Weekend series during the late 1940s, and I have seen the first Indianapolis Colts game and watched them clinch the AFC East championship. I had the privilege of watching Wayne Gretzky play for his first professional hockey team as an Indianapolis Racer, and I was present on the day that Joe DiMaggio retired from the New York Yankees. Last but not least, I had the privilege of watching Seattle Slew win the first leg of the Triple Crown, i.e, the Kentucky Derby, on May 7, 1977. Having stated some of the significant sporting events that I have participated in as a spectator and fan, I would have to admit that nothing in my mind compares to having watched Indiana go to the final four and win the National Championship in 1981, and watching them again (albeit on television) win in 1987 on a last-second shot. For someone interested in